So... This is Awkward.

By Timothy Tuttlesmith

Copyright © 2015 Timothy Tuttlesmith
All rights reserved.
ISBN: 1515329437
ISBN-13: 978-1515329435

Dedicated to a girl

I

The. Girl. Of. My. Dreams. sits across from me, her fingers wrapped around a craft beer and disturbing its cold sheen of condensation with watery finger trails.

Candlelight flickers across her face as she leans forward to sip her drink, her hair hanging down and casting moving shadows across her softly smiling cheeks.

She has a damned pretty face, but then she's T.G.O.M.D. so I'm bound to say that.

Those dark eyes suck mine in; I'm afraid to look away and I'm afraid to keep staring.

"So how many girls did you have to date before you found me?" she asks

"Errr... Too many?" I reply, breaking her gaze to look upwards and checking under my eyebrows as if my memories are somehow hidden there.

"Any crazy stories?" she presses.

"Definitely... But I never know where to begin..."

An Epilogue, but at the start

"Get on your knees!" I instructed, pointing to the floor in front of where Piper was sitting.

I had already stripped her of shirt, bra, and jeans, and this jettisoned clothing lay around the couch where we had been kissing and fondling a moment ago. Her exposed tits were modest but well rounded, and her nipples stood erect in the slight chill of my apartment.

The edges of her mouth betrayed the hint of a smile as she slid forward off the seat. "Yes sir!" she said, as her knees came to rest on the coarse rug in front of her...

My eyes were on her and not the rug. Its black and white zigzag pattern tended to make me dizzy, and the weed had already taken care of that. Her deep brown eyes were locked with mine and the rest of the room had taken on a warm-soft-transient-and-stoned quality that made it easy to forget where I was and exactly how I had got there...

*

I'd only just met Piper a couple of hours earlier. We'd exchanged small talk in a midtown wine bar, having decided on a Sunday evening rendezvous through a flirtatious exchange of long character strings. I had texted her a promise of *'a solid pre-Christmas ravishing'* along with a picture of a disturbing array of sex toys. Somehow this had tempted her out of Brooklyn and through that cold December night. All I had to do was walk west a couple of blocks to the nearest drinking establishment that still had a semblance of class.

*

"Give me your arms!" I said, producing a length of red cotton rope from a drawer.

She knelt upright offering me her limbs to bind. She was uncharacteristically quiet now the game had begun.

*

Before we had started getting amorous, Piper had been confidently chatting shit in her West Coast accent. It was one of those feminine but dry and low pitched accents that always seem tinged with hints of playful sarcasm. She wasn't afraid of saying what she thought either. After smoking up, we'd started talking about the pictures on my wall... "That one I took when I went to New Zealand a couple of years ago," I'd said, waving my hand at a photo of an appealing blue lake surrounded by lush greenery.

"Tell me about New Zealand," she had asked, or rather, demanded.

"Well I drove around the North Island first with some friends. Then I rented a car and drove around the South Island by myself, visiting a few people here and there..."

"No, TELL me ABOUT New Zealand!" she had insisted.

"Err...Ha... Ok I guess that wasn't very descriptive... I mean all the nature and wildlife is just so different there. I loved how all the birds sounded strange. Listening to the morning chorus made you feel like you were in another world, or some kind of prehistoric jungle..."

"That's more like it," she'd said, giving me a slightly doped out smile.

Finding myself in the groove of that memory I continued, "I think one of my favourite experiences was the first morning I woke up on South Island. I'd slept in my rental car, parked in this spot between the forest and the sea. It was great just waking up to the sound of all the birds and the distant waves from the Pacific Ocean. Anyway I went down to the beach to watch the sunrise, you know, as you do. It was like this sandy beach, with rocks and shit, and I was standing there, still waking up, taking in the smell of the sea and such... Then suddenly I heard this loud snorting noise right beside me, and I realised that some of the rocks were actually freaking sea lions! I was surrounded by these guys who were just hanging out on the beach, ready to bask in the morning sun. They didn't seem to care that I was standing there, so we just hung out and watched the sun come up together. It was pretty awesome."

"That does sound pretty awesome," she'd said, slouching backwards and staring at the ceiling.

*

Now I was wrapping two strands of rope around her arms, around and around and around. When satisfied, I took the two ends and threaded them between her wrists, completing what is known as 'a modern two column tie'. I tightened the cinch to ensure her hands couldn't wiggle free.

"Such a fucking boy scout," she muttered playfully.
"Hush you," I replied, tying the final knot out of reach of her fingers. There was enough rope left to act as leash to lead her arms by.

"Follow me," I said, leading her towards my bed, "but stay on your knees!"

She knee-shuffled across the floor, her bound arms outstretched in front of her as I kept tension on the rope.
"I've got a fun surprise for you!" I said, trying to sound just the right amount of menacing. I tied the rope around one of the bedposts and left her haltered there as I moved forward and started to pull back the black duvet.

"I told you I'd keep my toys out for you..."

I flung the cover aside to reveal my armoury of sex toys. I had spaced them out carefully to cover more than half of bed. There was a lot of rope for roping, a flogger for flogging, blindfolds for blindfolding, candles for candle waxing, a large hook with a ball on the end, (the purpose of which I'll leave to your imagination), clothes pegs for pinching (or hanging laundry, if I'm in that kind of mood), chains and padlocks for chaining and padlocking, a ball gag for volume control, a paddle for paddling, and a butt plug for making toast.

I let her take in the view. Piper's nervous silence persisted. We'd already agreed on the "traffic light" safe word system, saying 'red' meant 'stop everything', while 'yellow' would be interpreted as 'tone it down' and 'green' could be transcribed as 'shit yes, more of that!' At this point though, silence was all I needed to hear...

*

Piper didn't seem like the sort of girl to be easily intimidated. Like so many bright young things she'd moved to New York after graduating college, brimming with ambitious goals. A high flying job in public relations or journalism had been her aim and she'd gotten into a competitive PR internship, but had to work extra hours as a bartender to make ends meet. Eventually the public relations lost its charm and the bar job became her main source of income. Piper wasn't afraid of trying new ways to make money though. She'd told me that foot fetish parties were one of her more lucrative side ventures. Having guys pay her hard cash to kiss her feet or paint her toe nails was reportedly a lot less soul sucking than the regular nine to five. She'd met all kinds of guys through this business venture. Some were a little old and creepy but others just young and shy. Despite this variety of clients, she'd formed the opinion that having a foot fetish was subtly telling about someone's overall personality, and those relationships had always remained strictly professional.

Tonight, however, was for her pleasure. Even if she wasn't quite sure what form that pleasure would take... or how much pain would come first.

In terms of her specific interests, I'd gleaned that she liked both guys and girls[1], and she also preferred to be submissive, but it wasn't so much that she enjoyed pain and being dominated, but rather that she loved the idea of being the source of someone else's kinky pleasure, 'to be their personal fuck toy' so to speak. She found the idea of 'being used' was also in itself somehow a turn on, (although this was still dependant on the calibre of the gentleman doing the using).

She also loved getting fucked while high on weed. It was just one of life's simple pleasures.

---

[1] Apparently finding guys online who were interested in kinky sex with a girl is like grenading fish in a barrel, but finding girls interested in kinky sex with another girl isn't always so easy.

*

I loosened her rope halter from the bedpost. "Get on the bed!" I instructed

She hesitated as the sex toys were in the way, then stood up uncertainly and begun to clamber over them, trying not to kneel on the uncomfortable looking chains. However, her knees created wells in the soft mattress and their cold metal links slid down against her skin.

"Yes, I'm not sure I thought this through," I said. "Maybe the bed wasn't the best place to lay these toys out!" I hurriedly cleared a space for her amongst the various tools of stimulation and restraint.

"Where do you want me?" she asked
"Just here, on your hands and knees," I replied.

I tied the rope binding her wrists to the metal rail at the top of my bed frame. This, however, didn't leave enough slack for her hands to actually reach the bed. "Well... elbows and knees!" I corrected.

Clearing some more space amongst the chains, impact toys, and penetration devices, I joined her on the bed. I had picked up some more rope and I was about to start tying her legs when I noticed something.
"Oh, we'd better get rid of these first!" I said, looping my finger into the side strap of her undies, and yanking them down to her knees. With a little cooperative knee shuffling, her last item of clothing was cast aside and absorbed into the mound of toys.

I proceeded to tie her legs, but rather than just tie them together, I made her bend them at the knees and tied her upper and lower legs to each other. This had the benefit of significantly impeding her movement but also allowing more ready access to certain areas.

Ropes whipped back and forth as they were threaded and looped. While I was wrapping and knotting I realised I was working with somewhat over-frenzied concentration. However, I decided a little more calm and poise would improve the impression of dominance I gave off, and so I made a mental note to slow it down. 'Time to savour the moment' I thought, while sliding the rope over her hamstrings.

*

Piper had brought the weed at her own suggestion and we smoked it out of her little one hitter, (which in this case had been cunningly disguised to look like a regular cigarette). As one might expect from a West-Coaster she carried good weed. I don't smoke tobacco and when someone hands me a joint I often struggle to find the balance between inhaling a 'good dose' and sucking in too much so as to trigger a bout of purgatorial coughing. This smoke slipped down almost too easily though and my lungs weren't tickling at all after the first puff, so I assumed I hadn't inhaled properly.
I took a big second hit just as the room started to swim.
After a few minutes of staring blankly into space, I relayed the following report:
"Shit. I'm quite stoned now."
"Oh no, I've ruined you!" she said, laughing.

*

Recovered to a state of mild intoxication, I finished the knot securing her second leg in the kneeling position. Then for good measure I produced four Velcro cuffs from under my mattress and wrapped two around her lower arms and two around her ankles. She wasn't going anywhere.

I blindfolded her for good measure.

"Are you feeling sufficiently helpless?" I asked.
"Yes." she replied.

I caressed her hair, and then took a firm hold of it and pulled her head back for inspection. I leant in and kissed her on the lips. Just as her tongue began to touch mine I withdrew. Then releasing her hair I ran my hands slowly down her body until they reached her ass...

Some spanking and playful massaging later I moved on to fondling her breasts, cupping them as they hung beneath her.
"How sensitive are those nipples?" I asked, giving them a friendly pinch.
"Errm kind of? I don't know," she replied.
"Well, there's only one way to find out!" I said, picking a couple of clothes pegs out of the toy mound. "Now hold still!"

I peered underneath her, feeling a little like a mechanic inspecting a particularly sexy car. I positioned the first clothes peg over her right nipple and slowly let it pinch down, taking the whole tumescent nip in its jaws. She inhaled with a slight "hsssss" noise, but held still as instructed. I then applied the second peg to her left nipple in order to bring some symmetry to her pain.

In the darkness of her blindfold the pain must have seemed unrelenting and inescapable, but bearable enough not to say 'yellow'. Next she would have heard me rummaging in the toy pile, followed by the sensation of multiple flogger chords being dragged slowly across her back and ass - a tantalising warning of imminent pain. The caressing strands pulled away suddenly and then there was a threatening 'swish' as I brandished the flogger over my head.

I took aim.

*

The wine bar had been quiet that night when Piper had slipped through its heavy doors, escaping the biting cold and plunging into steamy warmth. I'd watched her scanning the gloom for me. Candles lit the tables and low hanging bulbs illuminated the bar, behind which a slightly plump barmaid said "Hi!" to my date with a cheerful southern accent, but before she got embroiled in bar side conversation I called out.
"Piper?"
She turned and spotted me, as I stepped out of my dimly lit nook behind the door.
"Hi!" she replied.

After a greeting hug, she slid onto the raised bench beside me and shed her thick winter coat. This bench had black leather upholstery and squeaked quietly as we adjusted ourselves in the candle light.

We talked, we laughed, we drank wine.

We got to know each other a little. Maybe at the time it seemed like we got to know each other a lot. However, now I look back through the fog of memory, I realise that 'little' may not be a small enough word.

Perhaps there is some deep tragedy in how close it's possible to be to someone in one moment and how far away they can be the next.

*

I fucked her enthusiastically. Her back and ass were crisscrossed with thin reddened lines where the flogger had already been to work. Some of these lines swelled slightly. A muted protest of the flesh. I held the flogger in my hand still, and lashed her occasionally to add some variety to the vigorous thrusting. My other hand grasped her hip, holding her bound form in place while she balanced on her knees.

As I fucked her I could feel her body changing somehow. After a while I could tell the geography I was ploughing was definitely different from the soft hills and valleys it had started as. Rather than being furrowed into submission the landscape seemed to be fighting back somehow... Maybe it had something to do with the weed, but I'd never been so acutely aware of these changes before. It was almost like there was some kind of internal lotus blossom unfolding. Although I imagined whatever was going on in there wasn't quite as pretty.

Regardless of its internal structure this engorgement egged me on. I sensed some fantastical orgasmic prize was close at hand. Dropping the flogger I grasped both her hips and focused all my energies on fucking her hard... and then harder, and harder, and harder, and harder, and HARDER, AND HARDER, AND HARDER, AND **HARDER, AND HARDER, AND HARDER, AND...**
And then little bright dots started to swim through my vision and the room started to spin.
'Shit... that's not good,' I thought to myself.

"Just need to take a time-out here," I said suddenly, withdrawing and reaching across to the bed stand to grab some water. I gulped it down and shook my head rapidly to fight off the dizziness.

After lying motionless for a while I realised Piper was looking at me with a somewhat quizzical expression.
"Sorry about that. The room started to spin. I thought it was best to take a break instead of passing out on top of you." I said
"Seriously?"
"Yeah, thought it was the smart move, considering you're somewhat immobilized right now."
"Errr... Yeah, I'd have been like 'What the fuck!' "
"I mean I've never passed out during sex before, but that weed was pretty strong and I got a little carried away there."
"It's ok," she said, clearly unimpressed.
I continued to lie beside her.
"Are you ok tied up there? Just gonna take a quick breather."
"I'm ok," she said. Then, after a minute of consideration, "Actually could you take these pegs off my nipples? They hurt quite a lot."

"Ha, sure," I said. I obliged her and then lay regaining my strength for a while longer. She remained tied, but kind of slumped over to her side as far as the rope and straps would allow
"Did you cum back there?" I asked
"No, not yet," she replied.
"Oh," I said, slightly disappointed, "I thought I felt something going on down there, but I guess not."
"I mean, I was enjoying myself," she reassured me.

I'd slept with a decent/indecent number of women thus far into my young adulthood. Before I moved 'across the pond' I could easily count the number of girls I'd sexed on one hand, but now I'd been living in New York for a little over a year I had exhausted all fingers and thumbs, and having run out of accessible digits I'd also decided it was slightly crass to keep a running tally of 'conquests[2]' anyway.

Despite my wealth of recent experience, spotting a bona fide female orgasm still foxed the hell out of me. I know the signs to look for - the contractions, the arching back, legs squeezing together, the tight grip of the fingers, the limp placidity that sometimes follows, and of course the vocals. However, the confounding factor is the sheer variability of my sample group; some girls would make deeply orgasmic sounds, coinciding with peaks of physical activity several times during sex. I'd finish, thinking a job had been well done, and then consider moving into spooning/napping mode. Then though I might wonder why the prospective little spoon kept humping my leg so enthusiastically, only to discover that they remained unsatisfied, and so napping had to be further delayed.

On the other hand there were the girls who fucked quietly, didn't seem to slow down, speed up, or go limp at any point, and just maintained a steady state of moderate enthusiasm, making me think there was some threshold of arousal they had not yet reached. However, during a breath catching period I might nervously inquire: "Did you cum yet?" and they might then make a quizzical face, responding along the lines of; "Yeeaah... Like five times!' [3]

---

[2] I also hate referring to those I have been intimate with as 'conquests', as if there was somehow winners and losers, when mutual fulfilment seemed like the most sensible goal. This squeamishness over vocabulary might be somewhat at odds with what I actually do to my 'conquests', but you may continue to observe that I display a range of apparent contradictions.

[3] Of course there was also the fraction of the data pool that went un-

Before getting back to work on Piper I grabbed a second bottle of water from the kitchen fridge. I downed most of it for good measure, but the dizziness had passed, so I pulled her back up onto her knees.

"I might just have to keep you like this for my personal entertainment," I said, as I began to fuck her again. I still took occasional swigs of water, and administered the odd spank with my free hand, defying all assertions that men can't multi task.

Just a finger's width of the refrigerated H2O left. I upended the bottle over her back. She gasped with surprise and arched her spine, a futile reflex to the cold insult.

I continued to fuck her.

"Thought you might want cooling down," I commented snarkily.

Now her nipples were peg-less I took full advantage, reaching underneath her with both hands and squeezing her tits hard. I playfully bit into her back and shoulders, leaving red circular teeth marks.

My bed slowly migrated away from the wall due to all the surplus kinetic energy. Approaching climax now with my hands on her tits and my arms under her body, I lifted her up, pulling her against her bonds, and then forcing her backwards onto my cock. We both grunted and gasped while my bed slats and metal bedframe all played their own violent concerto.

---

sampled; i.e. the times when I'd decided napping was just too attractive an option, and the 'did you cum?' question went unasked.

*

I flushed the condom down the toilet. I KNOW I'm not supposed to do that. Mostly I use the bin, but the idea of it sitting at the bottom of a bag in my kitchen gives me shudders sometimes. I then returned to my bound plaything and lay beside her, staring into her eyes some more. She could see the question pass across my face.
"What is it?" she asked.
"Oh just wondering if you enjoyed yourself back there," I muttered uncertainly.
"Are you kidding?"
"Kind of... Well not really."
"My god, you're such a girl!" she mocked

I wasn't sure how to interpret that answer to my somewhat vague question about her orgasm, so we fooled around a little more. Eventually I lay back exhausted and said, "I don't think I'm going to cum again. Shall we call it a night? You can crash here if you like."
"I don't do crashing," she said, but lay beside me a little longer.

As she untangled her underwear from a small pile of chains, I offered to put some clothes on and come wait for a cab with her.
"Why would you do that?" she asked, slightly abruptly
"Just offering."
"I think I can manage."

We exchanged a last brief kiss by the door of my apartment. I wanted to say, "Let's do this again sometime!" but stopped myself, wondering if I'd stand a better chance of seeing her again if I acted like I didn't care about seeing her again.

For a moment I stood motionless just inside my apartment, listening to her footsteps padding away down the hallway.

I let my apartment door swing closed slowly under its own weight.

I could hear the elevator making its little "ding" noise down the hall.

Then there was a loud 'THUD' as my door came to rest in its frame, and the latch engaged with a final metallic 'click-clunk'.

Prologue

Dating in New York is hard.

This is my personal conclusion; you can stop reading now if you like.

Admittedly I am still single as I write this, and somewhat jaded by personal experience. Perhaps by the time I finish this project I will have happened upon a lasting romance and my life will be full of metaphorical rainbows, daisies, fluffy animals and all the rest of that shit. However, I doubt an account of New York dating written in a state of contentment and with a well-balanced mind would be that entertaining. Thus I decided to start writing this thing while still engaged in the fray, and I guess we'll just see where it takes us.

So, yes, why should you continue to read these ramblings of yet another strange individual talking about how girls are confusing, and how he learned new things about them, and how those things still don't make any sense? Good question[4]. Erm... Well for one there will be some humorous accounts of kinky sex later. Everyone loves humorous accounts of kinky

---

[4] I'm not sure how useful this series of stories could be as a source of dating advice. I have developed no clear strategies for how to be better at picking up women. If there are any meaningful lessons to be had here you can figure them out for yourself. Many lessons from these accounts may well be painfully obvious to you the reader, but have so far thoroughly eluded me. You may even find yourself yelling at me "What the dickens are you doing sir! That is a poor choice of action!" In a similar way that I would yell at a cute blonde in a horror film not to wander alone into a dark basement ("Stay put and alert the authorities!" I shout as her hand tentatively reaches for the door knob). Bear in mind, however, that I probably cannot hear you yelling at me through a book... and your neighbours may be trying to sleep.

sex, right? I can't promise that this story will have a satisfying ending though, because I haven't got that far yet.

I suppose it's about time I gave some introduction to myself.

I am English. I am a scientist. I have a PhD from Oxford University. I am five foot ten. I suck at sports with impressive consistency. My main hobby is photography, and I sometimes do other artsy things (like attempting to write books). I am thin. My face is probably average looking (as far as one can objectively judge one's own appearance... I mean girls don't recoil in horror if I catch their eye, but second glances are rarer than I'd like). I am pretty open-minded sexually and I have a few specific interests which I'll get to later. I like playing computer games and watching movies. Oh, and I sometimes have panic attacks when dates are going well, which manifest as sudden feelings of nausea, often followed by my rapid disappearance to the nearest lavatory.

In summary, I have a few things going for me, a few things against me. The whole date-induced-nausea thing I guess is a little more unusual. It certainly adds a wildcard element to any given dating situation[5]. Fortunately these attacks seem to get rarer the more I date, so I can't claim them as a major handicap, or reason for my present singleness. They did,

---

[5] *Grossness warning- apparently some people are more freaked out by vom than kinky sex, so I'll endeavour to confine details of my panic attacks to pre flagged footnotes*- Yes, my panic attacks may be reminiscent of Stan in South Park- I would like to proudly declare that I have never actually thrown up ON a girl, I've always made it a safe distance away from said girl, and almost always made it to the nearest water closet / discrete bin / secluded flower bed... There have been a few notable exceptions of which I will spare you the details. However, even when deployed subtly, a mid-date barf is not exactly the sexiest move to pull out of your hat.

however, sabotage a number of romantic encounters in my formative years, meaning that I arrived in New York never having had a serious relationship, and generally under-experienced in the arena of pursuing women. (Or to be more accurate, I was under-experienced in the arena of pursuing women *successfully*.)

The whole English accent is meant to be worth serious dating currency over here, which I won't dispute. Although I suspect New Yorkers are a little more acclimatised to an array of exotic sounding accents, which dilutes my appeal. I also have a PhD, which if there was any real justice in the world would be valued a lot more than it is. Sadly though, the fact that I moved to New York to work in academia on a relatively meagre salary seemed to effectively neutralise the letters I can put in front of my name, especially when I'm competing for female attention with bankers, lawyers, illuminati members, and other individuals who can actually afford to live in this city.

Anyway, you probably get the picture by now. I'm a scrawny and nerdy Englishman with hit or miss social skills. I have never read any dating books, although under advisement I did once purchase "The rules of the game", but I did not get past the first chapter. This failure to read any kind of self help guide may be related to my general disdain for instruction manuals, a desire to take short cuts, and a preference for figuring stuff out by trial and error (mostly error, it turns out)[6].

In this account I am setting myself a few ground rules that may be helpful to explain. First, all accounts are based as closely as possible on real events and real people I met. Actual things that happen out here in the world are often much more

---

[6] Note: this is not the approach I take to actual BDSM stuff, safety first being the motto there!

unpredictable and entertaining than fiction. However, one caveat is that most of these stories are told from memory, which fades all too easily, and so to avoid having to constantly qualify these tales with sentences like "I think I said something along the lines of..." or "Then I vaguely remember her saying something about ...", I'll just reconstruct the stories and conversations as coherently as possible, but I may in fact get them completely wrong.

Ground rule number two is to maintain everyone's anonymity. This should have various moral and ethical benefits. To ensure this, I will change various details about the girls to give as much backstory to them as possible without revealing genuine clues as to their identity. I imagine most of the dates will be able to recognise themselves though. I just hope they don't try and kill me as a result.

One final note regarding time. It is strange how, looking back, different life events all seem to become a disconnected soup of occurrences. It's not always easy to remember the timeline of my New York dating. I am also often simultaneously pursuing dates with multiple individuals at any one time. I find this confusing enough as it is, and so to simplify your reading experience I will condense and rearrange the stories to try and focus sequentially on each individual in an order that best reflects 'the evolution of my New York dating story.'

Well I think that's the rules covered. Please ensure your seatbelts are fastened, your tray tables are secured, and your seat backs are in the upright position. This flight from London Heathrow will be departing shortly. We should be arriving in New York's John F Kennedy airport a little after 5pm local time. We do hope you'll have a pleasant flight.

Chapter 1 - Getting dates strategy 1- Be myself!

At the tender age of 26 I arrived in New York, about a week before Hurricane Sandy. Making a fresh start in a new country, with a new job, and knowing very few people, is not an experience that is enhanced by a severe natural disaster. Like all New Yorkers living in the blackout zones (in my case midtown Manhattan), I could yarn for a while about how this experience was both weird and really freaking inconvenient. However, at no point during these shenanigans did I befriend any attractive ladies, and so I did not get to embark on any sultry misadventures while stranded in the apocalyptic darkness of a city laid low by the forces of nature[7].

I mention the Hurricane as I think my experience of moving to New York has been transformative in many ways; I grew up in the English countryside surrounded by vast fields and very few people. I then hung out in Oxford for a bunch of years, which is a nice green and leafy town with easy escape to the countryside for taking in the fresh country air, eating picnics, drinking Pimms, and watching cows doing cow things[8].

Then I moved to New York. I'm not sure "green and leafy" are the first words that spring to mind when trying to describe Manhattan. There are also, like, no fucking cows. I mean I don't want the reader to get the impression I have some un-

---

[7] However, I doubt any sultry misadventures would have been helped by the fact I hadn't showered in days and my studio apartment reeked of urine as the loss of water supply had made my toilet unflushable. If I can make one prediction about the apocalypse from my hurricane Sandy experience, it's that it will not be sexy.

[8] Cow watching might not be considered a major Oxford pastime, but it's nice to have the option.

natural cow obsession, in fact I generally try to avoid any proximity to these smelly (and occasionally murderous) bovine monsters. However, the total absence of cows feels like a very clear Oxford-New York difference that is often overlooked[9].

Anyway, since my arrival, this city has assaulted all my senses, my abilities, my ambitions, my inner feelings, and my very sense of self. It's as if my personality has entered some kind of accelerated evolution driven on by the ceaseless torrent that is New York life[10].

So when friends offer me the sage old dating advice of "be yourself", I'm not really sure what that self is anymore. One trait I seem to consistently demonstrate is a tendency to be over honest with people. This is perhaps an advantage when attempting to write a dating memoir. Unfortunately it is not always advantageous when trying to project the appearance of a successful, masculine, mentally together, and sexually experienced human being, mostly because when I arrived in NY I was none of those things. However, honesty does have the advantage of 1) being easy to remember, and 2) being an attractive quality in itself (or so I am told).

Anyway, the first dating strategy I went with was just to put myself out there and hope that the girl of my dreams would turn up and be charmed by my self-deprecating humour, suitably enhanced by my English accent and winning smile

---

[9] I did see a pig on a leash in the East Village once... but that was a pig... not a cow... so basically what I'm saying is that this footnote really has no relevance at all.

[10] Perhaps NY is kind of like a metaphorical herd of bloodthirsty stampeding cattle and my personality is like the short sighted and arthritic old lady walking her stupid barky dog across their pasture during calving season.

(but trying to remember to hide my slightly yellowed English teeth). Unfortunately though, girls of your dreams very rarely turn up all by themselves. Perhaps it happens on occasion, but you can't just sit in your room and hope they appear. No. To stand any chance of finding the girl of your dreams in New York, you have to go LOOK for her.

There is no shortage of places to look. Here is one popular search strategy:

- Go to a bar. Sit at the bar, make eye contact with attractive girl, say "Hi!" and then follow it up with more conversation. Eventually get her number and arrange further activities to support more conversation and win her heart (/emotional co-dependency).

Sounds simple enough, right? I think this is what most people do in New York. It seems to work out for them. However, for an Englishman (or at least for me), this is harder than it sounds. Firstly, in England we do not go to bars, we go to pubs. English Pubs are about as different to New York bars as you can get while still serving identical functions. In English Pubs, the only people that sit at the bar are weird alcoholic old men who want to harass the barmaids and maintain the smallest possible distance between themselves and the supply of beer. The only strangers you normally make eye contact with or talk to are the barmaids from whom you order your drinks and maybe the weird old alcoholic dude at the bar if he ambushes you and complains to you about immigrants, the weather, or some other issue that upsets him. (Perhaps mistaking you for the individual responsible for those matters?)

The outcome of this culture clash for me is that talking to strangers in bars seems like a highly unnatural undertaking. It wasn't entirely unheard of for me to initiate a conversation in an English pub with attractive stranger. However, a considerable amount of alcohol had usually been consumed beforehand. Then, after initiating flirtatious conversation with said stranger, I was often so surprised by my own brazenness that I quickly ran out of interesting words to say, and so aborted the chat up attempt to avoid further embarrassment. For my confidence level when I first moved to New York, meeting girls in bars was only really an option if other friends were to attend the bars with me so I could drink with them and not feel excessively self-conscious. Unfortunately "other friends" were somewhat sparse when I first moved to NYC, and none of them had much interest in serving as my wingman.

I have considered and invented a number of other woman-meeting strategies. Most of them remain untested (perhaps wisely), but I shall now reveal my number one secret best place to meet women in New York....

Drum roll...

The best place to meet women in New York is....

The Internet!

BOOM!

Embarrassed silence.

Ok, so perhaps this is not the most exciting of revelations, but it is thanks to online dating that I got dates with 38 different women in my first year of living in NYC. Admittedly many of these women I did not see more than once. Online dating has many advantages and disadvantages. It is fun meeting a bunch of people, many of whom you would otherwise be unlikely to cross paths with. However, I think there is something about the process of online dating that seems to inhibit the development of mutual "chemistry" and makes getting second dates, or building a lasting connection, that much more difficult.

That being said, it is an immutable law of mathematics that before one can get a second date, one must get a first date, so let's start there. Getting date one can also be challenging. To begin with, there are a bewildering array of dating websites to choose from. A key distinction between them is that some are free and some want to take your money.

I had already dabbled with online dating in England, driven on by the strong encouragement of an American friend and many lonely months writing my PhD thesis. I was initially not very convinced by the idea of meeting strangers from the internet, so I started with free online dating sites and I have still yet to use one that you actually pay for[11].

---

[11] Free dating sites make their money from adverts, often advertising other dating websites that you do have to pay for. Occasionally I have clicked some of the advertisements out of curiosity, they range from "Christian dating; meet your soul mate today!" to "Get laid tonight! These horny girls are hot for you right now!". It's safe to say that if an advertisement looks too good to be true on the internet, it probably is. I once signed up for a free account with a supposedly reputable dating site, and I was immediately bombarded with messages from extremely attractive women. However, to reply to these messages I had to pay the website money... My suspicions heightened I decided to set up a second free account with a different name and no picture, and I was immediately bombarded with messages from the same women. Either these are real girls that spend all of their lives enthusiastically messaging new members of the site, or computer programs designed to trick you into falling for them so some real person somewhere gets to take your money. Anyway I have stuck to free websites that don't trick me into trying to chat up computer

Once you have chosen your dating site, written your profile, and uploaded a few suitably attractive photos, (always worth getting second opinions from friends at this point), you then have to try and get yourself a date. It is well documented that it is much harder for guys to get dates online than girls. Online dating is also taken less seriously than 'real life' dating, and so the odds are very high that your carefully thought out message will be greeted with a wall of silence. This can be disheartening, especially when you're just starting the online thing, I certainly gave up on online dating a few times in England before I got my first Internet date. Eventually though I realised finding a match in cyberspace required a very different mind-set than I'd previously adopted; I used to have a tendency to fixate my hopes, dreams, and fantasies on very select individuals. However, fixating on internet girls you have never met and may never meet is a bad plan, and so to avoid regularly weeping into my keyboard, mocked by the silent image of the online date who would clearly become my soul mate if only she'd reply to my witty icebreaker about cats, I had to get over this individual focus thing. Once I transitioned to a more "high throughput" approach of sending short but individualised messages to a large number of girls, and then forgetting their existence as soon as possible, I began to have more success getting dates through the interweb. (I also figured out a few more tricks that I may reveal later.)

Anyway I am getting ahead of myself with this talk of "tricks". When I first arrived in the big apple I was still an online dating novice, but insufficiently confident to chat up real life strangers, so the Internet was where I began my quest. I wasn't quite sure what I was looking for on this quest, but I was fairly

programs, and "ok cupid" has come to dominate my New York dating experiences.

sure it was something that A) I was lacking, and B) would come in female form[12].

...Oh and C) at some point there would be sex involved.

---

[12] Well if as this account develops we discover I am in fact interested in men rather than women that will be a surprise twist for both of us.

Chapter 2 - First date in New York

After a month or so adjusting to New York life and recovering from hurricane induced post-traumatic stress I decided it was high time I got myself some dates. I updated my location on a couple of online dating sites to "New York", which resulted in a flurry of messages. Well, if you count three as a flurry.

To begin with I exchanged a few messages with a couple of girls on a dating website called "Ivy Date". This site was aimed at ivy leaguers and Oxbridge students/alumni. I know, it sounds terrible already, but I figured as I was eligible I should take advantage of it. Of course I never paid them any money, so I was limited to replying to the messages sent to me, or just sending creepy looking smiley faces to girls I liked.

I found myself in two conversations on this site. One was with a teacher in the upper west side and one was with a medical student out in Long Island. The conversation with the teacher seemed to go well, and we started arranging to meet up, until suddenly her profile disappeared and all record of our conversations vanished. This was odd, as she definitely didn't seem like a robot, or a figment of my imagination, but whatever reality she existed in it was now separate from my own.

Unperturbed by vanishing date number one, I setup a date with the medic from Long Island. We arranged to meet one Sunday afternoon for coffee. The location was set as the Ost cafe in the East Village.

This being my first New York date I was a little nervous, especially since this was probably my first coffee date ever and I wasn't sure of my ability to make conversation without the help of alcohol as a social lubricant. I avoided eating lunch to reduce the risk of any sudden nausea attacks. I dressed myself in my coolest looking jeans and least creased collared shirt, and opted for the slightly tatty and less insulated black coat over my giant red skiing jacket[13]. Before leaving my apartment I made my bed look vaguely presentable, just in case this date was so wildly attracted to me that after consuming a single cup of coffee she wanted to bundle me into the nearest cab and race full tilt back to my apartment so as to make sweet and aggressive love on the nearest soft furnishing. Of course, a messy bed could completely derail this fantasy, so to plan for this optimistic eventuality the bed was duly adjusted. I then left my apartment, locked the door behind me, and marched off down first avenue to meet my fate.

I was about 10 minutes early for my fate. Fortunately, Ost coffee had clearly anticipated chicken-shit Englishman who don't know what to do when arriving early for a date, and had helpfully provided a bench outside on which to sit. At this stage of my dating career I was unsure of the etiquette for waiting on a date to arrive. Waiting outside has several advantages. Firstly, you don't have to look like a weirdo sitting alone in a bar or coffee shop (I had yet to appreciate that this is normal New York behaviour). Secondly, you don't have to deal with "service professionals" solo and can wait to rely on the social expertise of whoever you are with to navigate you through the diplomatic minefield of ordering a beverage. Thirdly, if you or your date decides the place you chose off the Internet is actually terrible, you can go find somewhere less terrible, and you are not trapped by an already purchased drink investment.

Unfortunately, outweighing all of these advantages is the significant disadvantage that waiting outside on the sidewalk

---

[13] Yes I needed better clothes, but my pay cheque was delayed by hurricane Sandy... and I hate shopping.

makes you look like a loser. Especially if you don't even have a smartphone to fiddle with and are forced to stand there staring into space, or freaking out passers-by who you stare at when mistaking them for your date.

My assessment is that cool people wait for dates inside an establishment, perhaps having already purchased their beverage. Then if they are sufficiently confident in the execution of the sitting and drinking, the bar or coffee shop becomes "their" territory, giving them the upper hand in the game of dating and seduction.

At this stage of my dating career, however, I was not one of those cool "waiting inside" people, so I sat on my bench and pretended I was doing things with my shitty flip phone[14]. The autumn sun was nice though, and kept me warm despite the chilly November air.

Fortunately, not long after our scheduled meeting time, a girl appeared who looked suspiciously like the person I had been talking to on the internet.
"Jenna?" I asked
"Yes, you must be Timmy!"
"Yes, nice to meet you!"

At this stage of a date some kind of physical greeting is often customary, but different people have different expectations, which can quickly lead to awkwardness. At first it seemed to me to be a little bit strange to hug or kiss a stranger who you are just meeting in the flesh for the very first time, and while I am fine with physical contact, it's not something I really grew up with a lot of[15].

---

[14] I think the only time someone looked cool with that model of phone is when Walter White broke one in half in Breaking Bad...

I was uncertain what to do when this kind-of-short-and-kind-of-cute-girl came to a halt in front of me as I stood up to meet her. For the briefest moment we stood there face to face, the autumn sun illuminating a friendly smile on her face. Should I go for a friendly hug? Or European style cheek kiss? Perhaps a handshake? Ok, clearly a handshake would be weird. I glossed over my indecision with action.

"Shall we go in?" I said, turning towards the entrance behind me.
"Sure!"

She had a cheerful American voice, although "American" perhaps doesn't narrow it down much. Her family was from Long Island but she lacked some of the harshness you might associate with a Long Island accent.

I ordered a black tea and she got some sort of complicated sounding coffee (almost all coffee's sound complicated to me). She started to fumble for her purse.
"I've got this, don't worry," I said.
"Oh are you sure?"
"Yeah, no worries!"
"Thanks!"[16]

I can't remember if I put a buck in the tip jar, I'd like to think I did, but it's possible it didn't even cross my unconditioned English mind to tip someone who just dispensed a hot

---

[15] My dad still gets confused every time I try to hug him (we normally end up in some kind of weird half hug, half handshake situation instead).
[16] I'll save you an overwrought discussion on the etiquette of paying for things on dates for now... but yeah, I bought her coffee. Go me.

beverage, handed it to me across a counter, and half smiled. If I forgot to tip though, Jenna didn't seem to notice.

We found seats on the high stools at the thin table running along the window, with a good view of the street and various East Village passers-by. There was another guy further along the table who was wearing large ear-enshrouding headphones and diligently inspecting Facebook, oblivious to the first date nervousness unfolding to his right.

And then we chatted.

We talked about many things; why she wanted to be a doctor, what my research was about, how annoying Hurricane Sandy was, how Long Island had lots of nice green estates you can cycle around and was great for escaping the city, how she went to Yale and moved back with her mum as the cheapest living option, etc etc. I was pleasantly amazed at my own ability to make sustained conversation while sober with a nice girl who I'd only just met.

Back in Oxford it had seemed like alcoholic intoxication was some kind of prerequisite for finding romance. By and large, the English seem to have this complicated relationship with their emotions. We try our best not to show any sign of having them at all for 90% of the time, and then for the other 10% we get as drunk as possible and try and express alllll the emotions in one garbled mass of drunken debauchery. Then the next day we pretend that we can't remember any of it... and that we have no idea where all those road signs in the kitchen came from... or why there is a dead traffic warden in the bathtub.

You see, the English have figured out that, at least in England, alcohol can be used as an excuse that will get people to forgive otherwise unforgivable behaviour. Many Brits seem to buy into the dubious assumption that person X can be transmutated into a fundamentally different person Y by the addition of booze. Clear evidence may then be obtained that (person X + booze) = (a massive dick), but yet person X and their supporters get to legitimately claim that all their asshattery is solely the product of the booze variable in the equation. I'm very unconvinced by this line of reasoning. I have no doubt alcohol relaxes ones impulse control but those impulses still have to come from some twisted recess of person X's actual brain in the first place[17].

Losing a little bit of impulse control is definitely an advantage when trying to 'get it on' with a girl. Without alcohol, the 'English' as a genetic entity probably would have gone extinct centuries ago, and Oxford students would have nothing to do except study and have obscure academic arguments with each other. (Although I'm sure if given enough time they'd develop plenty of other destructive habits to deal with the ever-present fear of failure). Oxford is also predominantly a collection of nerds of one form or another, and as nerds have the tendency to overthink things and lack random social skills, this makes them especially reliant on liquor for expressing feelings of attraction. I was no exception as a student, and for a long time even trying to kiss a girl that I fancied seemed like the ultimate emotional gamble; completely unthinkable unless blotto.

However, despite the lack of social lubricant on my date with Jenna we managed to navigate around any awkward silences and I don't think I made too many weird or disturbing comments... at least not that I was aware of. Although I soon

---

[17] I'm not usually someone who acts like a dick when drunk... A tit maybe; I get louder (and arguably funnier) for a while, then as I get really drunk I get quiet and even more introspective than usual, which is when I know it's time to go and sleep before I fall over.

realised that my earlier bed cover adjustments were definitely over optimistic for a coffee date.

I did veer into slightly dangerous conversation territory at one point. While talking about her Jewish background and I asked, "What's your take on Israel?"... I don't normally make date questions sound like part of a lie detector test run by Mossad, but at that time Israel and Gaza were engaged in one of their little contretemps, and I thought it was a legitimate current event worthy of discussion. Admittedly "What's your take on Israel?" was a poorly framed question, to which she gave a suitably diplomatic answer. However, there was a definite cooling of the tone.

Having steered the conversation away from politics we chatted for a while longer, hot drinks long exhausted. My fancy nylon tea bag lay stranded at the bottom of my cup, its herbaceous contents drained of their tasty alkaloids, and, after a little while, I began to feel awkward that we were taking up much sought after sitting space in this busy coffee shop.

"When are you meeting your friend?" I asked. This seemed to precipitate the end of the date.
"Yeah, soon. I should get going actually!"

We got our coats and I walked her to the L subway stop. We exchanged a quick hug and I said something like, "Let's do this again sometime!"
"Sure!" she replied, "Bye for now!"
"Bye, have fun with your friend!" I called after her as she sunk down the subway stairs. The green metal work of the subway entrance severed our connection as I continued to walk along the pavement.

Those brief snatches of movement I caught between the subway railings were the last glimpses I ever saw of her. I messaged her on Ivy Date later that evening.

"*Hey, it was great chatting today! Did you have a good afternoon? I got my paper written so I'm going to relax and sort through some photos! Hope psych goes well, and let me know when you're next in town :-)*"

A day or so later she replied: "*It was great meeting you! The first day of psych was rather hectic- I'm hoping for the best though. I'll let you know when I make my way back into the city and hope you have a good week!*"

While it's possible she has not returned to Manhattan for over a year, I think it's more likely that this was just one of those dates where both parties "like" each other but don't really pick up on the spark that makes them start to "LIKE" each other.

Still, I met a girl, and I didn't embarrass myself too much. I'll chalk it up as a win!

II

"So, how are you still single after all those dates?" T.G.O.M.D. asks, somewhat pointedly.

What I should probably do at this point is employ some carefully crafted spin-doctoring. I can already see the doubt creeping through her eyes, perhaps she's thinking, 'Did all those girls turn him down? He seems nice but perhaps there's something else wrong with him.'

Maybe the smartest choice would be employ a robust counter offensive and to make out that I'm just really picky and none of those girls met my standards, and I'm still single because I rejected them all and not vice-versa. I mean there were several dating situations where this was roughly applicable. However, making out that this was the sole reason for my singleness would mean painting over many other less favourable situations with a fairly sizeable brush.

Even now it seems I still haven't quite shaken a hazardous tendency for 'being myself' in dating situations. And so I start summarising for T.G.O.M.D. my analysis of New York dating culture, along with examples of my successes, examples of my failures, and how I've struggled to adapt to the scene. All the while I continue to maintain a potentially foolhardy adherence to the truth.

...

"Yeah, I guess dating here can be pretty tough," she says, after my summary has concluded.

And now I'm wondering if answering truthfully was a big mistake. Will I soon be ill-advisedly explaining why I'm still single to a different girl, in a different bar, with a different choice of anecdotes? Might this interaction with T.G.O.M.D. become my new example of a time I failed at dating when I really wanted to win?

Chapter 3 - Tater Tots and Teeth

After a brief jaunt home for Christmas I returned to New York with a renewed enthusiasm for getting online dates. Equipped with a newly minted Okcupid account I vigorously set about messaging every attractive and interesting sounding girl to whom I could think of something witty to say. None of them replied of course, probably because I just messaged the really attractive and interesting girls who were already inundated with messages from wittier and more attractive fellows than myself.

A few messages did trickle into my inbox, mostly from girls who, without wishing to reveal the true depth of my shallowness, were a little hard on the eye. Initially I thought I should probably reply to some of these messages, as although I didn't want to consider intimate acts with the senders, they often seemed like nice people, deserving of some sort of response to their outreached hand of human contact. After all, when I started the online messaging thing I would have always preferred some kind of polite negative answer than the open-ended silences that comprised the average response. I'm pretty sure someone once gave the sage and socially conscious advice, "Do unto others as you would have them do unto you!"

This, however, is New York, where a more appropriate piece of advice might be, "Do unto others what they're probably going to do to you, but do it faster, before they get the chance! (Plus don't forget to weight the body before dumping it in the river)."

Anyway, after a few attempts at polite reply, I just let the messages sit and fester, expediting my guilt with thoughts such as, "I don't want to lead them on and waste their time", or "This is what girls do to me all the time, it must just be how it works!"

With some patience, I got into a couple of conversations with more promising matches. A girl called Susie messaged me, and it seemed like we shared some genuinely similar interests. She worked in science publishing, liked arty movies, and generally seemed to project cheerfulness and enthusiasm in her messages. She looked nice too, and so after exchanging some friendly banter we agreed to meet up at a bar in the Lower East Side one Wednesday evening.

The evening started with me getting on a bus. It was probably only my second bus ride in New York, but I miraculously got on one going in the right direction and it deposited me on Allen Street with plenty of time to spare[18]. It was January. In

---

[18] According to Google maps, bus was the quickest way for me to navigate to this part of town. Some Americans from a certain background seem to have this thing against buses, which I suspect might based on a prejudice that poor people ride buses. However, these same Americans will happily ride the subway... (well maybe not happily, but they'll ride the subway with a look of blank resignation at least)... despite the fact the subway costs the same as a bus, and contains pretty much the same poor people that are on the bus, but rammed into even closer proximity. I am a proud rider of NYC buses... sure I hate them, but I like to think I am devoid of class related bus prejudices. Buses really do suck though. To begin with they never turn up. Like ever. And then there are the "Special bus services" (SBS) that look as if they're going to stop, but instead just sail past you... laughing. Even when a bus finally does arrive it then takes forever to move anywhere, because traffic in New York is horrible. If you ever find yourself contemplating taking a cross town bus during rush hour I recommend either walking, staying home, or killing yourself immediately. It also takes forever because Americans seem to be allergic to walking anywhere, and keep pressing the stop button so the bus has to come to a halt every couple of blocks. We then must wait impatiently while several old ladies get stuck in some kind of war over who can get off the bus slowest and obstruct the largest possible area

other words, it was bloody cold. I was not waiting outside the bar for my date in this weather and so it was time to practise my sitting alone at the bar technique. Fortunately, it wasn't too busy so I found two stools and put my coat on one and my butt on the other. Eventually I managed to get the attention of the surly looking bar keeper (despite the forest of beer taps in front of me), and ordered a suitably foreign yet tasty sounding ale[19].

Having text my date to inform her I was sitting at the bar, lest there be some hilarious yet unfortunate mix up where she waited outdoors while I sat there gormlessly, I sipped my beer and surveyed the room. A few guys drinking at the bar, a couple of small groups at the tables, maybe a date going on in the corner, generally a nice quiet and relaxed vibe. I sat on my bar stool trying to look natural and relaxed. I thought about what I should think about to remain natural and relaxed. 'This isn't a big deal,' I thought, 'I'm talking to other girls on the Internet, if this doesn't work out it will just be good practice... and she does science things, we can talk about science things... Man I hope we don't just talk about science things... That would be really boring...'

Before I ran out of internal dialogue[20] Susie came through the door. I could tell instantly that it was her. The frizzy hair was a giveaway, along with the fact she was clearly looking around trying to locate me. The face seemed right too, although people never quite look the same as their photos when transposed into the three animated dimensions of real life.

---

with their old person baggage.
[19] Bearing in mind "Goose Island" and "magic hat" all sounded exotic at this point of my New York experience.
[20] I don't know if I've ever actually ever run out of internal dialogue...

I stood up from my stool to greet her and she spotted me straight away.

"You must be Timmy!" she said
"That's me! Susie I take it?"
"Yes, nice to actually meet you!"

As I was standing I went for a greeting hug. She reciprocated and we seemed to pull it off without any awkwardness. She was wearing one of those big black puffer jackets that compressed a lot on hugging, expelling the cold air trapped inside.

"You too!" I said mid hug, then pulled back. "What can I get you to drink? I'm afraid I've already made a start," indicating my quarter empty beer glass sitting on the bar.

"Well they do have a lot of nice beers here. Let's see..."

A couple of beers later and the conversation was in full swing. We'd talked about her job, science, my research, New York, Brooklyn, Hurricane Sandy, and how various TV shows were awesome.
"So how long have you been doing this Okcupid thing?" I asked nonchalantly.
"Well I first tried it a year or so ago... in fact that's how I met my ex-boyfriend!"
"Oh yeah? It does sometimes work then! How long did that go on for?"
"About five, six months. Yeah we got on pretty well for a while, but then I found out he was into some pretty weird stuff in the bedroom."
"Oh yeah?" I said, making a mental note not to bring up any of the weird stuff I was into in the bedroom.
"Yeah... no... you don't want to know!"
I totally did want to know.

"Yeah... I was not into that!" she drifted off.
I laughed and let it drop.
"So have you been on any other weird dates lately?"

Several beers in and my bladder was getting distractingly uncomfortable but I didn't want to break the conversation and held on.
Fortunately she blinked first and said,
"Excuse me a second I need to use the restroom!"
"Good Idea, I might follow you."
I realised that sentence was open to misinterpretation as I was saying it, and hastily finished it with:
"...after you come back!"

I seemed to get away with that nonsensical string of words.

Once our bladders were no longer the focus of our attention we decided to get another round.
"Do you feel like some food?" she asked. "I'm kind of hungry."
I felt sufficiently relaxed by both the alcohol and the company that I wasn't afraid of having any nausea attacks.
"Sure. I could go for a snack or something. What's good here?"
Her: "Maybe we could get some tater tots to share?"
Me: "I have no idea what those are."
"What? Really? You've never had tater tots?"
"Nope. We don't have those in England. Can I hazard a guess that potatoes are involved?"
"So, they're kind of like hash browns... but little balls of potato and onion."
"Well that sounds good. Let's get some of those!"

This was a good decision. Tater tots are another great example of unhealthy food invented by America. Somehow it feels like they were originally designed for children but are now voraciously devoured by American grown-ups everywhere. And with good reason; they go especially well with salt and beer.

After beer number three, my memory of our conversation gets a little hazy, but at some point we decided it was time to stop drinking and go to our respective homes. Stepping outside, the cold enveloped us. We crossed Allen Street on the white walk sign.

"Well I should head this way to get the bus," I indicated north, "Which way are you going?"
"I'm getting the subway back to Brooklyn which is this way," she said, indicating east.
"Well it was great meeting you!"
"You too."
A few seconds later we were kissing. I think she must have initiated it, or at least I don't remember moving in for it on purpose. I definitely wasn't a pro kisser then[21], but this smooch session surprised me with its intensity. There were was all kinds of tongue, lip, and teeth contact going on. It probably wasn't particularly elegant to an outside observer, but it was fun to experience first-hand. My hands were pressing into the back of her puffer jacket. Then as quickly as the kissing started it stopped again.

"Well! You have my number!" she said, starting to walk backwards in an easterly direction.
"Yup! Let's do something again soon!" I waved after her.

I felt good as I started to walk up towards the bus stop. This was partly down to all the beer and tater tots inside me, but it had also been quite a while since I had kissed anybody, and it was just the confidence boost I needed.

---

[21] I can't claim to have improved much with experience either.

To my eternal shame I started humming the tune to Katy Perry's "I kissed a girl and I liked it!" as I stuck my chin down into my scarf for warmth.

There was no bus in sight when I reached the stop, so I decided to walk up a bit further. I ended up walking the whole way home. The East Village was still a buzz as I headed north. People were going in and out of Laundromats. Some kids with NY baseball caps were shambling along the street smelling of weed. In one restaurant window, a tired looking waiter was serving a couple of patrons a late night curry. In another, two ladies were on the tail end of a bottle of red and gossiping with expressive hand gestures. A few bars blurted out loud music while bored looking bouncers guarded the doors. The city just felt alive, and so did I.

"I kissed a girl just to try it, I hope my boyfriend don't mind it..."

*

I had a second date with Susie. We ate nachos in a Chelsea pub and then went to see "silver linings play book", which is the perfect date movie with romance and a little bit of edge (well kind of). I think we both had a nice time, but in the soberer light of the movie theatre she perhaps wasn't quite as attractive and interesting as I had remembered from that first date. Afterwards we kissed on the side-walk outside the cinema but that drunken passion had been lost. We seemed to mutually stop texting each other after that[22].

---

[22] Although I have since been informed that apparently it's the guy's job to text first, unfortunately a lot of the time no one tells us guys these things!

She was a nice person, even if she wasn't really my type. I'd have happily stayed friends. However, establishing a friendship after meeting through online dating seemed a bit weird at the time, so I just let it fizzle out. Besides, other Okcupid things had started to take off, and I'm pretty sure it was Plato who said that "A bird in the hand is way less exciting than all those chicks hanging out in that bush over there."

Chapter 4 - Promise you'll call me!

This is a story about how I got laid one time. It might not be a very good story, although I think there are a few funny bits, but anyway I totally get laid at the end of it. I may have forgotten a lot of the details of the story as well, so I might just make some up, but the getting laid bit I will not make up, because it actually happened... like for real!

It began, like all the best love stories, with a conversation about Infinite Jest over the Internet. For those unfamiliar with Infinite Jest, it is a book written by David Foster Wallace, who is like a titan of modern literature (or post-modern literature or something... I dunno, look him up on Wikipedia). In summary, it is the kind of book that literary and philosophical types get excited over, probably because it is weird, depressing, darkly funny, and long[23]. I am not really a literary or philosophical type but I do occasionally like reading vaguely pretentious things that my philosophical and literary friends suggest. As it was one of the few books I had read recently and could talk about if pressed, I had listed it on my profile under the "favourite books, movies etc." section. This decision resulted in me receiving a message from a girl called Jessica, which resulted in a conversation, which resulted in a date, which resulted in me getting laid... (Did I mention that already?)

It was one of those online conversations where we'd sporadically send each other excessively long messages with sizeable chunks of life story, book analysis, comments on how New York is crazy etc etc. Basically, we were conducting several threads of conversation simultaneously, like they did in the good old days when people sent real letters on paper, and

---

[23] I seriously recommend it... if you like that sort of thing.

actually had time to write them. Jessica was a literary type who had studied English literature at an all-girls college, spent some time in Europe, and was now prostituting her literary talents to write copy for a vendor of women's undergarments.

Eventually we arranged to meet one Friday in the East Village, I suggested a bar called St Dymphna's as it was one of the limited places I had prior knowledge of. It was still January and it was still bloody freezing. My wardrobe had expanded since Christmas to include a smart coat worthy of dating in New York. However, this coat was nowhere near as warm as my bright red ski jacket. I was tempted to go for the bright red option but the smart blue coat won out when I realised I could combine it with a super thick wool sweater to keep out the perishing cold.

As I walked down First Avenue, the remnants of Friday evening rush hour traffic were still flooding past me, heading in the other direction. The headlights of passing yellow cabs illuminated the thick plumes of steam escaping from the drain covers and condensing in the cold night air. A typical New York evening.

I reached St Dymphna's a few minutes before we were scheduled to meet. The noise of many chattering voices spilled out onto the street and the door was surrounded by a huddle of smokers. It was busy. Perhaps this wasn't going to be the ideal spot for a quiet drink and getting-to-know-you chat. I wandered through the door to see the bar en-swathed by an impenetrable mass of bodies. There standing behind this mass was a girl in a red dress. We exchanged glances. She looked away. I did the same. Then after a few seconds, we both seemed to decide 'well that could be my date', and we looked back at each other.

"Hi, is it Jessica?"

"Yes."

"Hi nice to meet you, I'm Timmy."

"I guessed!"

"Do you want to get a drink here or do you want to go somewhere quieter?"

"What?"

"Shall we go somewhere quieter?" I shouted, "I know a place around the corner..."

"Okay. Sure."

We stepped back out into the cold and started walking along the sidewalk. Walking along a sidewalk wasn't quite the opening date activity I was used to and it took me a few moments to strike up conversation.

"It's pretty cold huh?"

"Yeah, they say it's going to snow soon."

After this shaky start we kept chatting as we walked the couple of blocks to Tile Bar. This bar had a more relaxed divey atmosphere than your typical East Village place, and generally older patrons. Perhaps not the most romantic of settings, but at least we could hear each other talk. I spotted two empty stools at the end of the bar where we made ourselves comfortable. Conversation flowed more smoothly with beers in hand. We talked about travelling. She'd done a creative writing course in the UK and also spent a year living and teaching in the Swiss countryside. I told her about my own travels, childhood camping holidays in various parts of Europe, and my incompetence with languages.

Her voice was lower than I had expected, with a slightly disconsolate tone, but quite easy to listen to. At least it wasn't as deep and depressing as some voices I've encountered. Jessica wasn't bad looking either. I tried to remember to make frequent eye contact. She was only slightly shorter than me, thin and well served by her red dress. Her face might not have resembled the standard definition of beauty that we are conditioned to by Hollywood movie stars and super models, but it still had its own unique attractive quality.

Somehow we got onto the subject of accommodation. This was a bad idea as she clearly needed to vent on the issue. A would-be-flatmate had dropped out on her at the last minute and had left her on a desperate hunt for someone to share her apartment with so she could afford to pay rent. This was clearly weighing heavily on her mind and I remember sitting there thinking 'Wow, we have really been talking about the same thing for a surprisingly long time.' However, rather than saying, "Yeah, this conversation just got really boring, can we talk about something interesting again now?" I just kept nodding and saying, "Yeaaah, that's really annoying!" at the appropriate moments. Eventually we got back onto more compelling conversation, TV shows, movies, feminism, how she juggled her feminist principles and writing copy for a lingerie company, etc. Strangely enough I don't think we got around to talking about Infinite Jest once that whole evening.

A couple of beers down and she said she had better be getting back to Brooklyn. It wasn't too late but it wasn't too early either. She insisted on "going Dutch" and splitting the bill, which experience has now taught me is something of a rarity in New York.

Outside the bar, my destination was north and hers was south. I offered to walk her to the Subway as I started to walk south with her.
"Oh no, I'll be fine," she said.
"You sure? I should probably head the other way then."
"Oh, ok."

We paused walking.
"Well it was nice meeting you!"
I hesitated a few seconds too long. She took a backwards step south. Then I opened my arms and went in for the hug... but I kept my face in the way of hers.

I kissed her. She kissed me back. There was something frantic about this kiss, no excessive tongue or teeth involvement, but a hurried intensity of lips pressed tightly together, moving as one.

...it broke for a second, she went to pull back, but we kissed again.

"Ok. Well. Call me!" she said, turning away sharply and walking south with surprising speed. She had the essence of someone who needed to get somewhere fast, even though it was like 11pm on a Friday night. I can only speculate she had a carriage to get to before it turned into a pumpkin.

"Will do!" I called after her.

I walked north, my heart beating a little faster.

There was a bus sitting at the stop. I got on board. Then I was perplexed to find there was nowhere to put my metro card, so I waved it at the driver.
"Mnnyou hve ta pay nnat Mahhchhin!" he said angrily.
"I'm sorry?"
He pointed off the bus, aggressively jabbing his finger.
That much I understood. I got off the bus, somewhat hurt by this interaction. This was the second time this had happened. What was with these mystery buses that refuse to let you on board[24]?

I continued walking up First Avenue as the bus closed its doors with a hiss and sped past me. 'Fine,' I thought, 'I'll just keep my $2.50 and walk! See how you like that Mr MTA man!'

*

After the first date we continued to exchange texts. Jessica found a flatmate that weekend (just in case you were wondering). We agreed to meet up again that Tuesday at a bar called The Room down on Sullivan Street. This time I beat Jessica to the bar, though it took me a little while to figure out how to get inside. There was a thick black curtain enshrouding the front door that created the strange sensation that I was entering some kind of forbidden or secret place, so instead of using the door I first tried to push open the big windows next to it.

Once I had figured out how to get into the bar, I surveyed the dingy interior in case Jessica was hiding somewhere. This place definitely had a romantic and sultry vibe, with candles, old wood finishings, and various discrete nooks and crannies to sit in and whisper sweet something's in your date's ear.

Nooks and crannies do make it harder to locate a date though, and I disturbed one couples private moment when I poked my head around the wrong corner.

Then I got a text from Jessica. "*I'm on my way!*"

---

[24] I learnt soon after that these were "Special Bus Service buses" where you have to put your card in a machine on the street first which gave you a little scrap of paper that you wave at the driver instead. This is not a complex operation, but is still confusing to an inebriated Englishman...

Well that settled that. She turned up shortly after and we got chatting again, occasionally repeating little bits of conversation from the previous Friday, but nothing too boring. We talked about family and siblings. She had a brother who was a professional mime artist[25] and had some complex open relationship with his kinky fiancée. This might have been a good opportunity to discuss my own kinky interests but I didn't want to spook this girl whom I seemed to be building a good rapport with.

After a couple of drinks we decided it was time to get some food. I think I'd explained my tendency towards occasional bouts of nausea but I felt relaxed with Jessica. We spent a little while stumbling around Sullivan St. looking for a place she remembered that turned out to be closed down, and then we ended up in some Thai place instead. There were elegant fairy lights hanging down from the ceiling and we had a six person table all to ourselves. I ate something with noodles and shrimps in, and it was good. That's the extent of my memory. Once we had eaten our fill I took the plunge.

"How are you feeling?" I asked.
"Good. Full!"
"Yeah, me too! Do you fancy getting another drink somewhere? Or... if you like... we could go back to my place? I have wine and stuff?"
"Sure. Let's go to your place."
"Cool! I'm not too far up the 6."

My Internal Dialogue:

---

[25] Ok he wasn't really, but almost as ridiculous sounding

'BOOM!! A GIRL'S COMING BACK TOO MY PLACE!!!!! A GIRL'S COMING BACK TOO MY PLACE!!! OOOHHH YEAAAAH!!! A GIRL IS COMING BACK TO MY PLACE!!'

Also my place was totally not on her way back to Brooklyn.

We navigated our way through the Bleeker street subway station and waited on the 6 platform side by side. The physical contact barrier remained unbroken. There was no holding hands or gentle petting. During a quiet pause in conversation, we both looked at each other and smiled, before looking away again. Of all our interactions, that image of her smiling on the subway platform stands out somehow. Maybe it was the slightly drunken glow we both gave off, or maybe it was something else, but either way it felt good to be alive in that moment.

Back in my apartment we chatted for a while. We sat close together on my couch. I started to think it was well past the time I should have made a move. She was lying back into the couch, while I was sitting up a bit looking down at her slightly. In a brief conversation lull I started to move my face towards hers. However, just as I got to the critical distance where it was clearly apparent I was going for the kiss, she started talking again.

And she kept talking.

I held my position... hovering over her face.

Her mouth continued to be occupied making words.

I replied with the occasional "Yeah" and "Mmmhmm", and relevant conversational responses.

She talked some more.

"Mmmhmm," I said. I couldn't back down now, I might not get the balls to move my face this close to her face again, and she wasn't trying to move away. She kept making eye contact, but she also kept talking.

'Is it rude to kiss someone while they're still talking?' I thought to myself.

My left arm was supporting quite a lot of my weight while I held this face hovering position... it was starting to ache and twitch a little...

She kept talking

"Yeah, I know what you mean," I said.

It seemed like we had been in this position since the dawn of time. The universe just existed in a steady state where she talked for eternity while I hovered in an uncomfortable position ad infinitum.

For a second she wasn't talking. She looked away into the distance, perhaps trying to think of something else to talk about. She looked back at me. I kissed her.

After a little while getting bolder with our kissing I began rubbing her thigh with my hand. Gently she put a hand on my chest and broke off kissing.

"Promise you'll call me ok? I don't want you to be one of those guys that just sleeps with me and never calls again, because that sucks!"

There was an intensity in her face and tone of voice that threw me for a minute.

I pulled back a little further.

Me: "Of course!... I mean I don't think I've ever not called someone... I mean I don't know what I'm looking for right now. I... Well I'm not sure if I'm ready for anything long term just yet..."
Her: "No. Me neither."
Me: "...But yes of course I'll call you! Or at least text you, I don't really like calling people..."
Her: "Ok. Good."

I started kissing her again.

While we kissed I began running my hand up and down her thigh, exploring my way towards the button of her jeans. Some awkward stripping ensued as my hands explored further... Multitasking fingering and taking off clothes is not easy to do gracefully, but then I wanted to keep her excited...
"Let's move over to the bed shall we?" I said[26].
"Sure," she replied, and I led her by the hand then flung back the duvet with an over-excited flourish.

She lay back amongst the pillows as I pulled her pants off over her knees. I began kissing my way up her inner thigh until I reached its terminus, and then I explored what was above that with my tongue. It had been some time since I had had that taste in my mouth, and it seemed a bit stronger than I remembered. I continued the tongue exploration for a little while so as not to reveal I was having a slightly grossed out

---

[26] I lived in a studio. It didn't have anything as fancy as a "bedroom".

moment. Then I slowly relocated my mouth downwards again, kissing her other thigh[27].

"You have condoms right?" she asked.
"Of course!" I said

Taking this as a signal to attenuate the foreplay I scrabbled for my bedside drawer. I tried to tear off a condom from the strip, but instead tore open the condom packet next to it, so I just used that one instead. I went to put it on... wrong way round... quick correction, hopefully before she noticed....

Sex commenced in the missionary position.... From the noises she was making it seemed to be hitting the spot... "Oh!... Oh god!... Fuck!...yes!..... oh careful...Oh...Oh... Oh god, Timmy!!"

I was enjoying myself too, although most of my dialogue was internal. It went something along the lines of:

'I'm having sex in with an American girl in New York!
I'm having sex with an American girl in New York!
I'm having sex with a girl in New York!
I'm having sex with a girl!
We're having sex in my bed and everything!
Shit that was a pretty intense noise she just made... Did she just orgasm?... She seems to be going slower now... maybe she orgasmed... I can't tell.... Maybe I should keep going for a while to make sure... I'm quite close myself though... Shit I hope she's not the overly clingy type... she scared me a bit with that "promise you'll call me" thing... Maybe if I give her multiple orgasms she won't leave me alone....Wow I don't normally get

---

[27] For the ladies reading I want to be clear that performing cunnilingus is something I usually enjoy, I just had a moment there!

close to orgasm this easily... Yeah I think she came back then right?... I'm gonna cum now... #@$$%$!

...

How long can I lie here with this condom on before it gets weird?'

*

We lay naked on my bed cuddling for a little while, although Jessica seemed distant somehow, as if she was mulling something over in her mind. Then she sat up on the edge of the bed and began fastening her bra.
"I should probably go," she said.
"Are you sure? You're welcome to stay the night."
"No, they'll give me soo much shit tomorrow if I turn up to work in the same clothes!"

It was coming up to 2am... it had gotten late with all that face hovering.
"Are you going to be ok getting back to Brooklyn?" I asked
"Yeah, I'll take a cab."

I also put on clothes and went down to wait on the street with her until a cab came. We shared a hurried kiss before she was whisked away in that yellow steel box. The cab turned left and went out of sight, leaving me in the deserted street with the cold making my hairs stand on end. I slowly took in a deep breath of the night air. Then I went back indoors.

*

The next day I messaged her as promised. I ended the text with:

"...maybe we can do something Sunday?"

Eventually she responded: "*Sorry, no, I don't think so. It's been nice getting to know you but I don't think this is going to work out. Good luck with everything.*"[28]

"*No worries, good luck with your stuff too!*" I replied

There were no worries because by this time I had begun seriously exploring dating strategy number two, and my New York dating experiences were about to get a lot more "interesting".

---

[28] This compounded my doubts about her orgasm and whether her experience of the sex was mediocre as intended, or just poor.

Chapter 5 - Getting dates strategy two - Be a kinky sex master!

Sex is pretty fun.

I gather that it's popular too.

However, just because something is fun doesn't mean it can't be improved upon.

I mostly have Okcupid to blame for my descent into widespread deviancy (well, aside from my own innate perversion that is), as in order to find dates with whom you share some common ground, Okcupid gets you to answer many multiple choice questions. Topics include; your political and religious beliefs, what kinds of food you eat, whether you like beards, how you feel about camping, etc etc. It also asks you a surprising number of questions about sex. These questions can range from the innocuous "Would you have sex before marriage?" to the less innocuous "Would you ever be prepared to cut someone during sexual play?"

When I first came across questions like "Would you rather be tied up or do the tying?"... I was a little surprised. At first I thought it best to skip these questions as A) I imagined a lot of nice dateable girls would be put off meeting a guy who has a penchant for either tying girls up or being tied down himself, and B) what if work colleagues/ future employers/ family members were to stumble across my Okcupid profile? I didn't know what would actually happen if information about my sexual fantasies escaped into the public domain, but it seemed likely that there would be negative consequences of some kind.

However, as I browsed through profiles, I noticed a large number of girls had answered a lot of these questions. I could only see their answers if I'd answered the questions myself, but if you answer enough questions on a certain topic, Okcupid creates a little bar chart graphing your "kinkiness" and "interest in sex" (amongst other, less interesting, personality ratings). In my endless flicking through online dating profiles, I came across quite a few nice, normal looking girls on Okcupid with very strong kinkiness ratings. This definitely caught my attention.

Even more unexpectedly, I came across various profiles set up by girls with the expressed purpose of finding kinky sex partners. I'd normally say that if something seems to be too good to true on the Internet, it probably is. However, these profiles really did seem genuine and not people out to sell sex. (Prostitutes must get enough business in NY without needing to resort to dating websites).

When I first saw these kinky profiles though, my reaction was "Oh no, I'm not interested in that."

...but then after a few minutes browsing... "Let's just take another look at that kinky girl with pictures in her underwear"...

..."Nah, that's definitely too good to be true... and besides I'm looking for more of an emotional connection than that..."

...Some more browsing, a few more messages sent to attractive chicks who never replied, and I found myself thinking, "... hmm I could totally go for some kinky sex right about now..."

So of course I eventually started messaging the girls with the kinky sex profiles too. I don't think I ever got replies from them at that point, perhaps because a nerdy English guy who hadn't answered any of Okcupid's sex questions wasn't exactly what they were looking for.

And so it came to pass that I decided to create a second, more anonymous, Okcupid account. There are several reasons I use to justify this, and which reason I lead with usually depends on the company I'm in. They are as follows:

1. I wanted to find out how other Okcupid members had answered various sex related questions without having to answer them on my normal profile and scaring off the sweet innocent types.
2. I wanted to experiment to see if it was possible to attract women primarily using sex as a lure.
3. I wanted to experiment with meeting people by sharing my most secret desires right at the start, in the hope that this would build better and more honest connections from the outset.
4. I wanted to find people to have awesome kinky sex with.

So I thought up a suitably cheesy profile name, set up my tripod and camera so as to take some pictures of myself without a shirt on, (tripod picture = way more respectable than a selfie snapped in a mirror). I cropped out my head to remain anonymous and then converted these headless torso pictures to black and white so they looked slightly classier.

Then it was time to write some words. Describing your own sexual desires in a way that sounds simultaneously appealing and non-threatening is a bit of a tricky balancing act. Especially when those desires involve BDSM.

Now I feel the time has come when I need to give you a little more detail on what my sexual interests actually are. In BDSM terminology some might consider me a "switch", which means someone who enjoys both the dominant and submissive roles. Originally, my fantasies were submissive in nature and it's hard to say when they first began. I haven't fully got to grips with the psychology of it (I'll ramble about this later), but I do know that I was tying myself up with dressing gown cords before I even figured out how to jerk off like a normal person.

For a long while these desires stayed private and reserved for 'alone time'. Then, when I was in my early twenties I met a girl who also had submissive interests of her own, and was bold enough to talk about them with me. Until that point I'd never really let myself consider dominating someone, but meeting a girl who was genuinely interested in submission turned my mind onto new fantasies of being in control, as they now felt somehow legitimised.

One reason I hadn't really dwelled on these fantasies before is that I imagined the 'Dom' or 'Top' mentality to be dangerously aligned with how I imagined the unstable mind-set of an abusive husband, rapist, or generally evil person. While I can't speak for everyone out there, my experience has been that these mind-sets are as separate from each other as oil and water. It might also be worth pointing out 'for the record' that, since I started exploring my dominant side, I have not felt the slightest bit inclined towards actually assaulting anybody. For me, a girl's consent to tie her up and cause her pain is the lynchpin that makes any given scenario erotic. There seems to be something in the exchange of power and trust involved that is crucial to the eroticism of BDSM, at least for me.

My instincts told me that if I wanted to get any significant interest in my kink profile on Okcupid I should advertise that I'm looking for girls to dominate rather than girls to submit to[29].

So I wrote a quick summary of my interests, stating quite clearly that I was looking for damsels interested in distress. From the 'looking for' options I selected 'short-term dating', 'long-term dating', 'casual sex', and 'new friends'. I made it clear that I considered myself a feminist and my desires weren't about degrading women, that I would never force anyone to do anything they weren't happy with, and that I could be thought of as a safe pair of hands to explore whatever fantasies a girl was secretly entertaining.

All the information I included was true, although I may have exaggerated my height to 5' 11 instead of 5' 10, and I left out most of the personal details that could give me away as a science geek[30].

I combined this spiel with the pictures of my torso, and then I released my new creation into the world. Putting my darkest sexual desires on the Internet got me a little excited, so I dealt with that. After flushing the tissues I switched off my computer and went to bed.

The next morning I checked my email. A few minutes later my brain exploded. Dear *'terrible-kinky-profile-username'* you have a new message from Ms-Melody[31]. I squinted at the attractive, if slightly pouty looking, thumbnail of Ms-Melody.

---

[29] Instinct based on my understanding that also that society primes many women for submission (probably) and the recent popularity of a reportedly terrible book that I have never read.

[30] Oh when I put "providing multiple orgasms" in the "I'm really good at" section this may have been based on a limited sample size... and the disclaimer "effects may vary from user to user" perhaps should have been added later.

[31] No, not a real username... at least not when I last checked!

Her other profile photos looked pretty attractive too, even if she didn't exactly look happy in any of them[32].

Her message read:

"I am quite interested in being dominated and the main thing that attracted me to you (or what I can see of you) is that you obviously know what you are doing, and understand the exchange of power is about trust etc... But I want to learn all about this, Id love to be your little slave ha"

"WAAAAAT?! THIS SHIT ACTUALLY WORKED?!?!" I said out loud... to an empty room...

After I had taken a moment to calm down, I showered. Then I went to work and resisted checking the account for the rest of the day. That evening I replied to Ms-Melody and our conversation carried on for the rest of the week. I don't think I had been that aroused by something on my computer screen that much since I first discovered porn on the Internet[33].

I told her various things I'd like to do to her. A couple of times she didn't reply for a while and I thought I might have scared her off, but she came back eventually, just blaming her quietness on being busy. I politely suggested that I wanted to chain her down, spank her, and drip hot candle wax all over her body while she was helpless to stop me. She seemed to react positively to this suggestion, and so I proposed that we meet.

---

[32] Her's was also a "normal" profile, not one of the casual sex ones I mentioned earlier.
[33] And damn that's a long time ago. It was back in the days of dial up modems, when it took an hour to download a 1 minute video, and everyone was naive about the curse of "Internet history".

This all seemed to be working far too well. However, at that point I had only been in New York a couple of months and I did not own either chains or candles, which somewhat limited my ability to realise this fantasy.

It was time for a trip to the hardware store!

*

I bought a nice big candle and some suitably pinchy clothes pegs without attracting anyone's suspicions. However, getting hold of chain was another matter.

Chain might be a controversial choice of BDSM restraint. It's less comfortable and less widely used than rope, and extra care is needed not to put too much pressure on any nerves in sensitive regions, such as around the back of the knees and front of the wrists. However, in my mind, there is something pleasantly permanent feeling about chains, as when combined with good padlocks and wrapped around a victim in the right way, there's really no getting out of them without a key or bolt cutters. Both the permanent feeling and uncomfortable nature of chains can add to their appeal, so long as you don't mind some suspicious chain shaped marks the next day.

Where possible, I like to test restraints and other tools on myself first, and I had happily been playing with chains for some time before I arrived in NY (of course, I've never explored complete self-restraint as it is both tricky and seems like a terrible idea!). Chains are also relatively quick to deploy, as snapping a padlock shut is quicker and easier than fumbling with knots and long lengths of rope. Anyway, to begin my New York adventures I decided to start with the chain.

However, buying chains from a hardware store can get a little awkward. I think there are very few innocent uses a guy in New York could have for several lengths of metal chain. Especially when he doesn't really look like a handyman. I invented an almost believable story though: First I wandered into the hardware store and surveyed the shelves. No sign of any chain. I sauntered casually up to this short guy who was standing around as if he worked there.

"Hi!" I said "I'm looking for a safe box, or some metal box that I can just chain to pipes or a radiator to keep documents and stuff in. Nothing that valuable."
"You wanna safe?"
"Yeah, or a metal box of some kind... and some chain to secure it with"
"Safes're over there. Chain is in the basement. Come get me when you're ready to get the chain. I'll need to take you down."
"Great thanks!"

I went off and made a show of inspecting the safes. They were all way heavier and more expensive than the sort of box I had in mind to cover my chain purchase. After a while I went back to the assistant at the counter where he was measuring out some aluminium pipe.

"You find what you want?"
"No, they're all too big, but I think I saw what I wanted online. I'll take some chain while I'm here though."
"Ok, one sec."

He led me to the basement, unlocking the cage like door at the bottom. He muttered something that sounded like a question.

"I'm sorry?" I said, but he ignored me and carried on into the basement, not saying anything else. Dusty shelves stretched off into the darkness sagging under the weight of piping, wood, and other construction materials.

"Mmhhmm," the store guy said to himself, again unprompted.

'Ok,' I thought to myself, 'I hope this dude isn't crazy and about to torture and murder me in the bottom of the hardware store... being tortured and murdered in a basement of a hardware store by a short guy who talks to himself isn't on my list of fantasies.'

"Chain... chain, chain, chain..." he said, "Shit where do we keep the chain?"
He looked up and down the shelves. I looked a bit too while making sure I stayed behind him with a clear path to the exit. Every now and then he grunted another "mhmm" or "yeah"
"Aha. Here we go," the dude said, pointing to a few spools of chain on a shelf under the stairs.
"What kinda size do you want?"
"Err I dunno, how much is it?"
"Oh it don't say... but it ain't expensive."
I pointed to a spool of lightweight but sturdy looking chain.
"That will do," I said, "Can I get two 6 foot lengths[34]?"

"K... so I'm like 5 foot" he said spooling out the chain and measuring it roughly against himself.
I nodded. He cut the chain.

"Mmhmm. Yeah that bitch is crazy!" he said.
"Sorry?" I said, really confused at this point.

---

[34] Two 6ft lengths weren't really enough, I ordered another 15 m off the internet a month or so later... It was much cheaper and less awkward!

He ignored my confusion and continued with "Yeah, her and Charlene were really going at it last night at Johnny's place." And while he was talking, he looked at me with a blank dismissive expression, as if he were talking to someone behind me.

Then I noticed the Bluetooth headphone he had in one ear.
"Oh, I seeee! Sorry!" I said, realising he wasn't crazy... just having a simultaneous conversation on his magic-ear-phone-device.

The shop assistant cut the second length of chain while continuing to talk to the ether about that mysterious "bitch who were crazy". He then led me out of the basement and handed the chain to the guy working the checkout.

The checkout guy then asked, "What number is this?"
"Oh... Shoot! Man I forgot to check, one sec..." Said the assistant guy, disappearing off back to the basement. I stood by the checkout counter. The checkout guy stood on the other side. The chains sat there in between us. I maintained the facial expression I like to call "polite English smiling face". I thought about telling the counter guy my story about how I needed to secure a metal box to protect some documents... but that I couldn't find a metal box... so I just bought some chain...

He didn't ask what I was buying chain for though, so I just stood there, smile affixed. Eventually the "assistant" guy returned and relayed a product number, (which could have been anything as far as I knew). Checkout guy entered the number into the machine. "That'll be 68 dollars" he said.

"68 dollars? What the fuck happened there? That dickhead over there said this stuff wasn't expensive!" I said... to myself... in my head... while handing over my debit card silently.

III

What is she thinking behind those eyes?

Her pupils are wide in the low light and we hold each other's gaze. 'Eyes are the window to the soul' said someone... Although this seems off the mark, because I know from basic biology that eyes are just a window to someone's retinas, which you only really want to look at if you're an ophthalmologist.

Still, what is it about her eyes?

Aside from iris colour, I think everyone's eyes are basically the same. People talk about eyes as if they are these tellingly descriptive things, 'you have kind eyes', 'you have beautiful eyes', etc etc. However, I bet you wouldn't have to put that many discombobulated eyes in a bowl before you lost track of which eyes belong to whom.

Perhaps it's their activity that really transfixes us; eyes betray our interest and intent as they move in our head, and we can't hide them except by blindfolding ourselves... or wearing sunglasses.

Bright dots of candle light flicker in the two glassy spheres recessed into the skull of T.G.O.M.D. as we try to inspect each other's retinas.

How long have we held eye contact now? I feel like I should stop, my own eyes may be betraying too much...

And yet I stare.

Chapter 6 - Close encounters of the casual and nervous kind.

Having foraged some rudimentary BDSM kit I tried to arrange to meet Ms-Melody in person. However, she was flighty and seemed more interested in texting than actually meeting in the flesh. Understandable perhaps, considering the nature of the game, but she wasn't the only person to show interest in my kinky profile.

I received a number of messages from girls of varying hotness (the message I got from the 40 year old woman who lived in Florida with her two kids took the prize for most awkward). I also messaged a few people myself, either girls who visited my kink profile of their own accord, or people who clearly displayed some compatible interests on their own page. Most of the time I would just send people normal messages, questions about themselves etc. I figured that all the stimulating information they could need was already on my profile and I wanted to avoid becoming one of 'those guys' who just go around sending inappropriate sexual propositions to girls (I've never actually met one of 'those guys', but I hear many reports).

One evening I noticed an attractive redhead inspecting my profile. Of course, I inspected hers right back. Noticing that she had a scientific streak I messaged her with a playful boast of "mad science skills".

She took the bait.

We talked a bit about psychology, and I confessed the experimental nature of my profile. I told her that I hoped that being open about my sexual interests from the outset would allow me to build better and more honest connections with people. We kept the conversation pretty clean to begin with and when I told her my name, she introduced herself as Emma. After a few messages I asked if she might actually like to see what my face looked like.

She replied: *"I'd love to see your face. Send whatever you want... anything I can reciprocate with?"*

"Reciprocate" was an exciting word to hear but I did my best to keep it together. I sent her a picture of me posing minus shirt but plus face, and in my response I calmly included the line:

"I'd be very interested in seeing more pictures of you... the more submissive and sexualised the better of course ;-)."[35]

That evening I returned to my inbox to find a message with an attached photograph. It was a mirror selfie showing Emma kneeling on the floor in a black negligee (with face carefully obscured by the positioning of the iPhone). No nudity, but more than enough to feed the imagination...

We began to discuss our sexual fantasies in more depth. She was most interested in the control aspect, imagining a scenario where she had no idea what was going to happen next, bound, blindfolded and generally physically dominated. She wasn't sure if she would buy into role playing and claimed not to have any real experience with BDSM. However, she was keen to hear what my imagination might come up with.

Asking me what my imagination can come up with is a risky business; I'm pretty good at inventing ideas that no one else

---

[35] What? You got a problem with the creepy winking face? The Semicolon, dash, and closed brackets keys have served me well thus far.

has thought of, but sometimes there are good reasons that no one has thought of them, or at least not expressed them out loud. A few scenarios were discussed. At one point I thought I scared her off when talking about chaining her up and shutting her away in a cardboard box with pre-cut air / access holes[36]. She got back to me eventually though, claiming just to have been ill.

I asked if she was ready to meet up, and she replied: *"...If we do meet up, which I am game for, my only request is that the first time be somewhere like a bar or something public - I'm new to this and have the requisite need to figure out if you'll sell my organs on the black market before we get down to it. That ok?"*

Me: *"I think figuring out whether someone is going to sell your organs before you let them dominate you is a thoroughly healthy instinct! You can choose the place, although you're not allowed to steal my organs either ok? :-)"* I replied.

Her: *"Glad we covered the "no organ stealing" rule. That's an important one. Sunday I'm fairly busy but Saturday afternoon I don't have much going on. Maybe a happy hour thing?"*

Eventually we arranged to meet at 5pm one Saturday at a bar called Session House near the Upper East Side. I walked the whole way there, not quite believing I was about to meet someone for casual sex off the Internet.

There was a layer of monotonous low cloud hanging over Midtown. It was also approaching twilight and you couldn't tell

---

[36] I had some furniture delivered... gotta do something fun with all those boxes!

whether the cloud was dark because it was going to rain, or because there wasn't much light in the first place. This created an eerie effect of not quite being day but not quite being night.

As I walked up 3rd avenue, I passed several smartly dressed waiters smoking cigarettes outside empty restaurants, steeling themselves for the evening onslaught of Turtle Bay hoi polloi. I reached the bar about 5 minutes early but there was already a short, cute, and red haired girl waiting beside the door engrossed in her iPhone.

"Emma?" I asked, stopping alongside her.

"Hi!" she replied, looking up from her phone with an expression of nervous surprise. She continued to hold her iPhone in front of her defensively, so I didn't attempt a greeting hug. Just a friendly smile.
"Nice to meet you! Shall we go in?" I said.
"Sure!"

Aside from the bartender the place was completely empty.

"Wow," I commented, "I didn't expect it to be this dead!"
"Ha, yeah I guess it's early."
"If this were England there would at least be some drunken students or some old alcoholic dudes around at this time."
"Really? You guys like to drink huh?"
"Yeah, we've got to do something while it's raining outside."

We took seats at the bar and ordered a couple of beers. The conversation got off to a sporadic start, one moment we'd be chatting away happily about New York, or science, or careers, or family, or some other everyday topic, but the bursts of conversation were broken up by moments of awkward silence. During these interludes we both looked around the bar, avoiding too much eye contact, remembering the main thing that had brought us to this place, and how much we already knew about each other.

"So yeah this is awkward isn't it?" I said out loud, to break a particularly long silence.
"Ha! Yeah it is a bit. Though I don't think there's a real reason why it should be." she replied.
"Yeah. I guess we're just conditioned as we grow up that talking about sex with strangers is somehow bad."
"Mmmm maybe."
"I blame the influence of misguided Judaeo-Christian cultural values on my subconscious. But then I blame them for most things!"
"Ha!"

This led the conversation into a brief discussion of religion. We were both atheists so no disagreements surfaced there. A bit more conversation and a bit more beer later we found ourselves in another awkward silence. I took a moment to really look at my date; she was probably the hottest girl I'd yet to meet through the Internet... and from all reports, she was interested in having kinky sex with me! I sat there thinking 'I should do or say something... argh... I don't want to fuck this up!"

The bar was still empty; both of us were still not talking and looking around nervously. The only thing breaking the silence was some generic indie music playing in the background. I started to feel myself tensing up. Adrenaline began to tie my stomach in knots. 'Shit, not now!' I thought. I closed my eyes and took some deep breaths, trying to quell the rising nausea in my chest.

"So have you got a list of New York things to do?" asked Emma

"Erm... I guess kind of," I said, starting to reflexively swallow the saliva building up in my mouth.

"I mean I guess I did a lot of tourist stuff when I visited before." I tried to focus on the conversation to take my mind off my rising panic.

"I've not been up the Empire State building yet actually..." I said.

...No. It was no good. I couldn't even think of conversation to make. All my attention was now focused on keeping my stomach contents in place. I had to get out of there.

"...Sorry, will you excuse me for a minute, I need to use the bathroom."

I stood up attempting to maintain an air of calmness. Panic nausea held my guts in a steel grip and was mercilessly raising pressure.

I hopped down the stairs to the toilets, hoping that my rapid descent conveyed 'buoyant energy' and not 'desperate haste' but once out of sight I burst full tilt into the gent's.[37]

*

A few minutes later I was staring at myself in the washroom mirror "Fuck me!" I muttered to myself.

Now, with an empty stomach, I quickly recovered to my normal un-panicked state. I proceeded to gargle a lot of water from the sink. I'd forgotten to bring mints with me, so any attempt to kiss my date would now be extremely ill advised.

---

[37]*Grossness warning* in the split second I was dashing for the bowl I asked myself the question: 'Am I going to make it? Am I in range yet? Fuck it! I'll aim while moving and hope for the best...'

Once I had collected myself, and checked my face and clothes for any stray flecks, I returned to the bar.

"Sorry about that!" I said, and then thought 'hmm it probably sounds a bit weird that I just apologised for going to the bathroom... should I tell her I just threw up? No of course not! Are you an idiot or something?!'

I took a quick swig of beer, hoping it would cover up any unpleasant mouth odours. Normal conversation started up again, I felt much more relaxed. There were even a couple more people in the bar now. We were drinking our beers slowly. At some point during the chit chat I told her the story of how I got locked in the basement of my building for half an hour while looking for a laundry room. She seemed to get a kick out of that. She told me a bit about law school, and we then talked about gun control. After this another awkward silence descended. I looked at her and smiled

"Yup it's still awkward isn't it?"
"Ha. It doesn't have to be!"
"Yeah I guess we're both new to this... I mean I had a normal date earlier this week and I wasn't nervous for that at all."
"Really?"
"Yeah, I dunno I guess you're the first person I've met from my kinky profile.... I mean nervous is perhaps the wrong word..." (It was totally the right word) "... but I'm not really sure how to start talking about this stuff with someone new, as I've not done this before... I mean, I've not met a stranger off the Internet before who was interested in kinky stuff."
"You haven't?"
I continued to fluster along: "... I mean like I've done various kinky things before... but only with people I knew pretty well beforehand... I mean, I know my way around the basics... so, yeah..."...I decided to stop digging.

"How about you?"

"Erm... Yeah, I guess it has been hinted at in previous relationships, but I'd like to explore it further," She said, her tone imbued with wavering levels of confidence.

I wanted to ask her more specific questions about her fantasies, but it was like my mind deliberately went blank. It seemed to be engaged in some sort of act of self-censorship that prevented me formulating any kind of clear question. Instead, the conversation diverted into talk about relationships and online dating, and how law school didn't really leave her much time for either.

Eventually our last dregs of beer were gone. This would have been a sensible time to get another drink, but instead I managed to accidentally kill the date... and when I say kill it, I mean like totally annihilate it:

"So what are you doing with the rest of the evening?" I asked.
"Oh I'm meeting a few friends later for drinks," she replied.
"Do you fancy another drink here?"
"Um, I'm ok. I mean do you want another one?"
"I don't mind... I mean if you like we could go back to my place. I have wine and stuff?"
"Errr..." *pause for consideration* "Perhaps not tonight?"
"That's fine, no worries... shall I get the cheque then?"
"Sure."

I looked at my watch. It was a little after 6. Stupidly early, but I'd just blundered my way out of that second drink.

As we stood waiting to cross the road a car drove past pulling a trailer. It had a length of chain dangling beneath it that was scraping along the asphalt and making a loud jangling noise.

"I'm not sure that's legal," Emma said.

"How appropriate!" I commented, "So, are you up for meeting up again sometime?"

"Yeah, let's do something again soon!" She replied, with apparently genuine enthusiasm.

I walked her to First Avenue where she was going north and I was going south[38]. I gave her a hug and kissed her on the cheek. She stood affixed to the spot, not reciprocating or recoiling, and then she turned and headed north and I turned and headed south.

'Shit,' I thought as I was walking back past the United Nations, 'I didn't even get her number!'

Later that evening I messaged her on Okcupid[39]:

"Great meeting you! Sorry I totally failed on the kinky chat front. I couldn't tell if you were ready for it, and it's kind of hard to transition into it naturally! Am I sufficiently non-threatening to get your number? Anyway I think I'm free most of this week apart from Monday, if you want to do anything..."

The next morning I eagerly checked my inbox.

Nothing.

---

[38] I thought about asking if she wanted me to force her into a dark alleyway and ravage her, but I decided against it. Besides it was early and there were people around...

[39] Over enthusiastic post-date messaging is perhaps a rookie error, and one I would make for many more dates to come.

As the day passed I found myself checking it at regular intervals. I hadn't done this with any of the previous dates. For some reason that girl had gotten under my skin and I really wanted to hear some kind of response.

Monday came around and still nothing. Being ill practised in the art of playing it cool, I penned another message:

"Ok so now I'm wondering what dangerous sociopathic traits I accidentally gave away!

There's probably no escaping the fact that Saturday was kind of strange... Turns out trying to just meet someone for sex is harder than they make it look on TV! Or maybe it's just me; any pointers?

Anyway you're hot and interesting, so if just meeting for sex is too weird for you, would you like to try dating like normal people instead? I would be up for that, although maybe I seem like too much of a weirdo now!..."

Send.

Tuesday and Wednesday passed. Still nothing.

By Thursday I had given up refreshing my Okcupid inbox and transitioned back to the depressing profile trawling:

Hot. Not hot. Maybe hot. Scary... in a slightly hot way. Hot enough. Jesus why would you even post that picture?

Then I got a message from Emma:

"No I'm so sorry I was MIA! Had a late night/early mornings at work and school for a few days. Didn't mean at all to leave

you hanging. Yeah it was strange but... to be expected, I guess! I think we should try again - I'm not dissuaded and haven't pinpointed your sociopathic nature yet."

This message made me irrationally excited. I could tell I liked this girl. Not only had she induced a mid-date restroom dash (usually a good indicator of 'chemistry'), but I also seemed to have become emotionally invested in an Internet conversation for the first time since I'd moved to New York.

Sadly though, after exchanging a couple more messages, I was left hanging again. Weeks passed and my missives still sat unreplied to. I figured I had used up the unofficial quota of messages that can be sent before one starts to sound like a needy/crazy stalker type, so it seemed I had no choice but to let it lie. The bottle of white wine I had put in my fridge before that first date continued to chill and my over-priced chains remained under-used.

For now.

Aside 1 - Why do people like BDSM?

I guess it's about time I addressed the elephant in the room.

Why do weirdos like me get turned on by BDSM[40]?

The simple answer is, "Because it's fun!"

However, I can understand that many people could find the idea of getting restrained, hurt, and ordered around to be terrifying and horrific. They could also perhaps perceive the person doing the restraining and hurting as a little sociopathically deranged[41].

I think the critical thing to appreciate is that BDSM is a game, it's not meant to be 'real'. It's possible that the more realistic it seems, the better the game can be. Just like the best films and TV shows are often the ones that are the most believable and realistic. Watching horror films is considered a socially acceptable and mainstream activity but, when watching these films, viewers are bombarded with unpleasant visual and auditory stimuli. Yet millions of us still pay to see them, perhaps because we get to explore these horrific situations while remaining safe in the knowledge that they're not really happening to us. BDSM on the other hand provides a more immersive experience, with physical sensations thrown in as well.

---

[40] And from my highly biased sample of the New York dating population there seems to be quite a lot of weirdos like me.

[41] For me personally, the enjoyment I get from dominating someone does not come from inflicting pain in of itself, but from being given both the power and the trust to inflict that pain.

While I think of BDSM as exploring a fantasy rather than living out a reality, from what I've seen on the interwebs it can sometimes be hard to see where the boundary lies. Also, depending on who you play the game with, it could be a lot more dangerous than going to the cinema. However, this is not meant to be a defence of BDSM, or a discussion of the dangers, just an explanation of where these desires come from.

I have heard a number of psychological theories that frame kinky interests as some kind of learned deficit. For example; an interest in bondage might come from not being wrapped tightly enough as a child, or that getting excited by pain and degradation might be a result of childhood sexual abuse, or even that people who explore kink may be compensating for perceived sexual inadequacy. However, most of these theories seem to be based on little more than psychiatrists' tendencies for talking bullshit because they think it sounds good[42]. In fact, a recent study suggested that people who practice BDSM in either dominant or submissive role may be more mentally stable than the average member of the general population[43]. Some of the more up to date literature suggests that many psychologists are now ascribing the attraction of dominance and submission to sexual arousal by hierarchical status[44]; the idea being that our evolutionary ancestors evolved to pursue sex with more dominant individuals who could secure the best

---

[42] Someone let Freud get away with it once, and look what happened.

[43] Of course there are always going to be significant selection biases to contend with when surveying people about stigmatized sexual behaviour. I don't claim that this study is correct, just that it exists. Reference is here: Wismeijer & Van Assen, "Psychological Characteristics of BDSM Practitioners" - The Journal of Sexual Medicine (2013) Volume 10, Issue 8, pages 1943–1952

[44] Jozifkova, E. "Consensual Sadomasochistic Sex (BDSM): The Roots, the Risks, and the Distinctions Between BDSM and Violence" Current Psychiatry Reports (2013) 15:392

food, protect them from predators, etc etc. This idea sounds like it has some merit, but it's an idea that still makes me a tad uncomfortable as I'm card carrying lefty who thinks social hierarchies are generally a bad thing, even if I'm happy to play sex games based around them.

I also don't think this hierarchy idea tells the whole story, so as I have a sciencey PhD, and I also like BDSM, I think this vaguely qualifies me to make up my own bullshit hypotheses on the subject. They run along these lines:

BDSM practices are not 'learned dysfunctions' but are instead nuanced expressions of the powerful dichotomy of fear and excitement that lies at the heart of human sexuality.

The sexualisation of specific BDSM practices is perhaps just due to classical Pavlovian conditioning[45], or a case of 'Monkey see monkey do'. I know my tastes have evolved with exposure to different images and situations, and when I first used to search for bondage porn on the Internet, the more sadomasochistic elements often disturbed me[46]. However, as I became desensitised to the 'grossness', I also began to get turned on by the more hard-core fantasies as well.

Apparently the seeds of our sexual interests are planted during childhood. The idea that early sexual abuse conditions people to like BDSM is an extreme version of this classical

---

[45] In case you're unfamiliar with Pavlov's work, in his most famous experiment he would ring a bell every time he gave a dog food and eventually the dog would reflexively salivate at the sound of the bell even when there was no food around.
[46] To begin with, I would fantasise more about being tied up myself. I just preferred looking at attractive girls getting tied up and dominated by other girls (which kept the weird looking male genitalia out of it!).

conditioning hypothesis, and to some extent it makes sense that a victim of abuse could learn to associate feelings of helplessness etc with arousal. However, I personally have no memory of being sexually abused, (despite going to a primary school run by catholic nuns[47]), and out of all the kinky people I've talked about this with none of them have described any childhood abuse (several people have clearly stated that they didn't experience it).

I've also met many girls who said that they only recently got interested in BDSM because it sounded like a fun thing to try out, and it wasn't something they fantasized about at all during adolescence. I suspect that even the most minor childhood experiences of power exchange can sow the seeds of kink that may then sprout later in life. Thinking back to my own childhood, vague memories surface of playing a game where we got hold of some rope and tied some girls to a tree. After we pretended to hold them hostage for a little while they got bored, escaped and did the same to us (we let them, because fair is fair!). I think we then got told off for playing this game by some adult authority figure, which probably only served to heighten the illicit thrill. Perhaps a mildly violent subtext to cute childhood games is all BDSM fantasies need to take root.

However, we find ourselves with a chicken and egg scenario: was I tying girls to a tree because I was excited by it? Or by doing the tying did I learn to associate that activity with proto-sexual excitement? I don't really know anything about how kids develop sexual thoughts. Some parenting sites tell me it starts surprisingly early... but, to be honest, I don't want to think about that too much! However, why should tying a girl to

---

[47] I've noticed a lot of kinky Catholics out there though. I can't draw any conclusions from such flimsy data but someone should really look into that correlation.

a tree cultivate my erotic development while doing something like homework with a girl do nothing? Kids do homework with each other all the time but I feel safe saying that BDSM interests are a lot more prevalent in the adult population than homework fetishes.

This brings me to my core idea; where the roots of BDSM interests tap into the molten core of what makes our sexuality function. Sex is kind of scary, especially when you've not done it before! Even without all of the complex social stigma and bizarre rules that various human cultures have invented to confuse the situation and generally discourage sex as a practice, it can still be fucking scary. Both parties are exposing themselves to another conscious entity over whom they have no real control[48]. Also, for coordination purposes, it often falls to one party to lead. This makes trust and power exchange a key part of consensual sex, even if the sex is gentle and tender, and you don't bite their nipples even once.

When first thinking about exploring sex with another individual, nervous fear and erotic excitement are intertwined, perhaps along with more complex ideas of surrender or taking control. It seems quite natural that we can learn to associate arousal with these abstractions, and when the idea of sex in of itself becomes more mundane, BDSM may help reconnect to these basic erotic urges.

It also wouldn't surprise me if the human neuronal wiring for sexual arousal is genetically and physiologically intertwined with our 'fight or flight' circuitry. Social behaviour in mammals

---

[48] I don't really want to discuss gender differences here, but it's not hard to see why the gender that tends to be smaller and generally more exposed to harm during sex might have an increased likelihood of associating submission and arousal.

is far from universal but sex has to be. Otherwise that particular species of mammal won't be around for long. Back when our solitary hairy ancestor encountered our other solitary hairy ancestor in a dark forest, its brain's first two thoughts were probably; 'Do I run away from it?' or 'Do I fight it?'... Thankfully for us, this creature then thought; 'I don't think I need to run away from it... or fight it... perhaps I should have sex with it?' Our DNA has been through millions of generations of these nervous animal encounters. It would seem to make sense for the 'Fight?/Flight?/Sex?' decision processes to have become linked on a biochemical level. Those animals that thought "Fight?-no, Flight?-no... meh whatever," missed a lot of opportunities to make offspring, and the horny critters that kept considering "Sex? Sex? Sex?" in the absence of a fight or flight stimulus might have wasted a lot of time humping inanimate objects. (Until that is they got eaten by a bigger critter who thought: "Fight?-Yes! Nom.")

It would be unsurprising to me then if the childhood games that most feed our sexual development often involve a careful balance of fear, aggression and excitement[49]. More complex fantasies might then evolve out of these games, no doubt fed by all the crude and bizarre sexualisation we encounter in advertising and elsewhere, and thus we end up with one kinky adult.

Also if you're aggressively told as a kid that doing certain things is really bad, or you find your sexual feelings stigmatised, that probably feeds into it as well. However, I'm

---

[49] Maybe the upfront kids who just play 'Doctor's and Nurses' (i.e. poking bits of each other's anatomy to see what happens) go on to develop vanilla tastes, while the more shy kids who disguise their interests behind power games and tying other kids to trees turn into kinksters... but I'm not sure if this is a testable hypothesis...

not really sure how to fit this idea into the rest of my somewhat vague and rambling hypotheses, so I'm just going to tack it on the end here and leave you with a conclusion! (You can tell it's a conclusion because I'm underlining 'conclusion' at the top, like we do in real science sometimes.)

Conclusion

BDSM is a fun game. At least it is fun for many people who have learnt to find it fun somehow. There may be a lot of non-traumatic ways one can learn to find it fun. I've even put forward some muddled reasoning as to how the simplistic blueprints may be in our very DNA. DNA may also have nothing to do with it, but this wouldn't change the fact that BDSM is fun[50]. Maybe you should try it sometime! (Or don't. That's fine too.)

---

[50] Regardless of this many people may find the very idea of BDSM offensive for potentially legitimate reasons, but if you are one of those people maybe you shouldn't have opened this book.

Chapter 7 - Snowflakes and Lipstick.

While I may have got a little carried away with my kink profile, my normal Okcupid profile was not forgotten. It wasn't long until I found myself in a nearby cocktail bar talking to a girl named Jennifer who was blissfully ignorant of my tastes in the bedroom. She helped manage a large department store in Midtown, and she seemed pretty smart and on top of things. She also looked pretty damn hot, probably a little out of my league, but with the English accent, Oxbridge education, and good conversation I managed to hang in there.

A few cocktails down and she said she had better go home as she had to work the next day. Outside the bar I offered to walk her to the Subway station. She accepted. As we were leaving the bar a few sparse snowflakes began to drift down. They were followed by a few more, and then even more. They started to settle in Jennifer's wool hat and collect amongst her curly jet black hair. The Empire state building looked down on us through the dancing ice crystals, lit up in its classic 'all white' look. I commented: "The Empire State looks good tonight... Sometimes I love how it seems to be always looking down on us New Yorkers; like some benevolent supreme being watching out for us..." (I may have overreached on the poetic front.)
"Ha, yeah," she said.

We reached her subway stop.
"Well this is me," she said.
"Cool. Well let's do something again sometime. Dinner and a movie maybe?"
"Sure that sounds fun," she replied.
I went to kiss her goodbye and it got passionate. I felt a bit like I was in some romantic black and white movie, or an Edward Hopper painting entitled 'kissing in the snow with the Empire State building in the background'.

"Ha, I got lipstick on you!" she said, running her thumb across the edge of my mouth.
"I'm not complaining!" I replied.

Dinner and a movie was set. Unfortunately though the movie I chose (with her input) was Zero dark thirty... I would say that Zero dark thirty is a good movie. However, it is definitely not a good date movie. As well as being about torturing and killing terrorists, it is also as long as hell.

After we finally escaped the movie theatre around 11:30 Jennifer wasn't interested in a nightcap and said she just had to get home and sleep. We went down into the Union Square subway station together. She was taking the four and I was taking the six; trains that both go from opposite sides of the same platform. Another long kiss, withdrawing for a second, and then a brief one to conclude. Once again there felt like there was something cinematic about the experience, perhaps it was just because she was a damn good kisser. Her train arrived first and so I watched her step through the sliding subway car doors. They clunked closed again with all the nuance of a guillotine, and Jennifer was sped away into the darkness, accompanied by the screeching cacophony of metal train wheels on tightly curving tracks.

Some part of me knew right then that I'd never see her again.

Eventually she replied to my text suggesting a third date:
"Sorry for such a late response! I've got so much going on right now. I feel like it's probably best for me to not see anyone right now. I think you're great though!"

It's ok. She thinks I'm great.

IV

T.G.O.M.D.'s hand rests there on the table, palm down. It's just close enough to her that I can't quite tell if it's positioned as a subconscious invitation… or just where she feels like resting her hand.

Do I take a chance?

Having reached up to absent-mindedly but not-so-absent-mindedly flick my hair, I land my hand back down and bring it to rest on top of hers.

She doesn't flinch. She smiles as we converse. Her thumb reaches out and up, then squeezes down on mine as my palm gently massages her knuckles. A simple application of pressure, but why does it feel so good?

Chapter 8 - Disturbing the neighbours

One Tuesday evening I found myself staring at a sign on the tumble drier...

"DO NOT ATTEMPT TO DRY FABRICS CONTAMINATED WITH OILS OR OTHER FLAMMABLE SUBSTANCES. THIS MAY RESULT IN FIRE"

"Hmmm" I thought...

"Does candle wax count as a flammable?"

"...It'll probably be fine," I decided, shoving my bed sheets in with the rest of my white and vaguely pale clothes.

"Besides most of the wax should have come off in the wash...right?"

*

On the Sunday two nights prior I had arranged to meet Allie. Allie was someone I had been chatting to for a little while through my kink profile. She was looking for a playmate -or 'partner in crime' as she put it- rather than a quick hook-up, which sounded pretty ideal to me[51]. Various photos and bits of titillating information had been exchanged. One Sunday afternoon she was shopping in the city and I managed to persuade her to meet me for coffee before she headed back to Queens.

---

[51] I had no idea what I was really looking for. I liked connecting with people, so ideally I wasn't looking for one night stands... but I wasn't likely to turn one down either.

I suggested a coffee place opposite the NY public library and I said I'd meet her on the library steps under a lion. (It would probably have been easier to meet her in the coffee shop, but meeting on the steps of the library had a certain ring to it.)

I turned up kind of early and waited around watching the fifth avenue comings and goings. A little while after I had bored of the stone lion's company, my date finally appeared.

"Allie?" I ask
"Yes," she replied.
"Nice to meet you!"

I boldly went for a European style greeting in the form of a hand-shake-cheek-kiss combo. However, this did not go well as she actively dodged my attempt to get near her face with my mouth, perhaps thinking I was trying to make out with her straight away. After this exceptionally awkward start we went across the street to get coffee, or tea in my case. (You should just assume this is what I mean every time I say "get coffee").

Conversation picked up and this time there weren't the awkward silences that occurred the first time I tried to meet someone though my kink profile. (The shot of whiskey I had before heading to the library steps may have helped with this).

We covered the basics of each other's lives; she grew up in rural New Jersey but had moved to the city and was making a living bartending in Queens at a Korean dive. She was only twenty one and had dropped out of college a couple of years back. I don't think she told me her exact reasons, but I remember something about boyfriend issues and a penchant for smoking weed several times a day (a habit she claimed to have largely given up).

She was definitely attractive; blonde, thin, and with a nice face. However, there was a subtle gauntness to her features that hadn't quite come across in her profile. It wasn't off putting at all but it kept her good looks in check somehow.

We talked a little bit about online dating and BDSM. She'd explored a lot of things with an old boyfriend and then they'd started fooling around with another girl as a couple. Apparently it was all good fun until her boyfriend decided to just date the other girl instead.

After I had made my way through my mini pot of tea, and she had finished her refilled cup of coffee, I suggested we get something stronger to drink. She agreed and we boldly set out into the wastes of midtown, guided by my smart phone's bar suggestions.

"Would you like to hear my English accent?" she asked, while we were walking.
"Erm... Sure?" I replied.
I immediately regretted this answer. It was a terrible English accent.

We decided to try the Park Avenue Tavern. After getting lost and wandering around inside Grand Central for a while, we eventually located the tavern a few blocks down. The place had a nice vibe, with plenty of dark wood, shiny brass and other elegant finishings. We got some food and a bottle of wine, though I stuck to a steak tartar appetiser so as not to test my stomach's panic reflexes too much.

The conversation kept rolling. Allie occasionally did this thing where she would excitedly tell me a random fact that was barely related to the conversation. (I'm guessing she originally heard them on NPR, or some other hip news source).

"Did you know," she would start, "that sharks can't actually get cancer?"

I found this quite cute, but unfortunately many of these facts landed somewhere between dubious and wrong, and I couldn't resist the urge to dispute them. (As politely as possible of course).

"I think I might have heard that somewhere, but I'm not sure I believe it. Cancer is such a complex process I'd be surprised if something as closely related to us as a shark could completely escape it. I mean our basic biochemistry is so similar."

Fortunately, she didn't seem to mind me doubting her facts... at least it didn't stop her offering them.

A glass and a half of wine down (she insisted on pouring for me), I asked: "So where do you think your submissive side comes from?"
"Daddy issues," she replied cheerfully and without hesitation.
"Oh really? Simple as that?"
"Yeah. I mean my dad was never around when I was growing up, so I guess I never had a male figure to look up to."
"Fair enough..."

After I'd talked about where my own interests might have spawned from, and a few other things, I popped another big question:
"Would you like to come back to my place after this? I'm not sure I've figured out the etiquette for asking that question yet. It sometimes seems a bit rude to ask on a first date..."

"Yesss, I might do."

"Cool."

I smiled calmly.

Back at my apartment

When we got back to mine I opened some more wine and we continued to chat.

Not far into the first glass of wine she asked, "Can I use your bathroom, I need to go pee!"
"Sure, help yourself," I told her, wondering why she felt the need to clarify what she was going to do in there.

A bit more wine and conversation later I asked; "So are you up for fooling around?"
"Sure."
"Are there any things that you don't like to do, that I should stay away from?"
"Not really. I'm open to most things, although I prefer not to kiss unless I'm properly dating a guy."
"Really? Doesn't that get a bit awkward?"
"Not really. I mean some guys get annoyed about it, but that doesn't stop them having sex with me."
I had moved in close and began running my hand over her jeans.
"I don't think it would annoy me, although I guess it's a bit of a reflex I'd have to resist. Is it just the lips? Can I kiss other areas?" I asked
"Sure."

I began to lean further in and bring my hand further up her inner thigh.

"I need to go pee!" she said, fleeing to the bathroom.

"Again?"
"Don't worry I'm not doing heroin in your toilet or anything"
"Ha, ok good to know!" I said as she closed the door.

When she re-emerged from the bathroom she was no longer wearing trousers.

While Allie's jeans had evaporated, everything else remained in place. She leaned briefly against the door frame, perhaps attempting to strike a seductive pose. It may have worked better if her thick cardigan and spindly legs didn't make her look so top heavy.

She picked up her glass of wine and wandered over to the window.
"You do have a nice view," she commented.
"Well you're definitely enhancing it," I replied.
I joined her at the windowsill and, standing behind her, I grasped her body firmly and pulled it back against mine. I ran my hand up her bare legs and then took a forceful hold of her crotch.

"Shall I bring out the chains?" I whispered in her ear.
"Mmhmm," she replied.

I walked over to the wardrobe and pulled out an innocuous looking cardboard box. I kicked it so it slid across the linoleum floor, then it toppled as it hit the edge of my rug, spilling its jangling contents by her feet. I walked back to her, took her glass of wine out of her hands and put it on the side table. Kissing her on the cheek and neck I ran my hands over her body and pulled her jumper and shirt up over her head.

"Get on your knees," I instructed.
She did as she was told.

"Put your hands behind your back."
She obeyed.
I wrapped a length of chain around her arms, around, and around, and around. Then I padlocked the two ends together, making sure they were tight enough so her hands couldn't wiggle free.
"Now you're mine to play with...
...But where to start?"

Seriously, I didn't know where to start... I was a little too excited over all the possibilities and I couldn't decide where to begin. 'Spanking,' I thought, 'let's start with spanking... everyone loves spanking!'

I bent her head down to the floor and took my hand to the curve of her smooth white behind.

She seemed to enjoy her spanking, but after a little while she complained,
"My knees hurt."
"Let's move to the bed then," I said, grabbing her elbow to lift her up and then flinging her face down into my mattress.

Wait, I thought, dammit I'm meant to be hurting her! Caring about her knees wasn't a very domly thing to do was it? Shit I'd better make up for that...

"But now you get the belt to punish your complaining!" I said, unbuckling it from my waist. Folding it in half I let fly at her bare buttocks. It made satisfyingly loud slapping sounds and she gasped as the blows rained down. However, she didn't tell me to stop.

I worked her like that for a little while, judging from her gasps how hard to hit. I could have hit harder... but it was only a first date after all! Finally I decided she had earned a reward, so I turned her over and stuck my hand in her panties, exploring her fully.

Leaning over her while doing this, my instincts got the better of me and I kissed her briefly on the lips. I quickly remembered the rules and begun to withdraw, but her lips followed mine. I pulled back anyway and then slapped her playfully in the face.
"Mmnhhh," was her only response.
I slapped her again and then, with my slapping hand, I pressed her face down and away from me, finger fucking her hard with my other hand.

"I need to go pee!" she said suddenly
"Seriously?"
"Don't judge me! You can leave my hands chained together though"

*

I lay on my bed listening to the muffled sound of jangling of chains coming from the bathroom as she tried to manoeuvre, followed by a flush. 'Well, this date is going well,' I thought to myself.

When she returned to the bed I told her, "I'm not letting you get away from me anymore. Time to chain you down!"

I lay her on her back and began to wrap chain around her right ankle.

"Oh wait. I should probably take your underwear off first," I said.

I hastily pulled down her panties[52] and flung them onto the floor.

"Now back to securing those ankles".

I wrapped and padlocked the chain around one ankle, then around several bars of my metal bed frame, then around the other ankle. I locked the last ankle in place with a second padlock, securing her legs wide apart. Then I did the same with her wrists, making sure to remove her bra beforehand. The chain made loud clattering noises against the bed as I threaded it through.

After I locked her last hand in place I took a blindfold and placed it over her eyes.

"Now you're completely at my mercy..." I whispered, running my hand firmly across her tits and down to her pussy, "... I can do anything I want to you and there's nothing you can do to stop me."

"I'm going to let you lie there and think about that for a while..." I said, withdrawing my hand and standing up off the bed.

In the darkness of her blindfold she must have heard the sound of a match being lit, and smelt the mix of sulphur and paraffin as I ignited the wick of a thick candle. She would have then heard the pad of my footsteps as I wandered away into the kitchen.

When I returned, she would have felt the mattress shift beneath her as I knelt on the bed, leaning over, pausing to let

---

[52] I still really hate using the word "panties", in the UK we say pants but I fear this' may confuse American readers...

her mind imagine all the possible painful sensations she might be about to experience... any second...

Next came the sting of cold wet ice running over her nipples.

"Nnuuhh," was the noise she made as I ran the cubes down her body and over her clit.

"CLINK CLINK CLINK... CLINK CLINK CLINK." was the sound the chains made against my bed as she strained against them... but there was no getting away.

When the candle had built up a nice pool of molten wax, I scooped the half melted ice cubes off her now wet body, and picked up the candle, hovering it above her.

"Are you ready for a little candle wax?"
"Maybe...?" came the uncertain response.
"Now this is going to feel like it's burning, as it's quite a high temperature wax, but I've tested it on myself, and it doesn't actually burn you."
"Can you do it from high up?" she said, "last time I did this I was rolling on ecstasy, and I didn't realize I was getting burned... But if you do it from high up the wax has time to cool."
"Sure," I replied, "but this wax didn't burn me so you should be good."

Perhaps I should have said "shut up and accept your punishment slut!" to preserve the mood, but you know, clear consent is just sexier.

I held the candle high above her belly and tipped it slowly. I tipped it a little further, then a little further... then a little further... Finally a thin stream of hot wax spilled out and downwards... splashing over the bed sheets beside Allie and missing her entirely. Apparently pouring from that height came with a significant accuracy penalty. A second pour from a little lower though and thin drips of white wax were soon strewn across her stomach.

"Uuunnhhh!... MMMNNHHH!!..." she vocalised as I laced droplets across her tits and down her legs.

"CLINK CLINK CLINK... CLINK CLINK CLINK," went the chains, as she writhed, trying to escape the inescapable molten balls of burning heat stuck to her skin.

Occasionally when she looked in too much pain I'd run my hand through the wax, spreading it out and dissipating the heat. Solid lumps of candle were now stuck all over her skin giving it a strange bumpy texture.

"...FUUCCKK!!" she cried, as I splattered a stream of wax along her inner thigh.

"Too intense? Do you want me to stop?"
"No... not quite," she replied breathlessly.

After a little more straining and waxing though she said, "Ow, can you loosen the chains on my wrists? They're really hurting."

"Sure," I said, fetching the key and un-padlocking one hand then the other. Before I could grab it the chain slid away under its own gravity.
"CLINK CLUNK CLUNK CLUNK CLINK CLINK CLUNK CLINK CLUNK CLINK CLINK CLINK...." escaping through my bed frame and onto the floor.

I retrieved it and began attaching it to her wrists again, but loosely this time. The chain was making plenty more CLUNKs and CLINKs while I adjusted it. Then suddenly a loud THUD. THUD. THUD. Echoed through the wall.

"Uh oh," I said, "sounds like we've pissed off the neighbours."

I finished re-securing her wrists as quietly as possible. Wincing at every clink and clunk the chains made. I tried to think of any innocent explanation I could give for these metallic noises coming from my flat at 1 am. I drew a blank. Being a vaguely considerate human, I looked around for something to cushion and silence the chains against the metal rails of the bed. My own underwear was the first thing I saw, so I wrapped it around the chains and hoped for the best.

Trying to get back in the mood I began slapping some of the wax off Allie's stomach and thighs, and whispered to her, "Are you ready to get fucked?"
"Yeess," she replied (in what may have been her mock English accent, I couldn't be sure).

Condom in place, I maneuvered myself between her wax covered legs, which were still spread wide by the chains. I began to fuck her, slowly at first then quickly increasing the pace so as to administer a solid ravaging.

We were reaching a good animalistic rhythm when she gasped, "Wait, ow! Stop!"
"What is it?" I said, stopping straight away.
"The chains hurt too much. Can you untie me?"
"Just the hands?"
"No all of them, they're pulling on my ankles as you're fucking me."

I dutifully released her from her bonds, leaving the chains to hang from the bed so as not to disturb the neighbours further.

"You ok?" I asked, as she rubbed her wrists.
"Yeah, I was enjoying pulling against them up to that point."

We fondled a little. I tried to get back into it but struggled. Ever since I had grasped her by the window my erection had been a solid rock of inspiration. Now though it had vanished without a trace. Perhaps it was feeling guilty for overdoing it and hurting its new plaything on her chains, or it was embarrassed for waking up the neighbours with suspicious chain noises. Either way it stubbornly refused to return.

Defeated I snuggled with Allie under the duvet until we dozed off.

At some point later in the night I awoke to find my erection had firmly resurrected itself with renewed enthusiasm and, after some tumbling around under the covers, we fucked like regular people.

That morning Allie showed me how to make scrambled eggs (apparently you put milk and cheese in there too instead of just stirring some eggs in a pan... who knew?!). Then she left to head back for Queens. A few minutes after the door closed behind her I threw up in the toilet. I'm not sure why I threw up then, it was just a thing that happened.

I hung out with Allie a few more times after that, and lived a few more good stories. We were always clear that it was just a casual thing, and that we were both dating other people. Then one day she just stopped replying to my texts, and that was the end of that.

Encounter at my mail box

A few weeks after that date I was checking my mail box on the ground floor, just like I do every day. A lady, whom I'd guess was in her early 30s, with brown hair and a vaguely annoyed looking face, came in to the mail room and stood beside me. Figuring I must be in her way I moved to the side.

"Sorry," I said, in my stereotypically English way (we like to apologise for our existence... it's a thing we do).
"Thanks," she said, unlocking the mailbox for apartment 10T.

'Huh... I'm 10S,' I thought, 'that would make her my neighbour. I wonder what side of me she lives on?'

It's quite possible she also noticed the mailbox that I was checking, and figured out exactly which apartment I was in. We silently boarded the same elevator to go up to our apartments on the 10th floor. However, for some reason she pressed the button to stop at the 6th floor and got off there.

As I walked alone down the hallway to my place I checked the number of the apartment from which the angry THUDs had originated.

'Yup. 10T. Oh well, I guess that explains that one!'

Chapter 9 - Oxford dating strategies: A retrospective

So at this point I think it's fair to say that my approach to meeting women had veered down a dramatically different path to the one I had been trudging along for most of my young adulthood. I feel I should contextualise just how significant a gear change it was for me to meet a girl for the first time, take her home, and chain her up for my pleasure. This sort of thing did not happen to me at Oxford.

Perhaps it might have happened if I had moved in different circles... or looked in the right places... or just grown some significantly larger balls[53]. However, with a few minor exceptions, my balls spent most of my student years locked in a dusty box somewhere with a sign on it that read, "Steady now!"

I remember when I was going through a mildly self-involved artistic phase; I had an idea for a painting that would be entitled 'The perfect gentleman'. This piece would feature a naked man who was castrated, but holding his dismembered member in his hand, and thrusting out towards the observer. I know, pretty deep huh? I think it is pretty amazing nothing ever came of this artistic phase. I was clearly ahead of my time.

Anyway I guess if one peels back the many nuanced and undeniably brilliant layers of symbolism present in that picture that I never actually painted, it could be interpreted that the artist (i.e. me) saw a clear contradiction between being the 'good-guy gentleman person' that he thought society expected of him, and the 'horny fucker who actually got laid dude' that it seemed advantageous to actually be.

---

[53] That time I got the mumps notwithstanding.

Basically it has taken me 26 years to realise how little society actually expects from me[54].

Being an only child with parents who were born at the end of the Second World War probably had something to do with this delayed realisation. I guess they were pretty difficult to impress and had standards for me that were consistent with their own generation, but out of sync with the standards set by people who grew up actually buying food rather than trading in rationing coupons. They were still good parents by any standard, but they had lost touch with how young people tended to behave and interact about the time 'rock and roll' became a thing (I'm not even exaggerating). This led to a shortage of usable advice when it came to girls. For example when I was about 13 I somehow managed to get a first date with a girl[55]. I told my parents this fact, and in response they gave me the sage advice of: "Have you checked her parents are ok with this?"

...

Having assimilated this curve-ball I eventually summoned up the courage to ring the girl in question, using the number she had scrawled on a then-treasured scrap of paper. Despite it being the 90s we still had one of those old rotary dial phones, like the ones you see in old movies (sometimes they're red and important looking but ours was beige and yet still somehow yellowing[56]). Genuinely 'dialling' a number is much more time

---

[54] "Society" and "the opposite sex" are perhaps interchangeable in this sentence.

[55] How I got this date is a long and embarrassing story that I will not go into here. Needless to say it did not involve any great acts of self-confident seduction on my part.

consuming than the standard 90's practice of 'buttoning' one, but despite the mechanical investment of yanking the metal circle around for each number I still bailed on my first attempt to ring this girl. I hung up the receiver before engaging the final set of cogs required to dial the number '9'.

I gathered all my nerve and ratcheted in the numbers, including the intimidating, near 360 degree, turn for that suspenseful 9.

After a few rings I was connected and an older female voice answered the phone.
"Hello?"
"Hi, is Alice there please?"
"One second. I'll go and get her."
(I guess that today's 'youngsters', with all their mobile phones and internets, will never get to experience the true awkwardness of having to interact with a girl's parents when trying to arrange a date. Damn technology is awesome.)

After Alice came on the phone there was some incredibly awkward chatting. The highlight of which was me dutifully following my parents advice and asking her, "Are your parents ok with us going on a date[57]?" She wisely concluded the conversation with: "I don't think this is such a good idea, but I'll see you at school!"

And that is the story of how I fluffed my first date!

---

[56] They had definitely invented phones with buttons many, many years before, but sadly my parents were not the type of people to throw out a perfectly functional phone.

[57] Writing about this is much more excruciating for me than any other part of this book, by the way.

My dating retrospective may have overshot a little here, so before we get bogged down in the fetid swamp of my angsty (yet decidedly uneventful) teenage years, let's get back to the creaming spires of Oxford[58].

When students first arrive amongst the quaint but imposing towers of ancient masonry that comprise the Oxford skyline they share a number of common experiences: first they are shuttled to their new room, given various introductions, and otherwise made pleasantly acquainted with their new Harry-Potterish environs. Then, once their parents have waved a fond farewell, the drinking starts in earnest. For this is the start of fresher's week; the annual rite of passage where new students are indoctrinated into Oxford life. This is achieved by generally encouraging them to socialise and make drunken fools of themselves. As well as all these fresh faced lambs to the slaughter, fresher's week also attracts some lecherous college veterans. These old timers are battle hardened from their own first year experiences, and they are keen to get into the pants of the freshers before they realise that drinking a lot results in bad decisions, and that those bad decisions are often assholes[59].

Sadly/happily I never got to be anyone's bad decision during freshers week. Even now I find something vaguely/decidedly repulsive about the whole predatory male undercurrent that flowed through those seven days. Back when I was a student, the idea of casual sex with a girl I didn't know held little appeal, regardless of how closely she resembled a sea lion pup in a nature documentary about killer whales. Sure, I sometimes thought that a bit of impulsive steamy action might be fun, but

---

[58] This witticism is shamelessly stolen from the mysterious 2010 "sex editor" at the Cherwell student paper.
[59] The phrase 'sharking on freshers' was the common parlance for this activity.

I had also noted that many of these unplanned drunken unions did not seem to come without emotional strings. This could result in ill matched and often toxic relationships, and if I was to going to try and have sex with someone, I wanted to sleep with someone I liked. I certainly didn't want to find myself in a relationship with someone that annoyed the shit out of me, trapped there by guilt and a desire not to hurt anyone's feelings. I guess I was just a romantic like that.

This line of reasoning, combined with the panic attacks that struck whenever I got close to kissing someone I actually liked (and the fact I was at Oxford, so I had to work a lot in between the excessive drinking), is my excuse for not losing my virginity until my early twenties. (Although I also don't think I should feel the need to make excuses; the stigma associated with being a virgin is incredibly dumb in the same way it's stupid to stigmatize being a 'slut', regardless of gender. In fact the world might be a much better place if we all accept that it's fine for anyone to be either, or anything in between.)

As Oxford students, we didn't really do much dating, or at least not many of the people I knew did. I mostly met girls I liked through large social interactions involving groups of friends. This then allowed me to subtly get to know girls under the guise of friendship, so I could then make an informed decision whether I really wanted to ask them out or to attempt mouth collision.

However, after numerous years of being ignominiously relegated to friend zone, I came to the firm conclusion that trying to be friends with a girl first is a fucking terrible strategy[60].

---

[60] "Nice guys come last" is a popular saying that I gather has been polluted somewhat by 'male rights activists' and their ilk saying it with their mouths. I don't think it's entirely true; actual 'nice guys' still

To begin with once you're friends with a girl, and you decide you like her, this makes it ten times harder to summon the nerve to actually ask her out, as now you've got far too emotionally invested. Also, attempting to stick your tongue in her mouth when drunk may also bugger up the friendship. Sure it may have worked for Chandler and Monica in 'Friends', but I've noticed a lot of things work for people in TV are often less likely to succeed in the real world... telekinesis being another thing that keeps letting me down.

Being in the 'friend zone' is a pretty shitty place to be. Not only does it strip you of all the weird 'mystery' and 'edge' that for some reason chicks reportedly dig, but it sometimes puts you in the position of 'the pseudo-brother' where you have to deal with a bunch of other crap. This may include having to cope with the object of your all-consuming-desire frequently talking about guys she likes, i.e. one of the 'edgy' and 'mysterious' dicks out there who she actually wants to have sex with[61]. (Or a

---

come before whiney guys that complain about coming last because they're nice guys when they're actually total douches. 'Friend zone' is another term that has drawn some flak from some feminist circles, but to deny the existence of this particular form of purgatory just seems bizarre. Sure, being put in friend zone doesn't necessarily give anyone the right to berate the friend-zoner, but sometimes one person likes another person but that person only wants to be friends. It's just a thing that happens and can't really be described as anyone's 'fault', just an unfortunate imbalance of chemistry and/or circumstance that can have painful emotional consequences for both parties. I get the feeling that even genuinely 'nice' guys rarely come first though. If I was ever a genuine nice guy once upon a time I would blame my getting left behind on getting stuck in a cycle of low confidence and being too nervous to make moves on girls before it was too late.

[61] I seem to have opened an internal can of bitter and cynical worms by reflecting on this. I apologize. If you do find yourself in friend zone though, one piece of advice: NEVER EVER EVER TRY TO GET A

perfectly normal guy that will be transmutated into a dick by your internal furnace of jealousy.)

So after many years of testing this friend zone BS I began to realise it was really just a much smarter emotional gamble to collide mouths first and ask questions later[62]. The persistence of my virginity was also not helped by a certain cluelessness that rendered me oblivious to numerous romantic opportunities that I still occasionally look back on and kick myself for. I think my blindness to female interest can be blamed on my lack of confidence and a failure to fully appreciate that, as the guy, I was almost always expected to make the first move. Sexist as that is, it appears to be the economic reality of the culture we live in.

This is not to say that during the 'friend zone years' I didn't try other strategies for the meeting of girls. Nights spent drinking would sometimes culminate with a visit to one of Oxford's nightclubs, perhaps the most common places for student romances to germinate. Unfortunately, Oxford nightclubs were pretty universally terrible. For example, a popular one I often attended was nicknamed "Filth" but was supposed to be called "The studio" (which is what you'd call it in front of your parents if they asked about your plans for the evening). However, all the students called it Filth, as it was the name of one of their club nights that had just stuck[63]. Filth was not a

---

GIRL TO LIKE YOU BY SENDING HER AN EMAIL TELLING HER YOU LIKE HER. It may seem like a good way to get all your thoughts in one place and present a cogent and intelligent argument as to why the two of you should date. Unfortunately I'm pretty sure no one ever got laid by presenting a cogent and intelligent argument as to why they should get laid..

[62] Though all the time I wasn't having sex I may have been significantly overestimating its value as a romantic adhesive.

[63] 'Filth' eventually closed down, because that's obviously what should

classy establishment. To begin with it was located on the top floor of what Americans would call a 'mall'. "Oh a roof top club!" you might be thinking, "that sounds nice!" You would be wrong.

To get to Filth you had to first walk through the eerily empty atrium of Westgate shopping centre, complete with shuttered shops and weird acoustics. Then you had to go up some anonymous back staircase, which also led to a multi-story car park (in case you wanted to drop your shopping off first). On peak nights, the queue for filth would snake down these stairs, and your heart would sink with the realisation that you were now going to have to spend a long time standing around without anything to drink. Once in the queue, your luck might further decline when you found yourself standing next to that weird awkward guy you were kind of friends with by proximity and with whom you were now forced to converse. Meanwhile a little way ahead of you some member of the rowing team might be chatting up the girl you were kind of into.

The 'BOOM, BOOM, BOOM' of distant club sounds could be easily heard over the chattering of the queue. The weird awkward guy tries to explain neo-liberalism to you. (Just because you're drunk, doesn't mean you've stopped being at Oxford.)

Eventually though, the queue is negotiated. You wave your driving licence at the bouncer and are ushered into THE CLUB. There were no rooftops to be found in the studio, or even windows for that matter, it was just a large and very dark room with flashing lights, loud music, and alcohol[64].

---

have happened according to capitalism, but yet I still feel saddened by this.
[64] They did try to create a VIP area for a while with weird semi-

Possibly the most noticeable feature of Filth was its carpeted floor. It was not noticeable to look at, just a grey black colour that blended with the darkness. However, every so often one would be standing in certain areas and then realise that your shoes had somehow become stuck there. This was because, over time, sufficient sugary beverages had been spilled on the carpet that it had become like one of those adhesive bug traps, capturing those undergrads lured onto it by the temptations of sex and booze. You could usually break your feet free with only a little effort, but this was not a nightclub you wanted to fall down in.

Once you had fought your way to the bar and consumed enough alcohol to forget one's inhibitions it was time to hit the dance floor. This is where shit tends to get real on the whole smooching and inappropriate physical contact front. While I found it a fun place to bust some moves with friends, the dance floor was not my seduction venue of choice. Although I may have had some moves (even if they tended to consist of randomly flailing my limbs in whatever direction came to me at the time). Apparently though, if you do enough erratic but confident gestures, other drunken people will be confused into thinking you know how to dance.

Even if these moves succeeded in attracting some female attention on occasion, I still struggled to capitalise on this by moving into physical-contact-dance-mode. With girls I knew I could sometimes get in 'the zone', but cozying up to a stranger for ye ole bump and grind was another matter. Even when plastered, I just felt like some kind of talking ought to happen

---

transparent curtains and beds to sit on. I think it's testament to English reserve that I never actually saw anyone having sex on the beds. It did seem like an open invitation after all.

first, but when I tried that I could never hear shit over the blasting music.

I may have diligently busted my moves in the middle of that dark and sticky meat market, but I rarely had the balls to place a bid. The few encounters I did have in Filth (and its less sticky competitors) were normally with wasted girls who lunged at me before my dodging instinct kicked in. Mostly though, the evening would be spent dancing with friends, fighting to the bar to buy drinks, standing around awkwardly, and then wandering about wondering where the friends I was dancing with earlier had gone to. Finally I would reach the 'quiet introspective drunkenness' stage and realise that I no longer wished to dance, but really wanted to sleep, so fuck this whole sweaty charade I'm outta here.

My feet would make solitary echoing sounds as I walked back down the stairs and past the shuttered shops. A couple might be drunkenly making out in one of these not-so-private recesses. Perhaps she was pressing him into the slats that were protecting the entrance to Sainsbury's. Or maybe he was pushing her against the metal meshwork in front of JD-sports, her fingers grasping into its triangular links. He though, was never me.

Sometimes my steps would sway a little as I escaped the purgatory of the Westgate centre, relieved at my return to the real city. Oxford's cobbled streets always had an air of reassuring permanence. It didn't matter how many kebabs were splattered across them, or how many stiletto heels dug into their polished crevices, they would endure. When it rained (which was often), those cobbles would reflect the yellow-orange street lights and shine like the scales of some great sleeping dragon. Sometimes I'd stare at those street scenes for a while, entranced by the golden light dancing in the falling raindrops. Then I'd curse that I hadn't brought my raincoat and make a run for it.

Chapter 10 - A cold wind blows in Brooklyn

Another Saturday in February and again you find me in a cocktail bar on a first date. This time I have ventured outside of Manhattan to an out-of-the-way cocktail bar in Williamsburg called "The Shanty". The drinks are strong and the company delightful. Her name is Catherine and she's a biology teacher who I met through my normal profile. She has both the looks and the charm, and something about the way she talks reminds me of a previous crush. I couldn't quite place it, but it may have been the way she put on a slightly different voice when telling an amusing story... a sort of dramatic lilt; " Aaaannnd ttthhheeenn THAT happened!" It was quite endearing.

We talked a lot about our shared love of nature and nature documentaries and I confessed that when I was a kid I wanted to grow up to be David Attenborough. We also discussed online dating a little. She had avoided answering any of the sex related questions on Okcupid. I subtly mentioned that I may have made a secret profile to see how other people answered them, but didn't give away much more than that.

Three or four drinks down and it was getting late. Catherine thought she'd better get going or her housemate would be worrying that I'd raped and murdered her. She also wanted me to finish her Sazerac on her behalf. I took a few sips to taste it, then I downed the rest in one with what I hoped was manly gusto.

I started to regret my manly gusto almost immediately. "Wow that was strong!" I said, clearing my throat a little, but avoiding any fits of coughing.

As we left the bar we were hit by a gale force blast of insanely cold winter air.

"Jesus it's cold!" I gasped.

We made our way towards the Lorimer St. subway stop, the wind buffeting us and chilling me to the bone. In this sort of situation, alcohol normally serves as a kind of protective jacket, dulling your awareness of the cold. But the wind was so intense that it instead became the focus my booze addled consciousness. I could still feel the Sazerac in the back of my throat.

I really liked this girl Catherine. We seemed similar in a lot of ways, not all of which I could put my finger on. In that quiet Brooklyn Street I wanted to stop in the shelter of a parked van, pull her close, then slowly bring my lips down towards hers and hold them together while we absorbed each other's warmth, resilient to the hostile elements.

Instead though, I fell behind a few paces and vomited in someone's recycling bin[65].

It was fairly quick and clean in its execution, but sadly it did not escape Catherine's notice.
"Are you ok?" she asked.
Earlier that evening I had explained that I used to have these panic nausea attacks but optimistically declared that "I seemed to be over them these days".
Clearly I was not over them, and a bin of recycled cocktails stood testament to that.

---

[65] I'd say that one was about 80% panic attack, 20% downing the Sazerac. Even though I was a bit drunk at that point, I don't normally throw up from alcohol, except perhaps when I down it really fast, and then I think there is also a panic element to that.

"Yeah, sorry about that! I feel fine now," I said as we continued towards the subway before parting ways.

*

Somehow despite this display Catherine agreed to meet me for a second date. Explaining to her that she should take my vomming as a compliment as "I only throw up around girls I like" may have helped my cause, and she agreed to meet me again for dinner and drinks. This went better, although at the end I did have to hide in the toilets of 'proletariat' for a little while staring down another panic attack. The toilets in question were illuminated by a single red light and had wallpaper that looked like it was covered in vintage pornographic images. This didn't really help. However, I managed to hold onto my dinner and produce a large belch instead, after which I felt instantly better.

I kissed her goodnight that time.

The third date was where it all went wrong. The activities themselves were actually quite romantic: visiting the Frick collection one Sunday morning, followed by lunch at the boathouse in central park, finishing with a walk through the park. (This romantic series was mostly by accident rather than design, the only planned part being the Frick).

However, Catherine seemed nervous and distant, especially for the walk through the park. I didn't see any opportunity to make romantic moves, and at the end we just said goodbye with a hug at the subway station. Apparently she needed to get home to do laundry. Maybe it was the fact I had offered to have her over and cook dinner that made her nervous. She perhaps sensed that I was hoping to sleep with her soon, although sex didn't often enter our conversations. Maybe because she seemed too lady-like or I was too afraid of scaring her away.

Anyway, a few days later I got a text saying that she *didn't think the chemistry was there.* I thought about sending her a bold message from my kinky profile, but I decided that would probably freak her out and maybe get me a restraining order, so I left it alone. We met a few times as friends later in the year, but it didn't go any further than that.

Chapter 11 - Nah you're one of the good ones

A kit of pigeons bursts through a gap in the towering masonry of two Murray Hill apartment buildings. They turn as one, wings lit up orange all of a sudden by the dusky light beaming between some red brick high-rises. There is something about seeing a flock of birds that always makes my heart leap; that sense of agency to the whole. The flock seems to be one thing, and yet it is many things, and at the same time, nothing at all.

This is a big group. They're flying fast and seem agitated. Perhaps they're trying to evade a falcon or some other invisible predator. The flock turns again, sinuous. The ones at the back seem to turn first, yet those at the front know to turn too, and the leaders become the followers and the followers the leaders. The light has been lost from their wings now and, instead of being a cloud of bright specs against dark brickwork, they have become a swarm of flapping black dots against the yellowish blue sky.

I lose them behind the buildings and walk on a while, my concentration returning to the street.

Then they are back again, slower now, flying low overhead. Close up, I can see the variations in their plumage and there's no doubt they are a mongrel bunch. Some are the standard dark grey of city pigeons with iridescent flashes of green and purple around their necks. Others, though, have white feathers sticking out here and there, and some of them are more white than grey. I suspect that somewhere back in that flock's ancestry some perfect white dove strayed too far from home and had her cloaca despoiled by some big city brute[66].

---

[66] Of course it could have been the other way around, but somehow that doesn't sound as fitting.

They're coming to rest now, whirling around the roof of a brown stone, each bird hovering in to perch along the parapet and then jostling amongst themselves to peer down into the street. The flock is disbanded and all they are now is just some birds on a roof.

A garbage truck blares its horn with an uncalled for intensity. Apparently the taxi in front hasn't recognised the green light with the appropriate haste. With that awful blast of sound the flock is instantly reborn and swoops off over the rooftops once again.

Anyway, why am I standing in this street watching some birds fly about? I've got a date to get to!

*

By early March I had fallen deep into the Okcupid rabbit hole. Far too many evenings were spent aimlessly flicking through profiles, although rather than working on an efficient system of identifying and messaging potential matches, it had become more of a crazed addiction to clicking on the pretty face squares, giving stars to the ones I liked, and being ever watchful of my inbox.

"YES! NEW MESSAGE!" was my reaction to the latest [1] to appear in the inbox of my kinky profile
"DOUBLE YES! SHE'S NOT UGLY!"

The message read:

"Your profile has me pretty intrigued. You managed to be rather explicit about sex without sounding like a complete jerk about it. That's amazing and something I really appreciate...

It's a rare thing to find. I would love to see your face, however!"

"YES! I DON'T SOUND LIKE A COMPLETE JERK!"

I obliged her with a picture of my face, and various messages were exchanged. This time around there wasn't much discussion of our sexual interests or exchange of suggestive pictures (the novelty of that was starting to wear off anyway). I determined that her name was Josie and she was working on a nursing program uptown. I got her number and we arranged to meet for a drink at a bar in my neighbourhood.

The bar was busy as hell and, rather than deal with the scrum alone, I waited outside for Josie to show up. It wasn't long before a girl fitting her description appeared. She was relatively short. Long black hair ran down over her shoulders and pair of glasses with thick black rims decorated her face.

After a slightly stiff greeting we went inside and the hostess found us a table for two.
"What do you like to drink?" I asked, as we surveyed the drinks menus.
"I like wine. I don't drink beer though. It doesn't agree with me..." said Josie.
"Any particular types of wine you like?"
"I don't really know much about wine but I like red ones... and ones with a lot of fruit, and with like rich strong flavours."
"Yeah, I don't know much about wines either, but maybe you'll like a Pinot Noir? That tends to have a lot of rich flavours going on."

Asking Josie about her day led to a general conversation about nursing school. She was in the middle of an anatomy course where they were shown various bits of real human corpse.

Unfortunately, hurricane Sandy had really played havoc with their classroom, located in the basement of a now half deserted hospital building. This building had been flooded and currently only had sporadic power and other utilities.

"Yeah, it's not great," she said, "and there was this one practical when we got stuck in the room with the dead bodies..."
"What?"
"Yeah, one of my classmates went to leave and the door handle broke off in her hand."
"Shit! Seriously? Was there not some other way out?"
"No. We were stuck, and there was no phone or cell reception down there either."
"Man, that must have been scary. How long were you stuck down there for?"
"Like 40 minutes. Some girls were freaking out, and like banging on the door and yelling. It was pretty cold down there too. Eventually the janitor heard us and let us out."

Josie told this insane story in a kind of dry understated way, as if being locked in a room with a bunch of dead bodies was an everyday occurrence that didn't really perturb her that much.

Conversation continued. Her family lived in New Jersey, she loved riding motorbikes and listening to heavy metal. She also had a couple of clearly visible tattoos. Perhaps the heavy metal and motorbikes conjures a certain image of a wild and uninhibited biker girl. That was not what she was like. She wasn't really shy either, just a little on the quiet side, and we didn't talk about BDSM much on that first date, or discuss sex a lot either. Although we did talk about past dating. She used to go out with an Army Ranger for a while, then a member of the NJPD. I may have found this a little intimidating as I didn't exactly fit with a line-up of burly Americans who shoot people for a living. I also found out that Josie owned a bunch of guns back in New Jersey, and, when she described her dad as building motorbikes for a living, I immediately imagined a muscled tattooed gent who was handy with a tyre iron, and who might not react kindly to the kinky scenarios I was envisaging for his daughter.

While we were on the subject of "guys" she complained:
"There's this Mexican guy who works in the coffee shop at the end of my street. He kind of fancies me. It was good to begin with because he used give me free pastries, but then it got kind of weird and now he creeps me out... Now I have to cross the street so he doesn't see me."
"Really? What creeped you out about him?"
"I dunno. He just kept coming onto me, and apparently he was always asking my friend about me. I'm pretty sure he's here illegally. Maybe I should get him deported."
I laughed. It sounded like she was joking. I think she was joking...

As we ordered a second round of drinks, Josie confessed that she got drunk really easily.
"Cheap date!" I said with a smile.
"Yeah, I think there must me something wrong with me, but I sober up quickly as well, and don't normally get hangovers."

After the second glass of vino she reported that she was "Really drunk". This wasn't completely obvious, but she did keep doing this slow-blinking-and-moving-head-backwards thing, which suggested her alcohol inhibited brain was having trouble coping with all her senses.

While figuring our next move I said: "You can come back to mine if you like, I have wine... Or tea if you want to sober up."
"Tea could be good," she replied.

*

Back at my place I carried out my slightly complicated ritual for making tea. At that time I only had a tiny travel kettle which would take about 5 minutes to boil a single cup of water. My cunning strategy around this was to microwave the water briefly in a Pyrex jug, then transfer it to the kettle to bring it to boiling. (NOTE: don't fully boil water in the microwave as it might explode in your face... which is bad.). This ritual may have looked a little strange to an outside observer. Fortunately though, Josie was collapsed drunkenly on my couch, and just maintaining conversation through the kitchen doorway, oblivious to my bizarre methodology for tea making.

A few minutes later I passed her a cup of warm Tetley tea.
"This is English Tea," I explained, "I don't know what it is about English tea that makes it English, but it's just solidly English... I mean it's refreshing, comforting and invigorating in a way that somehow only English Tea can be. Probably because it just reminds me of all the times I drank tea in England and felt invigorated."

We talked some more about tea, and a range of other things. Back on the subject of online dating she described how she had mostly met a bunch of weirdos.
"How'd you know I'm not a weirdo?" I joked, "I could be some crazy psycho who's just lured you back to his apartment to murder you."
"Nah, you're one of the good ones," she stated in matter-of-fact tone.
"But how do you know?" I said smiling, hoping to build a little erotic tension.
"I can just tell," she replied, in the same confident tone while blowing on her tea to cool it down

No erotic tension to be generated there then, but it was pleasantly reassuring that this girl I had only just met seemed convinced that I was a good human.

"I dunno... you can't trust these Englishmen, you never know when we might try and colonise you or something!" I quipped.

"You're ok. You're here legally, not like those illegals."

'Huh,' I thought, 'I'm suddenly getting a bad feeling about this conversation...' but before I could interject and divert Josie went off on a little wander through anti-immigration land.

"If they can get into this country they get a sweet deal as an illegal immigrant. They get free healthcare, free schools, free food, free money... like a free ride that everyone else has to pay for. It's a big problem."

So I consider myself a pragmatist. I believe in having principles but I also believe in adopting the most sensible course of action to actually achieve the objective of those principles. In this situation though, I was not sure how to weigh the ethical positives and negatives of me getting laid vs. fighting perceptions that I believed to be false[67].

So, in order to respond to these statements that I profoundly disagreed with, I did this:

Precisely nothing.

I didn't challenge what I thought was a misinformed belief that illegal immigrants somehow have an easy life in America. I didn't address any of the broader questions of human moral

---

[67] I know, I'm a fucking bleeding heart socialist commie liberal. Deal with it.

responsibility for helping other humans regardless of what patch of soil they were born on. I didn't even subtly encourage her to probe her own assumptions without directly attacking her comments.

Instead I just said, "Uh huh."

And then I changed the subject.

And then I slept with her.

*

Josie had finished her tea and I asked, "How are you doing? Tea sober you up?"
"I think I'm feeling less drunk now. That tea definitely helped," she replied.
"Well then. I'd better take advantage of you before you sober up completely."

She smiled, still slightly slumped in the sofa, and so I leaned in and kissed her.

Her lips weren't particularly responsive but they willingly went along with mine. They had this slightly odd flavour, not unpleasant, perhaps a particular variety of chapstick I had not yet encountered.

She responded fairly passively to my advances, but before long I had stripped her of her clothes and she was lying under me along the length of my sofa[68]. One hand worked her pussy

---

[68] So for some reason I feel like I need to make some sort of excuse for all this talk about sex. These stories are not meant to be boasts, (although I hopefully include enough detail on my own fumblings to

while the other explored the rest of her body, slapping various bits of it to ensure she felt appropriately dominated. She made a lot of positive noises as I aggressively fingered and probed. Then to my surprise, after only a moderate amount of time working her like this I felt a climactic series of contractions inside her, after which she went a bit limp...

'Well that was quick!' I thought to myself. It turned out Josie was easy to please, which is always good for the ego. We hadn't really discussed her specific BDSM interests, so the toys stayed hidden on that first date and I focused on dominating her with my body alone. At one point I decided that girl jizz and my black fabric sofa didn't go so well together, so I tried to lift her up and carry her onto my bed. However, she displayed an understandable lack of faith in my upper body strength, and jumped to her feet before I could take her full weight.

On the bed I worked a second orgasm out of her with my hands and then began to seek my own satisfaction. However, sex with someone who orgasms easily does have some drawbacks. Her working up to the climax and the climax itself felt pretty damned great. However, just as I was coming up to speed she would then go limp and placid, and I would instinctively shift down a gear. Then the cycle would repeat with me not much closer to orgasm.

In search of my own fulfilment I turned her over onto her knees. She had a slightly odd tattoo of a bulging eyed tree frog at the base of her spine, which seemed to stare at me mournfully as I took her from behind. Perhaps in the UK we

---

make that clear). Nor are they meant to be erotica, though I do hope to instil some of the eroticism that was felt at the time. I guess they are just an important part of my dating story, and I want to tell as unflinchingly as possible.

might call this kind of tattoo a "tramp stamp" but I don't think tree frogs count as trampy... do they?... I mean at least it wasn't a butterfly.

I knelt upright watching myself going in and out of her, as I gripped her pelvis with both hands, the small amount of flesh on her hips squeezed out around my fingers, and I held her body firmly like this, forcing her backwards while I thrust forward, (though you probably get how sex works by now). She buried her head in the pillows, muffling assorted sounds.

'Well this is fun!' I thought to myself, widening my perspective a little. Temporarily observing the scene in the third person, I imagined myself as Christian Bale in American psycho, looking at himself in the mirror while fucking. I mean I imagined myself as Christian Bale without the muscle flexing and murdering... but then even with those caveats I didn't find the idea of being Christian Bale very sexy, so I went back to imagining myself as me.

I threw some more spanks in there while Mr Tree Frog looked on, though his red eyes grew no wider. Her skin was smooth and reddened evenly where it was struck, leaving nice red handprints. She came again and slumped forward in the bed. I lay on top of her, still thrusting deep inside of her, and breathing down hard on her neck. Then taking hold of her shoulder with one hand and her hip with the other I pulled her back onto her knees and kept up the full-throttle-fucking. Finally I lost myself in the influx of sensation and came with a grunting gasp.

She slumped back into the pillows and I collapsed beside her.

"How are you doing?" I asked.
"Awesome," she replied, "...I don't think I can move though."

Eventually she did remember how to move, and refusing my offer of board for the night she left my apartment with the suggestion:

"Maybe we can try the chains next time?"

*

One of the cool things about online dating is you get to meet a bunch of different people who you might not normally encounter, especially if you're a science nerd and spend much of your life confined to the lab. Maybe this sampling of diverse personalities is only fun if you're a little anthropologically minded, but aren't we all a bit intrigued by how other people in the world think and act?

When I moved to New York I was an explorer in an unfamiliar land and I wanted to get a comprehensive impression of the native inhabitants. Although the attractive female inhabitants may have taken priority just a little bit. New York certainly has no shortage of diversity; packed with all kinds of people, coming from all kinds of backgrounds, working all kinds of jobs, going all kinds of places, and dreaming all kinds of dreams. Oxford on the other hand is often described as existing in its own sort of bubble; a university city isolated from some of the economic realities that affect the rest of the UK, and mainly populated by a horde of students with above average intelligence and/or schooling. While diversity could still be found, the pulse of that city was dictated by the passing of the terms, and its tides of expression were linked to the phases of exams and finals.

There are many stereotypes about Oxford students that frequently surface in the UK media, the most popular one is that Oxford is dominated by elitist snobs who are all members of exclusive drinking societies that spend their time debating the best type of sword to open a champagne bottle with and the most effective ways to further defraud the working classes[69].

Fortunately, while I did encounter over-privileged and over-twatish individuals at Oxford with some regularity, they did not seem to dominate the student population. I made many great friends there whom I considered to be an interesting mixture of the fairly-down-to-earth or entertainingly-eccentric. However, none of these close friends belonged to any of the "drink port and urinate on the poor" clubs you hear about.

While I was an undergraduate, my group of friends seemed like a diverse bunch of characters, but they were all highly educated, mostly hard working, and mostly with parents from the English "middle classes". My friend diversity may have expanded a bit when I became a graduate student, but I was still in Oxford and I didn't appreciate how small the pond was until I was dropped in the ocean of New York.

Josie was a new and interesting fish. Definitely a variety that I had not come across in my little English puddle. However, just because her colours didn't match the ones adorning my own scales, it didn't mean that they couldn't shine with their own fascinating gleam.

*

Later that same week Josie came to my apartment after work and we chatted for a while over some wine. After a little bit of

---

[69] Drinking societies like the "Bullingdon club" for example that has moulded the privilege of far too many English politicians.

friendly kissing and petting, I sat up straight and looked down at her.

"Strip," I said, in a quiet but firm voice. She seemed briefly taken aback by the sudden change of tone, but obliged me and stripped down to her underwear, which I then further deprived her of.

"Stand up," I said. Taking her by the hand I walked her over to the end of my metal bed frame and slowly but firmly pushed her against it. My bed had convenient solid bars and knobs towering at each end (I may have purchased it with bondage in mind). The top horizontal bar at the end of my bed rested a little above Josie's belly button and I took her left hand and held it against it. Then I took a length of chain and began securing her wrist. "CLICK," the padlock closed, locking the bed, the tightened chain, and her wrist as one immobile unit. I moved onto the second wrist, the chains rattled as I wrapped the end around her soft skin and the hard metal. Another "CLICK" and both her hands were locked down. Her arms were spread open at about 45 degrees, as if she was about to greet someone with a low embrace, though of course embracing was now impossible for her.

Not satisfied with restraining her arms I knelt down and padlocked the end of a second length of chain around her left ankle. I threaded it noisily around one bedpost, then the other bedpost, and then back down to her right ankle. I wrapped the chain around it, making sure it was taught and forcing her legs apart, and threaded the last padlock through the leg-squeezing links.

With a final click she was all mine.

Running my hand up the inside of her leg I pointed this out to her.

She struggled a little to test the limits of her restraints, but found them to be unyielding.
"Better keep you quiet," I said, bringing out a recently acquired ball gag. Stretching it between my hands I brought it down over her face and pulled it back into her mouth. Her lips embraced the ball with a quiet guttural noise which you can only imitate if you try to talk with your mouth wide open and your tongue fixed in place.

To complete her feeling of helplessness I secured a blindfold over her eyes, placing her in darkness while she strained against the chains. I grasped her hair, pulling her head back while my other arm reached around and gripped her body tightly; reaching down my fingers toyed with the edge of her clit. Then I withdrew and let her hover in anticipation of what I might do next.

I brought my hand down firmly across her ass. The satisfying smacking sound reverberated around my otherwise quiet apartment. It was followed by more of the same, although each smack had its own slight variations in timbre; right cheek, left cheek, harder, softer, fingers open, fingers closed, all these variables made each thwacking noise its own unique symphony. The smacks were accompanied by Josie's quiet groans and exhalations, made unintelligible by the black plastic ball filling her mouth[70].

---

[70] If I was writing this as erotic fiction this might be a good time to include some saucy dialogue, perhaps uttering standard pornographic phrases such as "It's time for your punishment you bad little slut"... However, in real life I find this kind of dirty talk doesn't really come naturally with people you've only met a couple of times. As well as

My hands grew a little tired and her ass grew somewhat red, but I wanted to take her a lot further into pain land. I unbuckled my belt from my jeans and slid it out through its denim loops, enjoying the friction of it dragging around my waist. Folding it in half I drew the belt slowly across her ass and back, letting her anticipate what she was about to receive. Then I let fly.

The belt left thick red marks across her buttocks, back, and legs. She strained more against the chains in a futile attempt to escape her punishment, the gagged "Uuuggnnnhhh!!" and "Oouugnnn!!" noises she made grew more intense. I swung the belt harder and harder, working towards her limits.

Then, after one particularly aggressive swing of the belt a different, more desperate, noise escaped the ball gag. Her body recoiled hard against the bed and chains in a way that I could tell was driven by instinct rather than conscious thought. She exhaled with a hint of a whimper.

Although she didn't mumble the safe word or make the safe gestures we'd previously agreed on, I could tell some kind of pain threshold had been crossed. Maybe if she had been able to communicate more freely she would have wanted me to push her further, and I could have, but something about seeing that instinctive mammalian reaction to severe pain flicked a switch in my head. Previously my own excitement had been growing and growing with every strike, but as soon as I sensed that I had crossed a line innate feelings of empathy released an internal bucket of cold water, which manifested as an

---

running the risk of accidentally offending your playmate, I used to feel at risk of sounding silly and clichéd, so unless I was specifically inspired my sex dialogue could be pretty weak.

immediate loss of turgidity before Josie had even finished her whimper[71].

I took the belting back down a notch. Her reactions to the pain regained some poise, and my excitement returned. Once I was satisfied that my plaything had received sufficient punishment, I rewarded her with more conventional stimulation (i.e. sex!) Josie seemed to enjoy herself, still chained to the bed and slumping as far forward over the frame as the chains would allow. I couldn't quite get into the full swing of things myself though, as I had to squat weirdly in order to get in the right position (chaining someone in place does have its drawbacks), even when lifting her up off her feet so her whole weight was shared by me and the bed frame I still had to bend at the knees a little, so once Josie seemed to have solidly climaxed, I released her from her bonds, lay her down on the bed face first, and chained her in that position instead.

It occurs to me that I may be getting a little carried away with descriptions of our sexual antics... so for the sake of brevity I will not dwell on many more of the details. To summarise the

---

[71] Perhaps being turned off my inflicting serious pain is not consistent with some fantasies of how sadistic Dominant should be. I'll talk about 'labels' in the next aside, and I have never claimed to be a true "dom" or a genuine "sadist", either here or on my kink themed dating profile. Not that I wish to impose judgements on the right or wrong ways to go about BDSM, but it seems to me that while imagined fantasies of extreme abuse are all well and good, in real life people have certain physiological limits. Past these limits the bodies instinctive responses to pain might overrule all other sensations and excitements, regardless of how turned on someone is to start with. Of course these limits may vary wildly from person to person, and perhaps I seem overly empathetic to some, more conditioned, submissives, but I think I'd still rather be a bad 'Dom' than risk becoming a bona fide psycho.

rest of that night I next gave her the cold ice and hot candle wax treatment, followed by a more mutually fulfilling fuck session. By the end of that evening Josie was quite proud of the various chain marks she had accumulated.

After that our "relationship" continued in quite a straightforward fashion. Every week or so I would get a text from Josie asking how things were going. The resulting conversation would end in me inviting her over, or arranging to hang out at some point, which would almost always end in some kind of sex.

It wasn't JUST sex. On one occasion I helped Josie with her anatomy revision. I made her name nerve connections while she crouched on my rug, naked and on all fours. The belt served as punishment for hesitation or incorrect answers. This game would have probably been more fun if she hadn't memorised all the answers so well. In the end she only got a couple wrong so I had to punish those mistakes especially harshly. Needless to say, she didn't forget them after that! Also, occasionally we went out for drinks or something. Ok fine, it was mostly just sex.

A few more permutations of the chains were explored; I used them as a collar to lead Josie around my apartment like a dog on one occasion. Although that game quickly got boring when I realised I didn't really have anywhere interesting to lead her. "This is a cupboard," I said, "maybe I'll chain you up in here someday... but now let's go back to the bed".

Hog tying her hands to her feet was also fun, and this left me with a fair amount of excess chain. It was cold to the touch having been sitting in my flat all day without the heating on, and Josie complained about this. Having padlocked her hands to her feet, I dumped the remainder of the cold chain on her back. She gasped and I left it sitting there while I thrust my cock into her mouth.

In summary then, the sex was pretty great. However, I think it was clear to both of us that this relationship would remain a casual one. In many ways I found Josie quite a sweet girl; she was attractive and interested in science, she clearly cared about her family and those around her, she was honest and drama free, and she always replied to my texts reliably and promptly, which was a rare level of courtesy to find in NY.

There may have been some significant differences in the way we saw the world, especially when it came to politics. Perhaps I should have explored these differences more and pro-actively challenged her complaints about immigrants, social security, chemicals in food, Obamacare, grain based diets etc. However, I was always aware of the three guns she owned back in New Jersey (and her two ex's with job descriptions that included the use of deadly force), and I didn't really want to piss her off! It wasn't the imagined threat of violence that prevented a real relationship developing though, I never really felt that comfortable properly opening up to Josie, and even when she was shitfaced after her second glass of wine, she never seemed to really open up to me either. Despite all the weird sex, some intangible barrier between us remained unbroken. I kept seeing Josie casually for a while after we met and we switched to being platonic friends when she started dating yet another person who wears a gun to work. We're still friends more than a year later and I hope that doesn't change when I eventually summon the nerve to show her this chapter!

Aside 2 - On the subject of 'labels'

People seem to like sticking labels on each other, in fact it almost seems telling people they're a 'type' of person, or assigning one's own personality to a particular brand is becoming a modern obsession. Labels come in all shapes and sizes. You might say someone is an 'extrovert', a 'slut', a 'type A personality', a 'masochist', a 'liberal', a 'Republican', a 'control-freak', a 'border-line personality' etc etc. You might even get all wishy washy and type people by their astrological sign, or all pseudo-sciencey and assign someone a series of letters based on how they score on a personality test.

In some sense, using labels for people like we use labels for other objects seems like a reasonable way of making sense of the complicated world we live in. When interacting with our peers, it's useful to be able to predict how they will behave in different circumstances, and it's an attractive idea that you can pre-empt someone's future actions based on the limited things you know about them already.

However, I would like to propose that all existing systems of personality categorisation are pretty much always worthless bullshit.

While some labels may have value for quickly summarising a small number of personality traits, I think the general idea that personality types are a useful way of summarising people is like an infected thorn embedded in our social consciousness. It's a way of thinking that has been around for so long that we assume it serves a function and its merits are too rarely questioned.

I wonder if the popularity of labelling people is due to a human desire to be in control of all the information in our lives, and if we can't assign everyone to neat little personality categories this messiness makes some of us uncomfortable somehow. Perhaps some folks just need to put those rubber stamps on people, however inaccurate or misleading, just because they don't want to deal with the amount of thought required to gain a real appreciation of all the nuanced characters they encounter out in the world.

I think it's fair to use labels to summarise behaviours, e.g. saying things like: "Dave has a masochistic side", or "Jeannie was acting slutty last night"[72]. However, the critical thing is always recognising that a specific personality trait is just a small facet of any person, and to label a whole individual, e.g.; "Dave the masochist" or "Jeannie the slut" is a toxic way of thinking. Many people also lack a certain empathetic plasticity in how they deal with other humans, and once you assign someone a label it's as if they can somehow be written off; "Dave's a masochist. Masochists like pain. Something just fucked him up when he was young. I don't need to acquire any further understanding of Dave as I know what Masochists are like, therefore I know what Dave's like." Or more simply: "I don't like Masochist's, so I won't like Dave." It takes a certain kind of arrogance to make these assumptions, and it's an arrogance that I fear is all too prevalent. We should never underestimate someone's capacity to surprise us.

When I say personality categorisation is worthless bovine excrement, I'm not trying to imply that it's impossible to put people into loose groupings based on similar traits. However, what we need to acknowledge is that personalities are made up of a very large number of behavioural tendencies. People's

---

[72] The word 'slut' and prejudices against sexual active people deserve ranty asides all of their own, but for now let's focus on the general notion of labelling people.

tendencies then fall somewhere along various analogue spectra, and can often shift position unpredictably. As I see things this makes it completely impossible to draw solid lines around groups of individuals and tease them apart from the grand fractal tapestry of human nature.

Someone might argue that there's some usefulness in trying to make simplified 'digital' groups out of these 'analogue' mixtures, but in my opinion a filing system where someone can be in one folder one day and a different folder the next is a waste of time. Why not just give everyone their own folder? Then add notes as you get to know someone and not before.

I think it's particularly important to stay away from personality labels when dealing with sexuality and sexual interests, just because there are so many prejudices floating around out there.

For example, when I talk about sleeping with someone on the first date, often people imagine that I must have been on a date with a certain "type" of girl. Sometimes the reflex response is "I'm not sure they'd be my type" or "I'm not that type of girl"... Fine you want to get to know someone before sleeping with them, I can see many arguments to support that, and I used to think that way myself. However, fuck the assumption that there's a specific "type" of girl who will sleep with a guy on a first date. Also don't think for one second that promiscuous behaviour can predict one single thing about the rest of their personality.

Of the people I've been out with[73], and the small subset that I've slept with on the first date, I couldn't put any two of these

---

[73] The chapters of this book don't do any of my date's justice. I can only show you a few small facets at a time, and also it doesn't help

girls in one single personality category. In fact, there have barely been any similarities between them at all. Some might assume that my kinky sex profile might also attract a certain subsection[74] of the psychological strata, and that girls interested in being dominated might all have key traits in common. However, instead I have met a genuine diversity of individuals through my kinky profile. Several girls self-identified as "type A" personalities and considered themselves dominant in the workplace etc, but some girls were more quiet and submissive in their mannerisms. In fact most were just laid back normal people. Some dates might describe their personality as more dominant or submissive (as if they HAVE to be one or the other), but they often struck me as pretty well balanced. Thus, I have concluded that there are no hard and fast rules about the sorts of people interested in kinky sex, and no soft and slow ones either.

The general point of this diversion is to stress that everyone really is an individual. Our multitudinous human traits make it impossible to meaningfully categorise anyone as a 'type'. For some reason, people seem to like assigning themselves to categories. The simplest one being "Am I a good or bad person?" Fuck that shit, you're just a person, you can be a person who does good stuff or one who does bad stuff, and that can even depend on the kind of day you're having. You're just you and no label is ever going to capture that.

You may like this philosophy or you may not, but personally I can't help but think that all this human complexity makes the world just that little bit more exciting to live in.

---

that I forget a lot of the interesting details from conversations we had.
[74] Pun not really intended... but I'm going to leave it there anyway.

V

I'm not sure I believe in love at first sight and when I first met T.G.O.M.D. I did not immediately realise she was The Girl Of My Dreams. However, little by little, like autumn leaves settling on dewy grass, I began to experience a building feeling...

'I might just have something with this girl...' contributed my internal monologue, as my mouth occupied itself laughing at one of T.G.O.M.D.'s witty anecdotes. Three dates in now and the accumulating leaves of affection still hadn't been blown away by any gusts of sudden irresolvable incompatibility.

I was starting to hang on the arrival of her messages. She was sufficiently under my skin that if called upon I would happily perform some manly task to prove self-worth and romantic affection. Would I walk five hundred miles and then would I walk five hundred more? Well I'd probably attempt it, although I might start to question my decision after the first hundred miles or so.

My hand is starting to grow clammy as it rests on the table, still interlocked with hers.

Our drinks are almost empty and I'm trying to think of the best way to invite her back to my place, but without giving off the impression that I'm keen to leave and risking a premature end to a date that I'm otherwise enjoying immensely.

Chapter 12 - Harder!

For the start of this chapter we're going to have to go back in time to January, because that is when I first began chatting to a cute-bisexual-artist-student-Puerto-Rican-girl named Angelina[75]. We talked a bit about art and artists, and discussed the possibility of going to checkout MoMa together. She had messaged my normal profile, but her Okcupid personality-o-meter gave her a very strong 'kinkiness' rating, which seemed promising... so I gave her my number.

One Saturday morning I got a text:

"Hey, I'm on the train headed back to the city, what you doing?"

My afternoon was free so I agreed to meet up, but unable to decide what part of town we should rendezvous in I said that I'd come meet her outside Grand Central when her train arrived. I figured there must be somewhere good for a drink around there... "*Let's be spontaneous! :-)*" I texted.

I waited by the front entrance to Grand Central station. There were an innumerable variety of travellers coming and going through the station's doors. Unlike most public buildings that endure heavy foot traffic, this hub of American rail transport did not have efficient automatic door opening systems. It just had big heavy swinging wooden doors with shiny brass finishings that the Saturday travellers were having to battle with while towing their luggage.

---

[75] This message came before I had even got laid in New York yet, but this is a story that played out slowly and reached its 'conclusion' shortly after I met Josie, so that's why I am only telling it now.

Watching this war of Americans vs. doors provided sufficient entertainment while I waited for Angelina to arrive. The best bits were when two hapless folks would try and take on the same door simultaneously from both sides. They would then either neutralise each other's efforts, or propel the door with unexpected velocity towards the individual who decided to pull... This all happened despite the presence of large windows through which the assault-on-door could be easily coordinated, if only they had a little more awareness. I could probably reflect for several more paragraphs on New York door etiquette (or lack thereof), and its implications for social decline. However, we all have places to be and my date is meant to be turning up at some point in this story, so let's get back to her.

After a couple of texts to confirm which door I was waiting by, Angelina appeared, walking across the street. She was shorter than I expected and her nose and lip piercings seemed to assume more prominence than they had in her profile photos. Perhaps they were enhanced in real life by her bad-ass leather jacket. Still, I thought it was a hot look.

"Hi! How's it going?" I asked.
"Fine thanks," she said, while we hugged a greeting, "some homeless lady just told me I looked sexy... I always get come on to by homeless people for some reason."
"Ha, well I guess it's still a compliment. So do you feel like getting a drink somewhere?"
"Sure. Where's good around here?"
"I have no idea. This isn't a part of town I hang out in much. I'm sure we can find somewhere though. I figured we could give being spontaneous a try."

Sadly, as this date took place back in January, I did not have a smartphone on me as it was still somewhere in the postal system. Smart phones are very helpful to the process of being spontaneous as at the very least they give you suggestions for the best directions to be spontaneous in.

"Let's try down there," I said, pointing to a street running alongside Grand Central, "I have a good feeling about that street!"
"Sure," she replied.

A few minutes later we were staring at blocks of lifeless concrete and glass that mostly comprised office and parking entrances and stretched off into the distance, devoid of all personality, and, more importantly, devoid of anywhere that looked like it might serve drinks.

"Well this is a shit street. Whose idea was it to come down here!" I said.
She laughed.
We retraced our steps a little way, then I said "Ok this is the last time I try being spontaneous... Erm... over there is a tacky looking Mexican place we could try?" I pointed.
"Do you think that just because I'm Hispanic you should take me to a Mexican place? Huh?" She said, in what I hoped was a joking tone.
"Ha, no just seems like the only place on this street that might serve beer! Shall we try it?"
"Whatever. I don't mind."
"Let's take a look."

We entered the tacky Mexican place with neon margaritas in the window. The inside of the tacky Mexican place was also tacky. There were no other customers. We were immediately set upon by an enthusiastic waiter who hustled us into some seats and gave us menus before we could protest.
"So this place is... Erm... something?" I said
"Yeah, it seems pretty terrible," she said.

"Do you want to try somewhere else?"
"Yeah."
While the waiter's back was turned, we put down the menus and scuttled for the door.
"Well, being spontaneous isn't working out as well as I'd hoped!" I said, even though the humour of that comment seemed exhausted.
"I know this place down by Union Square. Do you want to head down there?" She suggested.
I was more than happy to let her take control of this so-far-disastrous date.
"Sure," I replied.

A short subway ride later we were jostling through Union Square towards what turned out to be a less tacky Mexican place. Maintaining conversation on the way there came easily enough, even if it mostly consisted of complaining about New York.

This Mexican place didn't have waiters. You just ordered food from a counter, or drinks from the bar. Having got some guacamole and chips we sat at a two person table by the window.
"Shall we get something to drink?" I asked, gesturing towards the bar.
"Actually I'm not technically old enough to drink yet. I turn 21 in March."
"Oh shit, sorry! I forget how crazy this country is about that. The legal age is 18 in England[76]!"
"Yeah it's 18 in Puerto Rico too, which is why I don't have a fake ID, but I drink all the time though."

---

[76] I also thought her Okcupid profile said she was older, but I decided not to say "Oh I thought you were older!" in case that sounded insulting somehow.

I'm not sure if I could get in trouble for writing about whether I bought beer for someone just under 21 in an anonymous dating book... but fortunately this is only a hypothetical question as I then purchased two non-alcoholic (but surprisingly beer like) beverages for us to drink instead.

We chatted over our drinks that totally weren't beer. I told her about my research and she talked about art school and print making. She found it frustrating not being able to just 'do her own thing', and believed that her art teacher had some kind of mild vendetta against her. I asked her what she liked to make prints of and she said a series of words that made no sense to me, then she clarified: "...it's like they're about imagined historical situations, but that never actually happened... and sometimes combining fictional characters..."
"Uh huh... I've not heard of that," I replied.
"Like for example I'm working on this piece right now where Malcolm X is being tortured by Hannibal Lecter at the battle of Gettysburg. I can show you if you like."
"Sure!"

She showed me a picture on her iPhone.
"Cool! That's interesting!" is what I said.
'My god that is comically terrible,' Is what I thought.
The picture consisted of squiggly lines that were barely recognisable as humans, let alone Hannibal Lecter or Malcolm X. However, despite never reading the dating rule book, I guessed that telling a date their artwork looks comically terrible is considered a faux pas... and maybe I just didn't 'get it'.

Some more rambling conversation later and we arrived at the topic of her piercings.
"Do you think my lip piercing is ugly?" she asked.

"No, not at all," I said, staring at it, "although does it not get uncomfortable? Like, doesn't it catch it on your food? Or does it get in the way if you're kissing someone?"
"No, not at all."
"Fair enough. I don't think I'll get one though," I said, smiling.
"Do you have any tattoos?" she asked.
"No, although I wouldn't rule out getting one... I'm just not sure I could decide on anything I'd want to have permanently drawn on me. How about you?"
 "Yeah I've got a couple, there's this one..."
She pulled up her sleeve and showed me a wilted rose on her upper arm.
"...and this one..."
She tilted her head to show me a beetle hidden on the back of her neck under her hair.
"... and then there's a big one on my thigh that my tattoo artist friend is still working on. It's going to be of my old cat sitting on his favourite chair. Here I'll show you."
She shifted in her seat, presenting her thigh to me, and then raised her skirt up to a slightly scandalous height in order to show me the large half-finished picture of cat and chair. I resisted the urge to look around to see if we'd attracted anyone's attention. It definitely would have been obvious that this girl was nearly showing me her ass in public.

Part of me hoped someone was looking.

After she lowered her skirt, a conversation about pets ensued. At some point I complained:
"There are so many people with annoyingly small ratty dogs in this city. They always seem to run out in front of my feet as if they're begging me to accidentally kick them!"
"Yeah sometimes I kick them deliberately," she said
"Wait... What?! Seriously?!"
"Well only like once... I was drunk!"

"Haha! That's... amazing?... If slightly scary..."

"I didn't kick it that hard... It was just in my way!... Although it did yelp a little though."

"Did its owner not get mad at you?"

"She was looking the other way, but she did give me an angry look afterwards. But whatever!"

"Wow... I'm glad I now know that you like to kick small dogs!" I said with a smile.

"I don't! Shut up. Whatever."

Weird as this date was, there was a pleasant transparency to it. As evidenced by her dog kicking story, Angelina had this unreserved honesty about her, combined with a certain amount of bad-ass aggression and perhaps some thinly veiled vulnerability; all of which made her easy to talk to. I told her about my occasional nausea attacks on dates, and the second sex profile I'd recently started on Okcupid. We related over our vaguely traumatic experiences in Catholic school and we discussed BDSM a bit as well, although we didn't go into our personal interests at that point. She also described an abusive relationship she had been in back in Puerto Rico. This seemed like a fairly amazing amount of sharing for a first date, but I found it hard not to respect her openness.

We both had friends in town to meet that evening, so as it started to get dark outside we agreed that it was probably time to head out. Angelina took the remaining chips and guacamole with us: "In case I can give them to some homeless guy," she said, and sure enough within a block there was some shabbily dressed chap sitting on the pavement who accepted her offering with an uninterpretable grunt.

We exchanged a firm hug by the union square subway stop, and then with a smile she disappeared down into the concrete guts of the city.

*

After my first date with Angelina we exchanged a couple of messages. Apparently she somehow got the impression that I wasn't really into her, so I had to assure her that I was (even if she did like to kick small animals). I tried to arrange a second date, but I didn't get any further response.

Finally I got an instant message from her: "*Can I see your kinky profile?*"

"*I thought you'd never ask! :)*" I replied, and sent her the link.

She seemed to like what she saw, and some back and forth ensued. She told me that she had made her own flogger and asked if I wanted to see it. Of course I said yes. The texted picture of the flogger excited me. The fact that it was draped over her bare ass in the image definitely helped.

Trying to arrange a second date still proved a challenge though. Many of my messages went unanswered for long periods, and I may have overdone the sex banter to try and attract her attention. After describing how I'd like to have her chained to my bed so I could work multiple orgasms out of her with my hands, she accused me of regarding her as an object and said she was reluctant to meet because she didn't think I respected her. Slightly perplexed by the change in tone, I assured her I did respect her, and I thought I was just playing the part I was supposed to play in the game I thought we were playing...

Confused and frustrated, I gave up the chase. Then a month or so later I got a message from her out of the blue. "*Hey*" it read. Not much to go on there so I ignored it. A while later I got a wordier message and we started talking again, but now the roles were reversed and she was pushing to meet me.

Eventually a Saturday came around when we were both free and a second date was set. Well, except it turned out she wasn't quite free. She actually had some friends in town but wanted me to come meet her anyway. It was never really clear to me what her plan was, but we found ourselves at the same union square Mexican place where we landed on our first date. She still had a friend with her but I thought I did a good job of dealing with this extra company and engaged them both in friendly conversation. Her friend then pointed out that Angelina and I were both being really awkward, and that we should stop being awkward.

Angelina informed me she had been out of touch partly because she had been busy dating a couple. She didn't seem to rate the experience positively, reporting that it had gotten weird when the guy seemed to be more into her than he was into his girlfriend. I didn't get a clear impression of what the couple was actually like from Angelina's polarized statements, but reportedly the guy was a muscle bound sports obsessed douche, and the girl was a psycho control freak.

Having successfully sowed discord in that relationship, Angelina had abandoned ship and now found herself back on the singles wagon, hanging out with me... and her friend.
"You look different to when I last saw you," she said.
"Really?" I guess I've had a haircut at some point.
"Do you think I look different?"
"Not really."
"You don't think that I look fat? I've put on a bit of weight."

I do not follow many rules when it comes to talking to women, but one I try to stick by solidly is to never ever ever be drawn into a conversation about their weight. That way madness lies. Talking about weight and body shape in the abstract is dangerous enough, but a conversation with someone about their actual body can quickly become a lose-lose situation. If you offer too much reassurance you risk sounding insincere and they might get angry at you. If you don't offer enough reassurance then they might think that you secretly think they're fat, and get angry at you. It's like walking along a knife edge, which actually is a knife edge. You can't stand on a knife edge. You'll just end up being like: "Ow! Why do my feet hurt?!... Ow! Why am I now cut in half?!"

It is possible that some part of my brain had already observed that Angelina looked a tiny bit sturdier than she did when we first met, but not in a way that had compromised her looks. My brain had filed this observation under "information not to bring up at any cost, even if asked about it directly".

"No, you look good," I said, "you've dyed your hair right? It looks redder."

See what I did there? See how I masterfully deflected the conversation at a critical moment to avoid a spiral into doom and despair? I know. I'm quite surprised at how suavely I pulled that off.

The three of us had been making what I thought was perfectly natural conversation for a while, but eventually her friend decided it was too unbearably awkward, and she left to go and catch up with her other friends who were in town.

Tiring of our Mexican locale Angelina and I wandered south into Greenwich Village. Now she was over 21, I used my lovely smart phone to guide us to a cool hipsterish place called V-bar south of Washington Square Park. A guy with a dense frizzy

beard served Angelina a glass of red wine and myself a hoppy beer. We sat at the bar. After chatting about her friends a little bit Angelina turned to me and asked: "Am I freaking you out?"
"No. Why?" I said. This question confused me, I imagine I pulled a confused expression in response. Apparently this looked like a freaked out face.
"You look freaked out. I'm freaking you out aren't I?"
"No.... I'm good."
"You just look like you can't deal with this crazy bitch you're on a date with."
"Errr, no. That's not what I'm thinking, though I'm not really sure how to deal with this particular conversation. What makes me look freaked out?"
"You just look nervous... like I'm making you nervous."
"No I don't feel nervous. I mean I don't feel like throwing up, which is normally a good indicator of when I'm nervous!"
"Still, I think you're a bit freaked out by me..."
If my confused face still looked like a freaked out face, then it probably wasn't reassuring her at that point.
"Well I'm not, but I don't know how I can demonstrate that to you"
"I don't know," she said.

There was a pause.

An idea occurred to me.

"Actually, I have an idea," I said, putting down my beer.

I leaned out of my bar stool towards her, ran my hand up through her hair, and bringing her head towards me I kissed her. Angelina didn't hold back engulfing my face in her lips, and somewhere behind the bar I got the feeling that a beard was judging me.

'Well that seemed to do the trick!' I thought. 'Thank god she's finally shut up about how I'm freaked out by her.'

We spent a while longer in that bar and Angelina said that some of her friends might come and join us, so we found some space at one of the tables. It began to get busy and loud. Kissing Angelina occasionally seemed to do a good job of keeping any awkward conversations at bay, and we chatted about hopes/dreams/TV/movies/art/dating/family/etc. After a couple of drinks it seemed like her friends weren't going to show up and that maybe I should be moving this date along somehow.

"Do you want to get another drink here? Or I have wine back at my place if your friends aren't coming?"
"Would you have me in your place?" she asked, sounding surprisingly sincere.
"Of course! Why wouldn't I?" I replied.

We walked back through Washington Square Park. Evening had not yet become night and various dark figures were still moving around its curving paths. Sometimes they were silhouetted against the park's great marble arch, which was lit up like the grand white doorway of a giant invisible house.

*

Not long after we had got into my apartment and I had handed Angelina a glass of wine she asked:
"Do you mind if I take my pants off?"
"No, that's fine by me!"
"I just feel more comfortable without them on."
"Sure."

So we were sitting on my futon chatting and drinking wine, Angelina now had no 'pants' on, (i.e. no 'trousers' on), and I could see her underwear sticking out from under her shirt. This was the new reality that I had adjusted to. Perhaps her removing her trousers was supposed to be the spark to ignite some fiery physicality, but she had been so matter of fact about taking them off as a means to make her more comfortable that I'd just continued with normal conversation.

At some point we transitioned to watching YouTube clips from obscure Puerto Rican cinema, and she transitioned to sitting on my lap. Having watched a scene about some pimps engaged in a knife fight over a particularly attractive hooker, I decided it was time to focus less on the computer screen and more on the ass perched on my crotch.

After some awkward kissing and groping on we slumped onto my bed. The rest of our clothes worked their way off and were flung back onto the recently vacated chair... or missed it and fell onto the floor.

Once Angelina was naked and I was down to my boxers, I rolled her over onto her front, exposing her bare ass ready for spanking. I struck her with my open hand and watched the impact rippling outwards and up into the rest of her body. It wasn't an exceptionally large ass, but there was enough junk in that trunk for it to show some good rebound, and a little bit of jello-like wobble.

"You're going to have to hit me harder than that!" she said, "I can barely feel it!"

With that invitation I didn't hold back and spanked her aggressively. She grunted and gasped with excitement, but then she retorted; "Is that the best you can do?"

I gave her a few more brutal swipes but even if her ass wasn't feeling it, my palms were starting to sting and curse me with each impact. She was really asking for it now. I decided to give my hands a rest and drew out a 30 cm plastic ruler from my stationary drawer. This made a sharper sound when it struck her buttocks, and the ripples moved faster and dissipated more quickly.

"Harder!" she said
I hit her harder.
"You don't have to hold back. I can take a lot of pain!" she added.

The problem was that I wasn't holding back.

I was surprised this wasn't hurting her more. I really put my back into it, striking her hard and fast, quickly switching between ass, back and thighs, then returning to her ass to give it a concentrated thwacking.

"Harder!" she grunted between gasps and moans. Suddenly, after one particularly furious thwack, there was a snapping noise and the last 0.6 inches of ruler broke off and flew through the air. It hit the wall and then fell down somewhere under my bed.

Pausing, I inspected the jagged end it had left behind. Deciding there might be some mild risk of ass impalement, I grasped it by this broken end instead and went back to work[77].

---

[77] On reflection my belt might have better satisfied her lust for pain, but it had fallen down somewhere and I didn't want to have to go look for it.

I had been pretty aroused since first groping Angelina on my lap, and I remained positively tumescent while exercising my ruler swinging arm. After a bit more tumbling and thumbling it seemed like an appropriate time to initiate intercourse.

This, however, is where I ran into problems.

It was safe to say that we weren't entirely sober at this point. Neither were we entirely drunk, but I wasn't in a place where I wanted to attempt any complex bondage, and rolling around on my bed with occasional spanking seemed like more than enough fun. Condom on I tried to locate my dick into the conventional dick accepting area. This proved more challenging than usual, and to begin with Angelina lay there submissively, expecting me to figure it out by myself. This is not something I would normally find difficult, but after the beer and wine there seemed to be a lot more folds and misleading crevices than usual. I double checked with my fingers. 'ok, I need to be aiming a bit further back, right... almost... no... Ok... There we go!'

At last, sex had commenced. Unfortunately though, my vagina locating difficulties were just the start of my problems. You see, somewhere in between the ruler breaking and intercourse making, my penis had started to get stage fright, and then when it had failed to find a receptive audience[78] on the first attempt, the pressure had really started to get to it. Even though it had now found the way in, I could tell that my erection was in a nose dive, its wings shredded by 50 mm cannon and fiery black smoke spewing from the engines.

---

[78] And by 'audience' I mean 'vaginal opening'... but you know... it's nice to keep some shreds of class.

A miss-timed thrust and out it came. My plane-erection metaphor slammed into cold hard waters of the North Sea with a wet thud, sending up a plume of ocean spray and discombobulated metal before sinking down into the ocean depths, never to be seen again[79].

Ok, so in real un-metaphorical life there was no discombobulated metal or plume of ocean spray (ew). However, what I had to deal with instead was one pissed off Puerto Rican.

"Afraid I'm having some problems here," I muttered.
"What? Unbelievable!" She said, in a less than encouraging tone.

I fiddled with the problem, and then Angelina fiddled with it AGGRESSIVELY (the image of her mouth tugging my right testicle out to its natural extent, while my penis remained stubbornly flaccid in the foreground is one that haunts me to this day). However, all was for nought.

"Ergh... come on penis, you're letting me down here!" I said... to my penis... out loud.
"I'm so offended! Are you not turned on by me at all?" she questioned.
"What? No, of course I am! Did you not see that I was turned on earlier?"
"Whatever. You're clearly not turned on now!"

---

[79] The first metaphor I was going to go with was "Like a bratty child unable to cope with the frustration of its tower of bricks falling over, my penis had thrown a tantrum and left the room, slamming the door behind it." However, I wasn't sure if there were laws against putting children and naked penises in the same metaphor....

This added drama was not conducive to my erection's return, and now I had to expend significant energy convincing Angelina that 'It wasn't her, it was me'. Pointing out that I had drunk a fair amount of alcohol, which probably wasn't helping, and also informing her that this had happened to me once before with another perfectly attractive girl, seemed to placate her temporarily.

"Will it turn you on if I use the ruler on you?" she asked
"Could give it a try," I replied, doubtful anything could bring my erection back onto the stage after its first performance had been so disastrous.
I lay on my front, naked and supine, and she slapped the WHSmiths "Shatter resistant" (but clearly not that shatter resistant) plastic rule across both my ass cheeks.

She did it again, and again. I grunted and gasped accordingly. It certainly hurt. This was the sort of thing I had spent countless nights of young adulthood fantasising about, one of many ideas that would percolate through into my consciousness uninvited when I was trying to sleep, and then force me to address my rock solid member just so I would stand a chance of dozing off afterwards.

There I lay. Getting spanked. One of many dark fantasies materialised... and yet instead of being overcome with arousal I was wondering how many stinging blows I should take before I'd tell Angelina that this really wasn't doing anything for me. I mean, it was still doing something for some part of my brain, but all the important bits of my subconscious that controlled the valves and pressure gauges had long since shut themselves away with a 'do not disturb' sign on the door handle.

Frustrated with my failure to respond to the ruler, Angelina resorted to sitting on top of me and humping me for a while. She ran her nails down my chest, digging in HARD.

"Mnnhhh!" I winced.
After a while she looked down.
"Shit, I really scratched you!"
"It's fine. It did feel pretty intense though."
"I've left some major red lines there. Sorry."
"That's ok. I guess I deserved it," I said with a smile.

Accepting that my penis had nothing more to contribute to proceedings, I had a new idea to potentially satisfy her and at least entertain me. I fetched a banana from the kitchen.
"I'm going to fuck you with this instead," I said.
"Are you serious?"
"Yup!"

I slowly slid it inside her. It seemed to be a pretty good fit, and I worked it backwards and forwards... "No... It just feels weird!" she said after a few minutes of being violated by my 19c grocery from Trader Joes.

Abandoning the soft fruit approach I tried to pleasure her orally. This was a failure as well. She discouraged me almost immediately by impersonating my expression with tongue distended, and claiming I looked grossed out and totally unsexy.

In the face of this unrelenting and un-constructive criticism I gave up completely. We turned in, but I consoled Angelina: "The last time this happened I woke up in the night with a raging hard on so I'll ravage you then."[80]

---

[80] She fell asleep pretty quickly, and I could tell she had drifted off by

*

Later in the night I awoke and my erection had returned in full force. I lay there motionless under the duvet pondering. 'On the one hand there is an attractive girl in bed with me who a few hours ago had been eagerly awaiting the return of this creature,' I thought. 'On the other hand she is asleep. There is also a chance that if I wake her to do what this organ is craving it might suddenly change its mind again.'

I decided I couldn't deal with the emotional fallout of waking her up for sex only to risk another return to flaccidity. And besides, I was sleepy!

*

The next morning, after some ablutions, I found myself sitting in my desk chair while Angelina emerged from under the duvet. Working herself upright, she retrieved and donned her underwear, then swung her feet out and down onto the floor. She sat motionless on the edge of my bed in her purple bra and turquoise panties and stared silently at me for what seemed like a soul questioningly long time.

---

her snoring. I had just dozed off myself when I was suddenly jolted back into consciousness by a terrifying growling-gargling noise. After a few fear-stricken moments I realised that it wasn't the sound of some blood-thirsty werewolf baring its teeth over me, but instead was coming from the unconscious girl I was sharing my bed with. I looked at her trying to figure out how a human could simultaneously make such a terrifying guttural sound and yet look so peaceful... Perhaps some kind of sleep apnoea? Was it a medical thing? Should I do something to prevent her from expiring? Fortunately after I made a coughing noise and poked her a bit with my knee she shifted position and the deathly growling changed back to annoying snoring.

"No? Nothing?" she asked.

Figuring she was referring to my erection I replied: "No, sorry... I think I'm just in a weird place right now."

As I walked her out I half expected her to leave in a huff but instead she said "Well if you just want to hang out as friends sometime let me know. I know some cool places downtown we could go."

"Cool, yeah. I'm not saying I wouldn't want to try this sort of thing again. I guess I'm just not in the right place at the moment. Let's stay in touch though!"

*

We didn't stay in touch though. Part of me wanted to message her just to see how she was doing but the other part was concerned that drawing out our connection could be somehow damaging to both of us. It seemed like drama was an intractable element of our interactions and, as other less dramatic things were working out for me, I left Angelina to figure out her own thing. I hope she did.

Chapter 13 - Getting dates strategy three - be myself AND a kinky sex master

I squeezed in a couple more dates into those final frigid weeks of winter. I had phone sex with one girl before I met her but then regretted this choice, as in real life she looked substantially different to her profile pictures... The second girl had pictures that didn't really catch my attention, but then she turned out to be super-hot as well as super interesting. Unfortunately, I was still distracted having kinky sex with Allie and Josie at that point, so I may have let a great opportunity for normal dating slip away from me.

For every actual date I went on, I always had to churn through multiple Internet conversations, attempting different witticisms and lines of questioning until I caught a girl in the right moment of excitement/boredom/frustration to come out and meet me. Through some of these online chats I learnt of various New York BDSM communities that held socials and group play parties at hidden venues. There was even an official BDSM club called 'Paddles' over in Chelsea. I was intrigued, but not especially tempted to join in as, at that time, the idea of kink being a secret shared by two (or maybe three) people was part of the thrill for me. However, I also discovered a site called 'Fetlife' which is kind of like Facebook for kinky people. It isn't really a dating site in that it's not designed to match people up, but rather it provides groups for interested people to discuss various different topics. It also lets people add 'friends' and share racy pictures of themselves and their partners in various stages of undress, bondage, and all out sex. Twas a most informative site! I was still using Okcupid to meet people but whenever someone deemed to share their Fetlife profile with me, it added a new and exciting dimension to our interactions.

In general, the whole 'having kinky sex with strangers' thing seemed to be pretty fun (at least it is when your penis works), and the couple of dates that had evolved into 'casual-sex-friend' things were also highly enjoyable.

However, it still felt like something was missing.

Yes, here is the shocking dogma-shattering headline: some men don't just want sex! Some of us actually seek 'emotional connection' or 'romance', or whatever you want to call that squishiness. Maybe this 'complexity' turns out to our disadvantage at times, but it is what it is, and come April I was as lonely as hell in the big city. Despite living in New York for almost 6 months, I'd made only a limited number of friends and I started to crave some kind of lasting romantic attachment all the more earnestly.

My fun and games with Josie had been halted by her new man, and Allie stopped replying to my texts after we smoked some weed, she blew me, and then I fell asleep. Having repeatedly tweaked both of my Okcupid profiles, they were attracting a steady trickle of interest. It seemed like using my 'normal' profile was probably the most reliable way of getting a real life date with someone I had plenty in common with. However, the downside to this profile was that I still didn't really have a clue how to do normal dating. Perhaps I was overly laid back and came across as friendly rather than seductive. I felt like I was also adapting my behaviour to match that of my dates and if they seemed shy it would make me shy, but if they were bolder and told me weird stuff, then I responded in kind. I was good at putting people at ease, but at the time I remember having a theory that developing 'chemistry' required a certain balance of amiable banter and rapacious 'edge'. This meant I didn't want to relax a girl so much that she lost the little tickle of adrenaline at the back of her neo-cortex[81], but then I didn't want her reaching for the pepper spray either. I don't think I ever proved or disproved this 'edge' theory but aside from meeting people through a kinky sex themed profile, I rarely figured out an effective strategy for introducing 'edge' to a normal date.

Another significant problem I had with normal dates is that I hadn't come across a smooth way to bring up the subject of sex. Perhaps with normal-dating-sex you are expected to just go for it; with the locking of lips and the invite back to one's apartment being a subtly disguised question. However, the problem with subtly disguised questions is that they often yield uninterpretable answers. "I'm not sure I want to come back to your apartment" may mean "I'm not sure I want to have sex with you" or it might mean "I'm not sure I want to see your place because it's out of the way and I need to get home and sleep". However, "Yes I'd love to see your place" might just mean that a girl would love to see your place and she's not tacitly agreeing to let you root her... I tend to err on the side of caution and take what people say as meaning what people say, but this ambiguity of sub textual clues meant normal dating was kind of confusing and confidence draining for me.

Having a kink profile on the other hand seemed like a good way to get all that awkward stuff out of the way first. The openness set an 'expectation baseline' so I didn't feel improper asking a girl back to my place on a first date... or running my hand up her thigh... or asking if she wanted to get strapped to

---

[81]There's some fairly solid research showing that people feel stronger feelings of attraction when 'excited' even if it's by an unrelated stimulus, like being atop a tall building: Foster, C. A., Witcher, B. S., Campbell, W. K., & Green, J. D. (1998). Arousal and attraction: Evidence for automatic and controlled processes. *Journal of Personality and Social Psychology, 74*(1), 86-101

my bed and spanked aggressively[82]... which is something I wouldn't normally ask a stranger on a first meeting!

However, my kink profile may have been a little overly focused on making girls moist and, while I'd met a couple of interesting people through it, the main thing I had in common with the first round of them (save perhaps for Emma) was an interest in kinky sex. I wanted more than that, but at the same time I didn't want to give up the sadomasochistic fun-times either. So I decided it was once again time to tinker with my online persona. Unfortunately, I have an aversion to deleting things that I already made (which is why this book is probably much longer than it needs to be), and so rather than edit either of my two existing profiles I started a THIRD profile and thus added an additional layer of dating complexity to my 21st century life. The aim of profile three was to combine the witty, self-deprecating and slightly nerdy personality aspects of profile 1 with the erotic temptations of profile 2.... and hope the resulting beast didn't break the Internet with its awesomeness. (Spoiler: It didn't.)

Another profile called for more pictures. I decided to stay clear of the bare torso pics this time, as some girls had told me that those were a turn off (but they'd said this was mostly due to the instant projection of narcissism rather than abject sexuality). The new photo I took of me brooding with a flogger maybe wasn't particularly subtle either, but I included my head this time and just photo shopped a Zorro style mask over my face to preserve some shred of anonymity. Next, I composed another concoction of profile sentences; the meat of the dish was a description of my kink vs. normal profile conundrum and how I was looking for a genuine match to explore a longer

---

[82] That's not to say I expected them to agree to any of this, I was just emboldened enough to ask the questions.

term relationship with. I stirred in a healthy dose of witticisms and seasoned heavily with references to bondage and power exchange. Then I placed the assembled words in an oven preheated to 400 F, cooked for 20 minutes, added parsley to garnish, and finally I dispatched this feast to Okcupid's servers to see what appetites it might stir.

*

Looking back at my life, I'm not sure at exactly what point I transitioned from only wanting to fuck people I already knew and was sure I liked, to anyone I found attractive and thought would let me. Perhaps I should mourn the death of that young romantic, but then again I'm not sure if my life would have been happier and more fulfilling if I'd put two bullets in him sooner. I don't remember making a conscious choice to become a man-slut, I guess I moved to New York and it just kind of happened. I certainly wasn't complaining, but I did hope I could find some middle ground between rampant sexual exploration and the pursuit of that one compelling individual who might 'complete me'. My new romantic fantasy might not inspire many Disney stories, but as I played my role of questionable-prince-charming I dreamed that I might meet someone relatively compatible, then after an enjoyable period of sexy fun and adventures we'd realise that we didn't irritate each other too much, and perhaps we'd enjoy hanging out so much that we would agree to keep doing it indefinitely! Oh and maybe they'd bring me tea in the mornings too, I'd know I was doing alright if someone brought me tea in the mornings.

Chapter 14 - A supposedly fun thing I may or may not do again

By the end of April the nut shrinking cold of winter finally slackened. Then, after only a couple of weeks of pleasantly rejuvenating spring freshness, the oppressive heat and humidity of the New York summer began to make its first aggressive incursions into the streets of Manhattan.

Unlike most weather, which one generally imagines being blown in from distant shores, Manhattan's feverish summer airs almost seem to rise up from the very core of the earth itself. This warmth first fills the deepest subway stations and then works its way up to ground level, bursting out onto the streets through vents and grates along with the putrid drain steam. It takes hold of the centre of the city first, as near the rivers spring breezes may just about hold back the tsunami of life sucking heat. Eventually though these breezes are routed, the heat's victory is total, and it drowns the city in a flood of dense suffocating air. Walking anywhere during the frequent NY heat waves can feel like swimming through an invisible fluid with the consistency of warm soup; as you move around you can literally feel the hot thick atmosphere sloshing against your face.

It was a Saturday afternoon in the beginning of May and I had to get to Brooklyn for -you guessed it- another date. At this point I had not really encountered the phenomenon of Manhattan air-soup and I left my apartment thinking what a pleasant sunny day it was, taking a cardigan with me just in case I stayed out late and it got chilly (I don't ignore everything my mother taught me.) As I got deeper into the city I noticed it start to feel warmer...

*

...A little over half an hour later I clawed my way out of the Bedford avenue subway stop, sweat drenched and gasping for air...

*

The New York subway is not really designed for comfort. The train carriages themselves are usually air conditioned, save the occasional car that can be quickly spotted in summer months by the absence of passengers[83]. The platforms, however, are another matter; the main ventilation they receive seems to be from the trains pumping the same dense subway air backwards and forwards though the tunnels in front of them like noisy and ineffective pistons. During periods when no trains are passing the air soup can quickly collect and pool.

That Saturday waiting for the 6-train had already been pretty grim, and I had realised the complete disutility of my cardigan. However, it was during the wait for the L train where I really started to question if I had stumbled into a lost chapter of Dante's inferno. This particular circle of hell was found beneath union square, one level down from the 6-platform. The L-train was delayed and the air soup had time to marinade. This invisible broth rose well over the heads of we

---

[83] Top subway tip; if a subway carriage is almost empty and the rest of the train is almost full, DO NOT GET IN THAT CARRIAGE. One does not 'get lucky' on the subway and there is always a good reason for and empty carriage being empty. Normally that reason is non-functional air conditioning, but I also once experienced a near empty carriage due to the extreme stench emanating from a homeless guy in the corner. The smell was so strong and unpleasant I can only hypothesise he had either soiled himself or expired, but I didn't want to get close enough to investigate. (Additional note: a trip in a stinky subway car is not a good way to end a date!)

the damned, immersing our reddened and sweaty bodies as if we were crawfish in a broiler.

An old Asian man was sitting on a tiny stool and playing some kind of stringed instrument that only had one string. As I am not musically talented I am not well placed to criticise the musical skills of others, but I felt this man's performance would have been improved if his instrument gave him more strings to work with, or, ideally, fewer. I couldn't tell if this musician was a demon sent to punish us penitent's, or a fellow trapped soul who had committed some great sin and had now been cursed by the gods to sit in this sweltering pit, only able to communicate through the high pitched screeching of that solitary taught fibre.

As the MTA wasn't even considerate enough to provide canaries in this oxygen depleted mine shaft I looked around to see if there were any old people who could serve the same purpose. There were none in sight. They probably didn't even make it down this far, I imagined their suffocated corpses were already lying prostrate a few levels above, perhaps collecting below the entrance stairs and being heaved into mine carts by dead eyed MTA employees who then wheeled them away for disposal.

After a while waiting for the train I began to feel dizzy and faint. I said I small prayer to all of the gods I didn't believe in: "If I die here on this hellish platform, please don't reincarnate me as that rat over there!"

Admittedly the rat I was referring to seemed happy, nosing its way excitedly around the fetid garbage in between the subway tracks, but I didn't think it was an existence I would adapt to well. Mercifully, before I lost consciousness I felt the gentle tickle of moving air on my cheek. BEHOLD! THE

SCREECHING WONDER OF THE AIR CONDITIONED SUBWAY TRAIN APPROACHES!

The train's doors opened with a delightful hiss and I pressed on-board, for once completely untroubled by my usual English concerns for politeness and respecting other people's personal space.

*

After I'd surfaced as a sweaty mess in Brooklyn I navigated the rest of the way to the Roebling tea house in a heat addled daze. The street temperature in Williamsburg was more bearable, but the beating sun still gave one the sensation of being gently roasted rather than aggressively broiled.

The tea house itself had a pleasant colonial vibe, with house plants edging large arched windows that let in plenty of light and illuminated the green and cream colour scheme. There didn't seem to be any air conditioning going on though, so I ordered a cool beer in desperation.

After a short time staring at the door a feisty brunette walked in with a twinkle in her eye... My date for the afternoon, and if I played my cards right, the evening as well. Her name was Caitlin and she worked in fashion. More specifically she designed women's jackets for bespoke outfitters. I know nothing about fashion, which I had already confessed to Caitlin in our messages, but after greeting her and apologising for my sweatiness, I tried to engage with her on the subject of clothing design.

I think I succeeded in talking about clothes... At least she did most of the talking and I nodded and asked appropriate follow up questions... I learned about many types and sources of leather, difficulties choosing zips or toggles, the trendiness of stitching patterns and various logistical considerations that had never crossed my mind when shuffling awkwardly past the women's clothing section in order to buy new socks with fewer holes in. I think I was able to convince both Caitlin and myself that I was interested in this subject and so she bubbled away in between straining her tea and sipping it with considered daintiness.

After a while I excused myself to go to the bathroom and while waiting for an entrenched occupant to vacate I gazed idly through the back door to the beer garden. Some hipster looking dude was about to sit down, but his ass caught the chair at a weird angle, and he fell onto the floor arms flailing. I chortled a little to myself. He seemed uninjured, but as he got up he stumbled and knocked the chair over... 'Seriously this guy is wasted' I thought, still stifling laughter. He picked the chair back up and went sitting down attempt number two, but again he failed and ended up on the floor. This was getting strange. Retrieving himself from the floor the hipster in question took a firm hold of the chair, feeling its back and seat with his hands as if to confirm it really was a solid object and didn't just exist in his imagination. He had friends sitting around him who seemed solidly amused but were not coming to his aid in any way... He sat down again, but this time he somehow put his weight overly far forward so that the chair tipped and shot out behind him, landing him square on his butt. His friends only laughed harder.

At that point I noticed him giving me a sideways glance... He also wore a cheeky smile that seemed out of place on a guy who had just fallen over four times in a row. 'This guy is faking!' I realised as he conducted some further chair based dramatics. He continued to cast glances at me in between his stumbles, and I began to get the awkward feeling that this tomfoolery was somehow for my benefit... The toilet sign flipped to 'vacant' and I scuttled off to attend to my bladder.

So yeah, that was an odd thing that happened. Not sure why I'm telling you about it... but then dates in New York don't always follow a consistent story arc. I was going to tell Caitlin about the fally-over guy, but I got distracted by other subjects as soon as I sat back down. Caitlin was the first date I had found through my third okcupid profile and we'd already talked online about her 'interests'; she was into being dominated both by her man and by her clothing, and by this I mean she owned a steel boned corset that she liked to wear firmly tightened. I had instructed her to wear this contraption to our date and she was displaying excellent posture as she sat there sipping on her tea.

"How does the corset feel?" I asked her.
"Tight... but good"
"Do you wear it often?"
"Not really, it's pretty new..."
"Still adjusting to it then?"
"Yeah, it definitely changes how I carry myself, and I have to breathe differently too... taking more short breaths as breathing deeply is hard."
"Huh, you're not going to pass out on me are you?!"
"Ha, no I should be ok"

Round one of beverages consumed, round two was ordered along with some snacks. Emboldened by beer one I pushed on with the topic that had brought us together: "So I was kind of surprised when you messaged me, I guess your profile was quite coy about answering the sex questions and we didn't seem that well matched..."

"Yeah, I think I come across more conservative than I really am. I don't know, but I think to be respected a girl has to come across as a lady in the streets but a freak beneath the sheets..."
"Yeah?"
"Yeah I think so, otherwise I think we are just considered like slutty sex objects..."
"I guess... although I think it depends on the guy... I mean I totally respect slutty sex objects!"
"Really? Do you just like to date slutty girls?"
"No, not specifically, it just doesn't affect my opinion of a girl if they have sex with a lot of people or not. Although... I mean maybe I'm drawn to less inhibited women in general..."
"I think you're unusual..."
"Maybe... I am pretty weird." I said with a smile
"I think a lot of guys have this idea that they need to get the nice sweet-and-innocent girl to be their girlfriend and take home to their parents, and then have the nasty slutty girl on the side that they fuck and live out their dirty fantasies with."
"Hmmm, maybe... I'm not sure I can think of any specific guys I know who think like that, but most of my guy friends are either kind of nerdy or married."

Our snacks arrived. I shoved a long, floppy, and deliciously greasy French fry into my mouth.

We talked a little bit about our living situations. She had roommates (or 'flatmates' as we call them in the UK so as not to give the impression that they share the actual room you sleep in).
"So do your room-mates know about your kinky side?"
"Not really, though I think they might have some idea... I live with one really good friend and we, like, share each other's clothes all the time, but I'm always kinda paranoid that she might be looking through my stuff one day and find my glass butt plug in the sock drawer..."

"Ha! Aren't girls' sock drawers sacred?"
"I don't know with her, but I hope so!"

Eventually, after much discourse, round two of drinks and snacks were consumed. I decided to test the waters to see where this date might be headed.

"Well I don't know if you have any plans for the evening... but you'd be welcome to come back and see my place if you like?"
"I don't know, maybe..."
"We don't have to do anything, we could just drink some more... or fool around, whatever you felt like!"
Her eyes scanned downwards and from side to side. The corset squeezing her waist was doing so much of my job for me.
"Yeah I guess we can do that..." She decided.

*

In the subway car we remained standing despite an abundance of empty seats. Caitlin grasped one of the metal poles by the doors and I stood facing her. Conversation lapsed momentarily while we were clattering though the long dark subway tunnel under the east river. My eyes met hers and then glanced to the side, but I forced them back to hold her gaze. For some time we stared at each other silently as our metal tube rattled through the subterranean blackness. Her eyes didn't shy away.

Slowly and deliberately I moved towards her, releasing my support rail and grasping the one she was holding. I slid my hand down that thin cylinder then settled my palm over her knuckles, gripping them tightly[84], and all the while I stared deep into those two brown encircled voids.

---

[84] Yes, I stole that move off Michael Fassbender in 'Shame'.

Wordlessly my eyes said to hers: "I'm gonna fuck you sooo hard."

*

The sun hadn't yet set and the air was still thick as we walked from the subway to my apartment. We had almost reached my block but I could tell Caitlin was flagging.
"Corset getting to you?" I asked.
"Yeah, can we stop for a second?"
"Sure..."

She steadied herself against some railings, her back towards them, and once again she trapped my gaze. This time I moved forward and kissed her. My arms held her firmly against the railings and her corseted body was pressed between me and the thin metal bars. Biology was taking its course, though perhaps a little too publicly...

"Let's get you inside..." I whispered.

We had barely gotten through the door before she pounced on me. After some foot-work, hand-work, and tongue-work, I found myself on my couch, straddled by an aggressive and enthusiastic date who was stripped down to her corset and humping my jeans while I spanked her.
"Yes! Yes! Yes!! Oh Timmy! YES!!!" she shouted.

I'm not sure if she reached some kind of mini climax, or if she decided she could no longer take the ass spanking I was giving her, but eventually she calmed herself and un-straddled me.
"I like being told what to do," she said.
"Oh do you?" I replied.
My brain thought: 'Shit, what should I tell her to do? Getting her to blow me seems a bit too unoriginal... errr.'

"Get on your hands and knees in the middle of my rug!" I instructed.

She obeyed.

Fun was had on the rug. After a little while I produced a toy that had intrigued me when I bought it but I had yet to test on a girl. The toy in question was a vibrating and inflatable butt plug. (I mean why get some boring static butt plug when you can get one that vibrates and inflates?) As Caitlin had already confessed the contents of her sock drawer, I guessed that she might be amenable to experimenting with this particular instrument.

It was a fairly intimidating looking device. The silicone plug itself had the usual tapering wine stopper-like shape, reaching a maximum width similar to that of a small cucumber or a large penis, before rapidly narrowing again for the comfort of the receiving hole. In other words it looked like a butt plug. However, coming out of this device was a short length of tubing and a wire. The wire connected to the vibration controller (containing two rechargeable AA batteries in this case, because in my opinion anuses should be vibrated in a rechargeable and environmentally friendly fashion). The tubing meanwhile went through a valve into a rubber ball that served as a hand pump (like the ones doctors use for measuring blood pressure), which allowed inflation of the tapered end of the butt plug. When pumped, it could expand to the size of a small lemon (or probably even larger if one was feeling reckless.)

"Does this look too big for you?" I asked.
"Oh, that's nothing!" she replied.
"Well let's get it inside you then!" I said[85].

---

[85] The butt plug was first placed inside a condom for obvious hygiene

*

A few minutes later I was fucking Caitlin doggy style with plug inserted, inflated, and vibrating. We were both having a solidly good time when suddenly there was an ominous "pop" noise... We both stopped still.
"Err... what just happened?" Caitlin asked.
I experienced momentary dread. Had something awful just happened? Had my date's anus just exploded? Did I even want to look down?

Fortunately, when I did look down, I saw that the rubber hand pump ball bit had just popped off the end of the tube connecting it to the butt plug. The pressure had clearly gotten to it.

Dread averted, we continued to explore a number of sex positions on the bed until I came with her underneath me and her legs on my shoulders. We both lay there, hot, sweaty, and exhausted. She finally took off her corset.
"I think I definitely cum more intensely when I'm wearing this," she said.
"Oh yeah?" I said, entwining my legs with hers and moving in for the spoon.

My arms reached around her and my hands squeezed her arms. She wasn't fat by any stretch of the definition, but her skin had this dough-like texture that yielded easily to the touch. 'My soft subby dough ball,' I thought as I held her tight.

The sun had set and through my open curtains I could see the blinking of a jet plane tracing a line across the dark purple sky.

---

reasons... Poop is icky.

A light switched on in one of the hundreds of windows in the tower block opposite but it was too far away to see if anyone was moving in there. The sudden illumination was the only clear sign of life amongst the patchwork of window squares, some light, many dark. We lay there naked behind our own dark rectangle. Someone with a telescope might be watching us... but they probably weren't. Besides, Internet porn has actual sound and better lighting.

After a little while, Caitlin said something like: "Just say if you want me to go."
"Oh no, the night is still young! Just let me recover for a bit and there might be a round two."

*

"Looks like our friend is back," I said, about half an hour later. Some humping and groping fanned the flames of excitement and woke us from our dozing.
"Anything you'd like me to do for you this time?" asked Caitlin.
"Erm, nothing specific off the top of my head. Anything particular you want me to do to you?"
"Fuck me in the ass?" she pleaded.
"Erm, ok... sure," I replied.

Awkward confession: I had not actually done anal sex before this date. That's not to say that it didn't appeal to me but I guess it was one of those things I never dated anyone long enough to work up to. Out of curiosity I had googled "how to do anal sex" at some point prior to that night and I remember perusing the 'beginners guide to anal sex' on the website of some men's magazine. Unfortunately, I think that this particular guide had been written by someone who had never actually had anal sex before. It certainly talked extensively about how you should make sure your partner is happy about it (duh), and gave sensible suggestions like testing her out first with fingers or small butt plugs, and to use plenty of lube. However, whatever I read definitely failed to stress the importance of making sure your partner is really fucking turned on immediately before you try to shove anything sizable through that sphincter. Cold starts are just not a good plan.

Caitlin had asked for anal sex, so anal sex she would get. It seemed like only good service to get on with it without beating about the bush[86]. I lubed up my condomed penis and it stood stiffly to attention awaiting this new mission into uncharted enemy territory. 'Alright men, we're going in!' I definitely didn't think to myself. I pushed Caitlin onto her knees...

...Greater than expected resistance was encountered... Should I just push harder?... I guess I'll push harder... 'For king and country!'[87]
"OOWW!" yelled Caitlin, recoiling.
"Shit, are you ok?" I asked.
She didn't reply immediately, instead curling backwards in a way that suggested she was not ok, and that her ass was really quite unhappy with me.

"You need to fuck my pussy before you fuck my ass," she whined quietly.
'Well, clearly this is something I should have known 5 minutes ago,' I thought to myself guiltily.
"Sorry," I muttered, "I guess I kind of killed the mood there."

After a few minutes, she uncurled and moved back in to cuddle with me. Cuddling evolved into fondling and fondling evolved

---

[86] Yes that pun was intended, and yes I am sorry.
[87] I did not actually think that either, don't judge me, I'm just going with the metaphor...

into sex. However, even if her butt had readied itself to receive guests after this standard fucking, I wasn't brave enough to risk another incursion.

*

Caitlin went home after round two. The next morning she texted me some pictures of some dark hand shaped bruises on her ass, which made me feel simultaneously guilty and aroused. Despite this arousal though, I didn't race to setup round three. Maybe it was because we were quite different people, or that something about our chemistry was off, or just that I still felt guilty for screwing up the buttsex.
After a bit of back and forth I texted her:
"*Well I certainly had fun yesterday, but maybe I'm not as strictly dominant as you're looking for...*"

The response came 10 minutes later "*I had fun too. I think I am looking for something else though. Someone more forceful,*"

And for my final reply I went with: "*Fair enough. Best of luck with it! I shall remember your bruised ass fondly.*"

Some memories last longer than bruises anyway.

Chapter 15 - The spread sheet

Summer advanced, the mercury rose, and my online dating continued to spiral out of control. I would find myself embroiled in phases of binge dating where I couldn't even keep track of who I ought to be messaging, sexting, or chasing dates with on any given evening. However, communicating with multiple girls at once probably wasn't helping my chances of actually finding lasting dating success with any one individual. Especially when I forgot to reply to their messages... Or never got around to asking them on a date... Or couldn't think of a good second date idea so never suggested one.

I would often scan back though my inbox and think 'Oh shit, she was hot, why didn't I get around to meeting her?!' Perhaps the best thing about dating in New York is the vast number of available single people, but the worst thing about dating in New York is almost definitely the vast number of available single people[88].

To try and bring some order to the miasmatic chaos of my dating life I had the cunning/awful idea of creating a 'dating spread sheet'. The main purpose of this romance accounting system was to keep track of who I should be messaging, but when setting up the various rows and columns I may have gotten a little carried away. Names and contact info went in the first two columns, but then I just kept adding. "Kinkiness" was next (just in case I forgot who was into what, or caused controversy by threatening to spank and ravage someone who had only seen my normal profile). Then the next column I

---

[88] Especially when you consider that there are also thousands of other single guys in New York who the girls you are trying to date could meet instead (plus a lot of them get paid excessively well and can take girls to nice places).

titled 'the plan/to do next', which was intended to remind me whether I should be texting them, sexting them, proposing drinks, sending them flowers[89], etc, etc.

The spread sheet continued its downhill trajectory; the next column I termed 'personality', as it's always helpful to boil someone's complex traits down to a few words in a small spread sheet cell[90]. Next I went lower with a column entitled 'sexiness'... pretty self-explanatory that one. Then I added three more columns: 'texts?', 'dates?', 'sex?'. intended for yes/no answers just in case I started to develop dementia or I became trapped in such an avalanche of pussy I was unable to keep track of who I had dated and slept with.

Then in the final column I wrote: 'this is a horrible idea WHAT HAVE I BECOME!'

I then deleted most of this girl-auditing system. I was fairly sure that using a spread sheet that gave numerical rankings for 'sexiness' and 'personality' would significantly accelerate my transformation into some kind of terrible person. Also all these columns were clearly far too labour intensive to fill in! I could use that time far better actually messaging potential dates, or even doing meaningful and productive things with my life.

In the end I did use the spread sheet for a while, but just to keep a list of names, numbers, and Okcupid pseudonyms for girls I was messaging, along with brief notes on whether they seemed kinky and if sexting seemed advisable. Names were then highlighted green if they seemed into me, yellow if they

---

[89] Yes I am joking about the flowers. Somehow I feel sending an Internet date flowers in this day and age is just one step closer to a restraining order.
[90] Note sarcasm.

seemed less interested, or other colours like red, blue, and purple, if those colours seemed instinctively appropriate at the time...

So it's safe to say I was going on a lot of dates. I'm tempted to say they all blurred into one, but that would be a dumb lie. Each date was a distinct and novel experience, none of which I really regretted (although maybe there were a few I would have avoided in retrospect).

Most of these encounters could probably be spun into interesting yarns but I'd like to finish writing this book before I grow old and senile while still making it clear to you, *mon cher compatriote,* the sheer number of dates I actually went on in my first year in New York. To these ends, I have composed a catalogue of ships I passed in the night. Some of these vessels I fled from, others I chased, while some merely floated past in calm waters.

One way or another though, most were forever lost in the fog.

Take a deep breath now. We'll get through this together.

*

Name	Joan
Occupation	Student: pre-med
Personality	Shy
Hair	Blonde
Kinky?	Interested

Other notes	Looking for something casual in between studies

This was a particularly awkward date. We met in Herald Square. I'd planned to take her to a bar but it turned out she was only 20 and didn't drink, so we somehow ended up in the Starbucks next to the Empire State building. This is not just the worst place to take a date ever, it may in fact be the worst place ever. Most of the fake wooden tables were occupied by dazed looking tourists and their offspring, and the only space we found was next to a table dominated by a snoring homeless lady. This dispossessed individual was squeezed into a corner with her various derelict possessions and just about hidden from the Starbucks employees.

Dates conducted next to sleeping homeless people are not a good dates. Joan was shy and awkward and after consuming our hot drinks I hastily concluded it with an 'I don't think this is going to work for either of us'. She nodded, we hugged, and then I ran off into the night.

Name	Jamie
Occupation	Med student
Personality	Peppy
Hair	Black
Kinky?	?
Other notes	Put up to dating by her friend

Good conversation in a wine bar, I was apparently her first online date and she congratulated me on not being a weirdo... It would have been a shame to ruin this by telling her how much of a weirdo I was. I probably should have texted her to try and set up a second date, but I didn't.

Name	Louise
Occupation	Lawyer
Personality	Friendly
Hair	Blonde
Kinky?	?
Other notes	?

More nice bar-based chatting but sadly she just wasn't really my type.

Name	Ellie
Occupation	Writer
Personality	Nerdy/Great
Hair	Brunette
Kinky?	Yes
Other notes	Allergic to latex

Explored two Midtown bars with a girl who had seen all three of my profiles before we met. She was nice and liked nature and nerdy things and wasn't ashamed of being just who she was. We ended up getting food and I didn't even have a panic attack. I invited her back to mine, because it seemed like the thing to do. I kissed her, because it seemed like the thing to do. I stripped her, strapped her down to my bed, and fucked her hard, because it seemed like the thing to do. I texted her to make sure she had a good time and got home ok, because it made me feel like less of an asshole.

Name	Nicola
Occupation	Waste management
Personality	Chilled
Hair	Light brown
Kinky?	?
Other notes	Disappointingly not in the mafia

More cocktails were consumed in the Shanty in Brooklyn. Nicola lived in Greenpoint and was driving so I couldn't really get her wasted. She was hot, sciencey, and quite tall. She also had a neat invention for a toilet seat to cure bowel cancer. The date ended with a nice hug by her car and I texted her to try and get date number two in the works. She never replied to me though, so if ever I get a chance to steal her toilet seat invention I'm totally gonna do it now.

Name	Abigail

Occupation	Screenplay writer
Personality	Sweet
Hair	Blonde?
Kinky?	?
Other notes	Southern belle?

It was a definite air soup day when I met Abby down at a bar called Drop off Service in the East Village. I'd been to this bar a couple of times and it had seemed date appropriate. Of course when I actually took a date there it was full of jock bros talking loudly in their American loud voices (as if volume can somehow compensate for a lack of interesting things to say). Consequently I had to repeat every other sentence I said to Abby, either because she didn't hear me or because I'd used some weird English expression she'd not heard before (and often both). This was another date that only led to a hug and an unanswered text.

Name	Siena
Occupation	Student
Personality	Self-assured[91]
Hair	Brown
Kinky?	Defo

---

[91] By which I mean aggressive and kind of bitchy

Other notes	Libertarian...

There are people who are cool, and there are people who are hard. Siena was the later. Of course, I first saw her hot profile pictures and after she 'liked' both my normal and kinky profiles I was champing at the bit to meet her.

In real life Siena turned out to be more built than I had expected. An Amazonian rugby player who looked like she could easily take me. All her proportions were still hot, they were just a bit more intimidating in real life. The stranger aspect to our date though was that it wasn't really a date. Siena was moving dorm rooms one Sunday evening and somehow persuaded me to come and meet her as she was finishing up. I agreed to this, so I guess I must have been keen, and I ended up holding various doors open while we pushed the last few trolleys of her jumbled possessions through the street, up some elevators, and into her new room. She was living in an all-girls college and I had to leave my ID with the security guard at the door, presumably to discourage me from raping anyone.

The 'date' then progressed to drinking red wine out of mugs in her new kitchen, surrounded by bare cupboards and empty dorm rooms. Siena was keen to tell me about the various wealthy guys she hung out with, some of whom had paid her to do things like slap them around in public. Most prominent among them was an investment banker friend of hers who lived in a vast upper east side penthouse. Apparently he shared this penthouse with ten different women, all of whom he was supporting financially, and sleeping with accordingly.

It wasn't hard to see that ideas of wealth and success intoxicated Siena (she had listed 'Fountainhead' by Ayn Rand amongst her favourite books. I really should have known better). I didn't have much to offer in the way of dizzying financial achievements (hell, I still shopped at Trader Joes even though it was a twenty minute walk away). My confidence was somehow drained in that stark white kitchen, with its cracked lino floors and humming fluorescent lights. I didn't really feel like dominating this date... or at least that's what I told myself after she had escorted me out with a kiss and I had collected my ID from the doorman.

Name	Suyin
Occupation	Being young
Personality	Crazy... and far too young
Hair	Black
Kinky?	Interested because it sounded cool
Other notes	Young young young, way too young. (By which I mean 19... She messaged me first... so that makes it ok right?)

I met Suyin one Sunday for ice cream in central park. We sat by the boating lake and chatted. (Maybe I was paranoid but there seemed to be a helicopter hovering over us the entire time). Suyin conveyed a considerable amount of energy in the way she spoke and it struck me that her personality lay several miles past kooky and not too short of lunatical. Suyin told me that she was under the protection of 'the skulls and daggers', who were apparently some kind of Hispanic gang in Harlem. I think there was also a good chance that she was a compulsive liar. While I may have left her with a friendly offer of future spanking, she was definitely too young for me and I decided to try and avoid dating 19 year olds in future.

Name	Malory
Occupation	Ballet dancer
Personality	Friendly and chatty
Hair	Red
Kinky?	?
Other notes	Suspiciously normal

I persuaded Malory to meet me for a late night cocktail when she was coming back from her friend's house party. She was warm, chatty, forgiving of my lack of ballet knowledge, and also hot. You could tell she was a great person to be around. Perhaps the sort of person that gets described as the 'life and soul of the party'. We kissed passionately on the corner of 3rd avenue and E33rd street. It must have looked passionate too because a passer-by cheered us. Now, whenever I walk past that corner at night, the memory of her kiss resurfaces, but sadly it was the only kiss we would share.

A second date was set but then rain checked. In the last text I had from Malory she said that she was sunning herself by a pool in New Jersey and coming back into town next week. Then she stopped responding.

Name	Brooke
Occupation	Psychology student

Personality	Friendly but somehow reserved
Hair	Blonde
Kinky?	?
Other notes	Didn't really drink (Only found this out after I got her to meet me in a bar)

While I took a deep slurp of beer number two, Brooke told me she didn't drink much because her father had been an alcoholic. Despite this she didn't seem to judge me too much for drinking when she wasn't and we went on two dates in the end. Both dates were followed by making out, but in a slightly awkward and stilted kind of way (probably because only one of us had been drinking). I was up for a third date, she was not.

Name	Valerie
Occupation	Games developer
Personality	Tattooed gamer chick
Hair	Black
Kinky?	Maybe?
Other notes	Only in town that night and on her way to London

A last minute rendezvous in the Park Avenue Tavern on a muggy Sunday evening. Thunder rumbled in the distance. Valerie had gotten there first and was already sipping a cocktail and looking hot at one of the bar's corners. I adopted a stool on the other side of said corner and hung my still dry umbrella on one of the hooks under the woodwork. She told me about Atlanta (where she was coming from) and I told her about England, where in 48 hours she would be landing. She refused a second drink because apparently she needed to go and meet her brother. As she slid off her bar stool a strange thing happened where she practically disappeared beneath the bar. At first I wondered if she had knelt down or something, but then she remained at that height and started walking. I realised she hadn't fallen over but was just incredibly short. Like, probably under 4 foot 10' and on some scale of dwarfism, short. This didn't make her any more or less attractive, it just shows that I don't pay enough attention to heights listed on people's profiles.

Name	Fay
Occupation	Job seeker
Personality	Sassy
Hair	Brunette
Kinky?	Yup
Other notes	Short shorts

Fay messaged me first on profile 3 with a sassy and rambly message about Englishisms and kink. I sassed her right back by pointing out that she looked like she was drunk in all her pictures and I couldn't tell if she was hot or not. She appreciated my snarkiness and threats of punishment, and before long I was waiting to meet her at a bar called the Belfry. Infuriatingly, she was more than forty minutes late and the

Belfry was rammed and noisy. I switched back and forth between hovering inside the air conditioned doorway and loitering outside on muggy 14th street. After 20 minutes the bouncer must have thought I was a weirdo. After 40 minutes I must have seemed certifiable. Eventually though, Fay arrived and I led her to a quieter bar around the corner. At least she bought me a drink to make up for being late. Aside from her lack of punctuality, she had a good sense of humour and before long we were making out on the plastic seats of the M15 bus, and heading back to my place.

I spanked and flogged Fay until her ass and back were thoroughly reddened; her punishment for keeping me waiting. After sex round 1 I let her have a go using the flogger on me while I was strapped down. She giggled a lot and eventually released me saying, "I prefer when you do it to me".

There was a definite spring in her step as I watched her leaving my place. Her denim short-shorts were swaying from side to side and riding up into her ass as it diminished down the hallway.

Name	Vicky
Occupation	Advertising
Personality	?
Hair	Brown?
Kinky?	?
Other notes	?

She smiled a lot and she wasn't ugly, but her three dimensional body and face weren't quite what I was expecting. I wasn't feeling it so I aborted the date after one drink with the cunning line: "I expect you'll want to get an early night for your run tomorrow?"

Name	Pamela
Occupation	International development
Personality	'Type A' or whatever
Hair	Blonde
Kinky?	Yes
Other notes	Seemed like a smart and together young woman

Pamela was a little older than me; 29 and staring down the barrel of 30. She had a theory that only douchebags like David Foster Wallace, but with careful use of both profile 1 and 3 I managed to persuade her to meet me for cocktails. She was charming and smart. I remember an in depth discussion on the on-going political turmoil in Egypt, and discovering a mutual fascination with the travels of Alexander the Great.

Talk of her tough-mudder experience led us neatly into her BDSM interests and I described how I was trying to learn some more complex rope techniques, the sort of convoluted and intertwined designs that wrap and immobilize the whole body. I could see a twinkle in her eye and a shudder in her hips as she talked about the designs she'd seen, and her hands traced imaginary ropes over her body. Despite this gentle suggestion, I failed to tempt her back to my place. She said she had to get up early for a run the next day. I kissed her briefly outside the bar. At first she went with it but then hastily turned to leave, saying "Text me!" over her shoulder.

I texted her on three separate occasions. The first two messages got no response... and the third didn't get a response either.

Name	Ophelia
Occupation	?
Personality	Boring
Hair	Brown
Kinky?	?
Other notes	Had nothing to say

One beer - Zero conversation.

Name	Ashley
Occupation	Social Media
Personality	Chatty, weird, super interesting
Hair	Brown
Kinky?	Interested
Other notes	English!!!

A girl with an interesting looking sex oriented profile checked me out. I started writing her a message, but just before I pressed 'send' a message popped up from her. This simultaneous messaging got us off to a good start and we exchanged banter on various subjects. For example, she told me how she once had sex in a church, and I told her a cautionary tale about my recent solo misadventures with duct-tape[92]. Banter transferred to texting, but scheduling an actual meet up was challenging as Ashley always seemed to be off doing something fun sounding.

The times we did meet were impulsive last minute affairs where I was in her neighbourhood and she happened to be free. The first time we met was for cocktails at the Wayland. They were good cocktails and Ashley was fun to talk to. I'm not sure how much of it was that I hadn't met any new English people for too long, but I liked Ashley's sense of humour, her openness, and her general enthusiasm for life. Her own lack of inhibitions made me feel safe in describing my various dating trials and tribulations and she was similarly forthcoming. I discovered that she had a penchant for group sex parties, which was a particularly interesting conversation topic and I learned many new things. For example I found out that Oxford students had their own group sex society[93], though it must have been a well-guarded secret to escape the ravenous Oxford gossip mill. Ashley also told me that during her student years she had sometimes frequented orgies hosted in luxurious London mansions and English country houses. 'Eyes wide shut' scenarios drifted through my mind. Group sex was not

---

[92] I don't think anyone noticed the fact I had remarkably smooth ankles for much of June...
[93] Tragically not called 'the Oxford group sex society'; that would be far too easy!

something I had ever sought out myself, but I couldn't deny that she had me intrigued.

When not talking about sex I also learned that Ashley was a fan of weird nature stuff. On her phone she showed me pictures of the various frightful insects and myriapods that she had found inhabiting her crumbling East Village apartment. After a couple of drinks she decided it was time to call it a night, and as we were leaving I tentatively proposed; "I mean you'd be welcome to come back to mine if you wanted to?"

"Oh no, not today. I was supposed to have a threesome yesterday, but I'm just all over the place at the moment. Sorry," she replied.

"Sure, no worries! Let's hang out again soon," I said meekly.

Eventually I caught up with Ashley again. We got fro-yo and chatted in Tompkins Square park while the fireflies were coming out. These brief flashes of green light above the dark grass almost seemed like ethereal spirits, perhaps trying to transmit Morse code from another realm.

Ashley somehow ended up buying my fro-yo for me as the result of an awkward checkout interaction where I offered to pay, but then she insisted I had bought drinks last time, and so I relented and she paid for both, but then I wasn't sure if she had just meant to buy her own... "Argh I'm so stupid!" I said out loud to myself randomly the next day, while pointlessly obsessing over this error. Perhaps I had been in New York too long and forgotten how English people are meant to do multiple rounds of insisting to pay for things? You know how you get those retrospective feelings of stupidity that randomly bubble up and make you want to spontaneously punch yourself in the face? Well for some reason this not-paying-for-fro-yo incident haunted me like that for many days, even though it definitely had zero influence on Ashley's desire to sex me.

While Ashley was confident and friendly in the way she talked, there was something slightly awkward about her body language that gave off a 'don't touch me' vibe. So I didn't touch her. The fireflies had more nerve than me though and one flew straight into her face. Having finished the remains of our melted dairy products, we fled the suddenly hostile park life. Ashley said that she had some more people to meet that evening, and so I walked to the L stop and we parted ways.

I badgered her by text for a while. Based on the last two meetings it seemed to be a matter of rolling the message die and hoping she was free that evening. Eventually though, she got bored of telling me she was busy; *"I'm flattered, but I'm afraid I'm just not interested."* was her reply to my final, and somewhat seedy, proposition. After a bit of pressing she revealed the main thing that turned her off about me (aside from texting her too much), was my teeth. She thought they could use straightening. Instead of being hurtful, this dental insult was a weird relief. I was happy that it was just a minor physical defect that put her off me[94]. I'd been experiencing a string of dating failures in June and July. I was beginning to worry there was something noxiously unappealing about my personality! Having been effectively closured, I thanked Ashley for her honesty and deleted her row from the spread sheet.

Name	Hermione
Occupation	Imports and exports

---

[94] Before you start picturing my mouth as a distorted jumble of dentition I would like to say that several independent parties have since rated my teeth as 'perfectly fine'.

Personality	No bullshit
Hair	Black
Kinky?	Yes
Other notes	Tall

More cocktails at my local neighbourhood speakeasy. Hermione had this kind of 'resting bitchface' expression that made her look annoyed whenever she was in a neutral emotional state (or at least that is what she told me). This stone eyed visage made it hard for me to tell when she was actively disapproving of what I was saying or just mildly interested. She stared at me with a particularly disconcerting 'open-mouthed-bitchface' when I rambled about my desire to have my brain cryogenically frozen and reconstituted as a computer (I don't remember how the conversation led to this). Needless to say, she wasn't on board with the idea.

Despite her confusing facial expressions we seemed to get on and have plenty to talk about including our kinky dating experiences. While on date number one, she reacted positively to the suggestion of a date number two. However, later she texted that I seemed like a nice guy but wasn't interested in getting freaky with me[95].

*

---

[95] I was starting to wonder if that cocktail bar was cursed. It seemed nice, intimate and classy but yet I never got laid when I took a date there. By early summer I was definitely starting to develop superstitions about particular venues, and trying to keep tabs on my success ratios for each one.

Did that list get exhausting? Imagine how it felt living it.

At this point it might appear to you, *mon cher compatriote*, that I was overdoing the whole dating thing a bit. This may be true but I had to do something with my time! I had started to make a few New York friends but I certainly didn't have a 'posse' of compadres. The friends I had made were either fellow NY stragglers or people who were ensconced within their own friend networks that I felt somehow invasive trying to infiltrate. There was no Central Perk for me to go and laze in with a group of amigos. There was no 'Monica's apartment' in which to gossip with shared acquaintances. There was no fountain to jump in pointlessly with a bunch of umbrella wielding besties[96]. It was just me... in my empty studio... with my pot plant and a pet firefly I'd named Boris[97].

So it could be said that I dated for company more than anything. As an only child I don't really mind extended periods of alone time, but the nascent companionship I felt on some first dates bleakened my otherwise empty social calendar. To quiet the discomfort I felt when second dates failed to materialise, the most effective distraction was to seek another first date. And so the cycle continued.

After its early blossoming, my sex life also seemed to be wilting in the summer heat (only 2 out of the 17 dates in this chapter were 'home runs', in case you weren't counting). Perhaps my new ambition to try and find a real match was part of the problem. I was keen to push for second dates and keep in

---

[96] This will definitely become a more surreal paragraph if read by future generations who have not watched 'Friends'.
[97] Well, Boris's light in my life existed only briefly, but it shone oh so brightly! (And also greenly).

contact with girls I'd met, but on the actual dates I adopted a relaxed approach and I didn't push girls to come home with me for sexy times, as I wished to appear like 'respectable boyfriend material' who wasn't just out to get laid. I suppose at that time I hadn't completely debunked my theory that genuine emotional connection might be best cultivated by careful courtship, and that romantic desires would be enhanced by a slow build-up of sexual anticipation over multiple dates[98].

However, one by one, all the interesting first dates I hoped to court and seduce slowly dropped away into a black hole of unanswered text messages. My 'building anticipation' theory of romance did not square with the data I was collecting from 'I want it all and I want it now' world of New York dating[99]. If I didn't sleep with a girl on the first date it seemed like my chances of seeing her again were dramatically reduced. This was especially true with the kink themed profiles, as I had several dates that seemed to go really well but I didn't sleep with them and then date two never happened. It was as if once the thrill of meeting a kinky Englishman for the first time had subsided then some critical frisson was irretrievably lost. Perhaps when these girls were given time to reflect, their nerves got the better of them, or they decided the mysterious phenomenon called 'chemistry' was missing[100].

---

[98] Sometimes it's funny to look back at how wrong you were.
[99] My keenness to maintain post-date contact may have also played to my disadvantage, perhaps making me come off as needy and lonely (which maybe I was, but I probably shouldn't have projected that!). On the other hand, I also wasn't sure if some girls just wanted me to chase them more, and if me not chasing them made them think I wasn't interested enough to be worth their time. Sadly, not getting replies left me no way of knowing whether they thought I was too interested in them or not interested enough.
[100] Personally I think there is an over-reliance on gut instinct or 'chemistry' in early dating decision making. I think a lot of people

The silver lining to all these low blows to my ego was that at least I was getting plenty of experience. Continuous and excessive post-date analysis was teaching me things, although what exactly I was learning would be kind of hard to condense into a lesson plan. Most importantly, the constant dating was conditioning my subconscious (and other socially relevant backwaters of my brain) to make the right moves and not the wrong ones[101]. I suppose dating is a bit like learning to play a sport; you can read books about it all you want, you can plan your actions to the minutest detail, but if you don't get out there and practice you'll just get knocked for six every time.

*

expect it to be there instantly and probably miss out on a lot of great opportunities to fall in love just because the first time they met a stranger a bunch of brain chemicals didn't fire in quite the right order.
[101] It also seemed apparent that I needed to be more confident and aggressive in my dating tactics. This might sound unpalatably close to the dating 'philosophy' expounded by certain noxious individuals who refer to themselves as 'pickup artists'. Some of these 'pick-up-""'artists""' teach that guys should be as manipulative, rapey, and consent violatey as legally possible in order to get girls into bed. This was a level of fucktardery I had no intention of exploring, and when I say 'I needed to be more aggressive' I'm talking about a subtle increase in aggression that could take the form of small differences in body language or how I said things. For example replacing the nonchalant "You can come back to mine if you like?" query, with more the more expectant question: "Would you like to come back to mine?" could easily tip the balance from a "not-sure" to a "maybe".

Name	Timothy
Occupation	Scientist
Personality	English
Hair	Brown
Kinky?	Serious weirdo
Other notes	Complains far too much about dating.

VI

Our hands part as we pass through the subway's clunking turnstiles. However, they soon find each other again and are reunited in this thick subterranean air.

'1. (6) Pelham Bay Park 7min', reads the green pixelated LCD that hangs over the platform. We walk along a little way to put some distance between us and the other bodies milling around the station. T.G.O.M.D. nestles her back into one of the H-shaped steel beams that keep the concrete mass of city above from crashing down on our heads.

There's a growing rumbling. A 4 train is approaching on the express track. Its lights are just starting to illuminate the square black columns that sandwich it between the 6 lines.

From her steel nook, T.G.O.M.D. looks up into my eyes. Both our hands are interlocked now and I squeeze her fingers tightly as I begin to kiss her.

The 4 train's screeching and clattering grows louder. I can feel the air moving on the back of my neck as our tongues make forceful contact. I grip her hands down by her sides and press her into that shallow metal alcove. My knuckles rub against the hard rivets and my chest squeezes against her breasts. Our hearts beat at each other as our lips fight for dominance and the high speed cacophony of shuddering-screaming steel on shuddering-screaming steel stampedes ever closer.

...

The express is passing us now and all other noise is blotted out by the awful ear-crushing roar. Carriage after carriage, all squealing, rumbling, and offending the senses. It seems like this train goes on forever.

I kiss her harder and I revel in the passionate thrill of every single second.

Chapter 16 - Taxidermy and Christmas lights

A Tuesday; I had snuck out of work early and I was loitering outside a bar called The Pine Tree Lodge, trying to find the optimum place to stand on the sidewalk so as not to obstruct the steady flow of commuters. Dozens of shiny shod and swanky sandaled feet trod past, pounding the melancholy grey concrete. This sullen landscape was livened only by the frequent dark blotches of petrified chewing gum. It's odd to think that all those black marks had accumulated over the decades, each one a record of some passing cretin who was too lazy to use a damn bin.

Manhattan sidewalks are one of those essential pieces of city engineering that are ever present but yet largely ignored. I mean, who gives a shit about grey paving slabs anyway? For the most part, New Yorkers can go about their daily lives safely paying no heed to the hard resilient surfaces under foot. Until, that is, they trip over them and find the ignominious (but still very solid) concrete heading towards them at high speed. Growing up in England, I remember playing the game called "Don't step on the cracks or you'll fall and break your backs!" The object of this game was to try and walk along the pavement without treading on the gaps between the paving slabs, (much to the annoyance of any accompanying adult who probably wanted to get somewhere).

At the time it seemed that this game had an absurd title, "Who trips on tiny pavement cracks?!" I thought. "Maybe miniature people with tiny feet?!" Of course, I had not visited New York, a city where, despite generating billions in tax revenues and being at the forefront of technological innovation, the task of maintaining a consistent, level, and non-hazardous walking surface is apparently too demanding. The giant slabs of sleeping sidewalk are left to slowly migrate over time (at least they are in some parts of town, don't let the nice flat sidewalks in midtown lull you into a false sense of foot security). Eventually, these shifting slabs create cliff like edifices at their junctions, and while the resulting escarpments are usually subtle enough to avoid the eye's notice, they can be easily high enough to catch a low flying foot and send its owner tumbling. I almost wonder if this patchy sidewalk maintenance is the product of some secret conspiracy to enhance the rate of natural selection in the city. Just like the suffocating subway stations, perhaps New York sidewalks are deliberately mal-aligned to kill off the weak and elderly and thus save social security dollars.

After staring at the sidewalk for a length of time that can only be described as 'excessive', I looked up to survey the passing commuters and to see if my date was in sight yet. 'Oh shit,' I thought, as I spied my bosses' secretary. She waved at me before I could pretend not to have seen her... She was a nice friendly lady, I could probably trust her not to rat me out.

I'd not been to this bar before. It looked kind of divey online but in a novel and interesting way. I had asked Millie (aka tonight's date) to choose from a range of drinking establishments but she had brushed off talk of cocktail bars and selected the 'dive' option. I was hovering outside just in case she had second thoughts on arrival.

Millie had found me through Okcupid profile 2 and already added me on Fetlife, so we were closely familiar with each other's interests. I suppose a dive bar seemed as good a venue as any for discussing them further.

I didn't have my glasses on, so while I was myopically scanning the passers-by I found myself staring at any approaching pedestrian who looked vaguely female with blonde hair.

'Is that her?' I thought.
'Nope, that eye contact freaked her out and now she's walking past me briskly.'

'Maybe her?'
'...oh no, that lady looks like she's in her 40's.'.

'Oh this girl looks like a possibility...'.
High heels, long legs, and a killer body in a business suit, all crystallized out of the mists of my vision. They were topped by two blue eyes staring right at me.
I held mine steady.
'Holy shit, Millie didn't look this tall in her photos,' I thought.
This blonde vision grew closer, still looking at me, becoming more defined. She was actually real and not just some mirage. It seemed like I had lucked out with this date...
I smiled...
She didn't smile...
I lifted my hand to wave...
She didn't slow down...
My eyes followed the side of her head as she walked straight past me.

'Either that's not her, or she just took one look at my face and bailed.'

I turned back around to find a different, and very short, blonde girl grinning at me.
"Hi!" said Millie
"Errr hi! Millie? How are you doing?!" I said, as my brain caught up with the situation.
'I guess this girl looks nice too,' it concluded, having readjusted its height calibrations a little.
'...Yup, those are some seriously blue eyes!'
"Does this place look ok to you?" I asked.

"Sure. Let's do it!" Millie replied.

As we snuck inside, we were greeted by a large moose wearing sunglasses. This was already not your typical bar ornament. The groovy moose was accompanied by an array of other taxidermied animals spread around the bar and oddly juxtaposed with cascades of fairy lights. These festive constellations of white, green, and red were wrapped around the dead animal heads, which somehow disguised their morbid nature. Until that is you looked closely at their faces and saw their dead glass eyes staring back at you.

The bar itself was adorned with drift wood lanterns and other rustic nick-knacks, and the laminated food menu's and other bits of dive bar kitchery fuelled an oddness that was somehow amusing.
"Well this is different!" I said. "What do you want to drink?"
"Beer is good!"

Having been dispensed two 'alpine lagers' from a no-nonsense barmaid with whom I certainly didn't want to pick a fight, we went in search of the beer garden that we had seen in some Yelp photos.
"Nope. That's just a room with sofas and a large water buffalo head," I said, having reached the back of the bar.
"Well those are the toilets... and that looks like the kitchen... Excuse me is this the way to the beer garden?" Millie asked a passing waitress.
"Oh we don't have one of those anymore," came the response.
Another lesson learned in not trusting the Internet. We settled ourselves either side of a thin table next to a wall plastered with book spines and fake log ends that were all covered in biro and felt tip graffiti.

"Well you can't claim I don't take you to romantic places!" I joked.

She laughed, and we proceeded to chat. Millie was a biochemical researcher and as this was a subject I knew a bit about we both got to geek out and complain to each other about the woes of doing science. She was in the middle of some Sisyphean experiment that she had been excited about initially, but had now either gone wrong or given a null result and she was faced with repeating the whole endeavour without even knowing what to do differently the second time around. However, despite our mutual complaining, everything Millie said projected a kind of cheerful enthusiasm. She talked about growing up in the Midwest, her close-knit family, and how she enjoyed doing amateur dramatics in her spare time. She quizzed me on England in turn, and how I coped with moving to New York, as well as grilling me for my best dating anecdotes.

As the alpine lager made itself felt, Millie excused herself to go to the bathroom. In her place, a long deceased racoon stared at me, poised on the mantelpiece as if running forwards. It was adorned in green fairy lights that partly made up for its hair loss problem.

Millie returned, we acquired more beer, and feeling confident in our rapport I asked "So, how have you been finding Fetlife?"
"Errr, kind of intense. I dunno, I think I might delete my profile. There are just too many creepy guys on there that just won't leave you the hell alone!"
"Oh yeah? I don't have that problem as a guy, and I think it's meant more for people in the scene to keep in touch and not so much for meeting people to date."
"I guess so. You sure see some pretty weird stuff on there!"

Our table had a long rail running underneath it that Millie was resting her feet on. While we talked I slowly moved my right leg to rest against her left leg, initially trying to make it seem as if it had always been there, but then massaging her leg gently so she knew this was not some accidental collision. Her leg did not flee, and above the table we continued to converse in the same tone as before.

"Have you ever gone to any of the BDSM social events or kink parties?" I asked.
"No, but I've thought about it. I don't know if I'd want to go to something like that by myself though."
"Yeah, as a guy I'd worry about looking like some kind of pervy creep if I went by myself."

Now my other leg closed in on her right; a classic pincer movement.

I continued to ramble: "I also have this fear that I'd not get on with other guys who claimed to be 'dominant'... though I dunno, I guess I just have an invented idea that I'd end up hanging out with a bunch of douches I'd have to pretend not to hate."
"Yeah, I'm sure you'd find people you'd get on with."
"Yeah, probably. Maybe we could go to something together sometime? Then we wouldn't be standing alone looking awkward!"
"Sure, I could be up for that!"

We sipped our beers and talked more until eventually conversation paused with both of us leaning forward over the table watching each other's expressions. Millie's legs remained locked between mine.

"So... what AM I going to do with you?" I said, smiling.

My knees squeezed in, applying pressure to the leg sandwich. I looked into her nervous smiling eyes of ocean blue... and then I leant forward and kissed her.

It ended up pretty passionate for a hands free kiss across a table in a near empty dive bar.
Withdrawing for a breather I said: "You're lucky you've got the table to protect you!"

Millie looked down, nervously biting her lip.

"So do you want to get another drink here or do you want to get a drink back at my place?" I asked
"Erm, I'm not sure if I should come back to your place. You should know I'm not the type of girl who goes home with a guy on the first date."
"No? I'm not sure there is a specific 'type' of girl that does that."
"How do you mean?"
"I mean I've met a bunch of different girls through my kink profile, and those I've slept with on the first date normally haven't come across as a 'type', or like 'slutty' or 'trashy' or anything. Mostly they seem pretty smart and together in fact."
"I guess I can see that," she said sceptically, "but you have to understand us American girls are deeply influenced by the rules our mothers teach us, whether we admit it or not!"
"Oh yeah, what are the rules? I should really learn this!"
"The rules are like. 'always wait for a guy to call you first', or 'always let him pay', or 'never let a guy go too far on a first date or he won't respect you', you know, stuff like that!"
"I see. This is useful information!"

We talked a little bit about heeding and rebelling against parental advice, my legs still squeezed hers and my hand played along her outstretched arm.

"Anyway, wouldn't you judge me if I came home with you on a first date?" she asked me.

"No of course not!" I said, sincerely, "I think a girl should just feel empowered to do what she wants. If she feels like having sex with a guy on the first date, then she should do that, but if she doesn't then she shouldn't. It's her life at the end of the day, so to hell with whatever our fucked up society thinks she should do."

"But if you had sex with someone on the first date wouldn't that make you less likely to want to go on a second date with them?" Millie asked

"No, not at all. To me whether we have sex really doesn't make any difference to how I see someone. In fact in my experience with my kink profile I've probably had more second dates with girls I've slept with on the first date. Though that's possibly just because girls get cold feet after the excitement of the first meeting a kinky guy has passed."

Millie replied with a "Hmmm".

I put my recently emptied glass to my mouth in the hope more beer had somehow materialised at the bottom...

There was no magically appearing beer.

"So what do you think? Another drink?"

*

Back in my apartment we fell together onto my bed. My hands ran up under her shirt as I pushed her back into the billowing duvet. They grasped and squeezed at her soft body, pausing only to fight with buttons, clasps and other obstacles that insisted on getting in the way.

As I was feeling her up Millie muttered: "You should know I usually find it super hard to climax."

"That's ok, I like a challenge!" I replied, grasping her wrists and pushing them against the mattress.

"Mmnnnhhh," was her response as I began kissing and biting her neck.

My hands and mouth went to work... then after a little warm up I asked "Shall I strap you down? I can do it so that you can escape if you want."

She looked momentarily conflicted, then nodded her head.

"But you're not allowed to murder me!"

"Noted: no murdering."

"Oh and you have condoms right?"

"Of course!"

I reached above her and rummaged under the mattress, producing one padded Velcro cuff which flopped onto my sheets.

"Wow, do you just keep these under there the whole time?"

"Yup," I said, rummaging for the second cuff.

"But what if you have friends over?"

"Well that's why they're hidden under the mattress!" I said, thrusting her wrist out above her and wrapping the padded material around it.

An excited whimper escaped her mouth as I secured her second wrist.

"I'll leave them loose in case you want to wriggle out and hit me, ok?"

She nods.

The leg cuffs needed some adjusting to account for my new toy's short stature, but all her limbs were immobilised quickly enough. Having a girl naked and at your mercy just never gets old.

*

After I had apparently risen to the challenge, I unstrapped Millie and we cuddled for a while. I got up to get water, and as I abandoned her there lying naked amongst my sheets, she whined: "Owww I kind of like you now."
I smiled at her. For some reason that sentence didn't fill me with any significant amount of terror.

"And you're a good kisser too," she said, after I'd returned to the bed and our lips had played together for a while.

It was still early. Yellow evening light was streaming through the window and catching Millie's hair as she kept kissing and toying. She worked her way up on top of me. Shit, I love evening light, and when a naked woman is straddling you and inundated with that fiery glow... well, it creates a scene more beautiful than one ought to rightly wish for.

As I lay there Millie slowly rubbed herself up and down me, teasing me back to excitement. My outstretched hands came across my belt amongst the disrupted sheets. Time to punish her for this wickedness! As I lashed her butt she arched her head backwards open mouthed with surprise. Her face came back smiling, but smiling the kind of eyebrow-raised smile you give someone when part of you isn't sure if you should actually be mad at them, but the rest of you can't help but grin.

I took a second swing at her, but this time my aim wasn't so good and my belt landed lower down hitting the back of her leg. Unfortunately for me, most of the kinetic energy from my swing was focused at the very end of the belt, which wrapped around Millie's leg, flew through the gap between her thighs and hit me square in the balls.

"OOOmFFF!" I exhaled, lips pursed and cheeks ballooning outwards. My nuts hastily retreated inwards and my knees and legs jerked upwards as if to effect some instinctual but futile testicle protection.
"Are you ok?" Millie asked.
"Just belted myself in the balls... don't mind me!"
"HAHAHAHAHA!"
"Thanks. I appreciate your sympathy!"
Millie continued to straddle and tease me. "That's pretty embarrassing for you, haha!"
This insolence incensed me to take another, particularly vicious, swing at her with the belt.

I thought I aimed higher this time.

It transpired that I had aimed at exactly the same spot.

"OOOUGNNNHH!" is an approximation of sound I made, accompanied by even more pained facial expressions.
"Again?!" Millie exclaimed in disbelief.
"Jesus!"
"Are you ok?"
"Ergh, I'm out of the game!" I said rolling over into a foetal position.

If at first you don't fail hard enough, fail fail again[102].

---

[102] Life lesson: never try to belt anyone's ass when they're sitting dangerously close to your testicles.

*

To: *'Millie okc'*
Message body: *"Have you any structured plans for your afternoon? I'm thinking you should get some work done... Then come over here for me to have my way with you... Then we can get takeout. :)"*
SEND

BEEP BEEP...
"This sounds like a splendid plan [...] I'll do whatever you tell me! ;)"

*

And so I tempted Millie into my lair for a second time.

I could smell alcohol on her breath as she kissed me, and when I asked her if she'd been drinking she admitted shyly, "I may have had a quick margarita at a bar near here."

It's funny how hard it is to see yourself as others see you. I'd certainly never imagined I was sufficiently intimidating that someone would feel the need to drink before coming to meet me. However, I felt there was something decidedly sweet about this admission and it pleased me, though I wasn't 100% sure why.

"Sounds like I need to catch up with you then! Do you want a beer or something?"
"Need some courage of your own huh?" she teased.
"Oh, did you want to jump straight into being dominated then?!" I said, grasping her wrists and pushing her down into the couch.
"Errmm... I'll take a beer." she recanted.

After our refreshments, my evening's entertainment consisted of chaining a naked Millie to the bed on her hands and knees. The hard metal links held her wrists and hands together as if in prayer, and locked them to the top of my bed. Her ankles were wrapped and fastened individually, and spread apart just the right amount. Further loops of chain passed around her knees to keep them where I wanted them. I kept chaining until I exhausted my supply of padlocks. Millie could only hope that I didn't lose the keys.

No escape routes this time. She would have to take all that I made her endure.

My open hand, my flogger, and my belt were her main tormentors that evening. They mocked her small white body, held powerlessly by interminable links of chrome plated steel. Perhaps this was my revenge for her laughing at my self-inflicted misfortune on our first date (my own tender parts stayed well out of harm's way this time around), or perhaps I just liked hurting her. She did keep trying to impersonate my British accent after all, and that always brings out the sadist in me! I put a ball gag in her mouth so she couldn't sass me further. It was undoubtedly for her own good.

I fucked her and flogged her back. Some particularly loud, animalistic grunts and groans could be heard through the gag as we got going. They worried me for a moment, but as they repeated themselves I was reassured by their consistent structure and the subtle undertones of pleasure[103].

Later we ate Chinese food[104].

---

[103] She did not resort to the "Jazz hands" safe-word/gesture.
[104] What it lacked in quality it made up for in monosodium glutamate.

*

Millie left that same evening, she was still in one piece, if a little chain marked. I cleaned and stowed my sex toys and then finished packing my suitcase. I had a flight to England to catch the next morning.

One of the many drawbacks of living outside your home country is that you have to spend all your holiday time going back there just to reassure various friends and relatives that you haven't forgotten their existence, and ensure that they haven't forgotten yours.

I'd taken a gamble and added Millie on Facebook before I left. She seemed sane, and I didn't think there was too high a risk that she'd turn out to be a psychotic type who, if spurned, would send incriminating messages to my friends, or post jealous rants about BDSM on my wall, or boil the pet bunny.

I spent a couple of weeks back in England and exhausted my official holiday quota[105]. While I was there, Millie kept in close contact at first, but then she seemed to grow distant. I can't deny there was a knot in my stomach when I got back to America and she told me she was seeing someone, and that it was getting serious. I didn't feel excessively jealous of her new man though, not even when pictures of this grinning couple started to scroll through my Facebook news feed. My stomach knot resolved itself soon enough and, before long, I had two new dates lined up for that week. However, a sense of loss still lingered at the back of my mind. Millie was someone who it felt good to be around and her boisterous personality had further

---

[105] American institutions aren't exactly generous with their holiday allowances.

demonstrated to me that it's possible to be a loud American without being obnoxious or annoying.

Whatever we shared on those two sweaty evenings, I don't think it was nothing.

Perhaps it was only just short of something.

Chapter 17 - Why do you build me up? Buttercup?

It's a Wednesday, and another evening home alone. My air conditioner is whirring like a diesel train but I can still hear the occasional sirens passing below. Of course, these sirens signify nothing more calamitous than the fact I am still living in New York and that the dramas and tragedies vested upon some other bees in this hive are continuing with their regular frequency.

Some of my neighbours were having sex earlier, although I couldn't tell which ones. I could just hear the ethereal sound of a thudding bedstead and 'auh auh's drifting in from somewhere that wasn't here. The faint smell of tobacco smoke has also been subtly infiltrating my room, creeping in via some vent or other and producing whiffs that remind me of my Nan's house. Just faint hints of that stale life sucking odour, but they're still maddening.

I feel trapped. Trapped in my apartment by the suffocating heat outside. Trapped by the four walls around me and the photographs stuck to them. Trapped by those over-familiar memories. Trapped by my computer screen and its endless streams of recycled information and pretty thumbnails of girls I'll never meet. Trapped by the maze of towering concrete, glass, and steel that surrounds me, stretching as far as the eye can see. Trapped by this city's endless possibilities and all the things I could be doing in this moment, but the knowledge of which only serves to shrink the walls around me. I long for green open spaces, but even if I were suddenly transported into the depths of some wilderness, I know that something in my mind would still remain closed off, because there are bars between me and what I truly desire, and tonight the whole world has become my prison.

I wouldn't say I've ever really suffered from depression, unlike most of the other residents of this city I've never seen a therapist and never been prescribed pills to re-tune my brain. For the most part, I like my brain as it is and I am averse to having it fiddled with. That's the English way I suppose. Perhaps I was brought up to be the 'strong silent type' as Tony Soprano would put it (or at least the silent type... I haven't worked out in a while). There are times though, such as this evening, where you find me sitting here alone in my room, times where I feel like my whole motivation to "be" has just been drained out of me. And so I sit here emptied. And I stare at nothing...

I mean I wouldn't say I'm actually depressed because I get the feeling depression should involve more 'pain' in some form or another. Right now I feel more of a numbness than anything. Perhaps I would characterise this as more of a 'depression-lite'; a state of mind where one realises that all potential endeavours are too unlikely to succeed, or require far too much effort and emotional investment for the rewards on offer. When the risk of falling prey to failure's knife seems too great, then doing nothing can just present itself as the most logical option because it carries the least risk of disappointment. All the numbers in balancing this equation of risk vs. reward are subjective anyway. I suppose it's just a certain loss of hope that makes you see how hard the scales are tipped against you.

'What has precipitated this evening's descent into personal oblivion?' I ask myself.
'Come on, you know full well the answer to that!' I reply to myself.

It's not my failures at work, although that part of my life has been consistently demoralising since I left England, but today wasn't remarkable. I spent it setting up experiments rather than observing their uninterpretable results. No, this evening's gloom has been precipitated by the slow collapse of yet another house of dating cards, and there standing out amongst the settling rubble is one particular queen of taunted hearts. Her name is Ramona.

Fucking Ramona.

We should be on our second date right now, that is if she hadn't gone so silent all of a fucking sudden.

I check my phone again, in case I had been selectively deaf and not heard a new message arrive from her. There's no envelope symbol to be seen, not even an email one to give me a millisecond of false hope. I open up our text conversation, you know, just in case she has sent some kind of ninja message that slipped into my phone without raising any alarm... No... Nothing... (I guess they still haven't invented ninja SMS yet).

I've scroll up through our conversation to the topless picture she sent me some time after our first date. There's no real purpose to this ogling. I guess I'm just checking to see if she really did send that picture to me and it wasn't all just some cruel trick of my imagination. No, there was that skinny body and those pointy nipples crowning her modest breasts. The size of her rack didn't matter one bit; I wanted all of her just as she was.

But right now I'd settle for a damned reply.

Fucking Ramona.

Sometimes I wonder if there's a team of assassins hunting down all the first dates I get on really well with, and taking them out one by one. I suppose the FBI should have checked their Okcupid accounts and spotted a pattern by now (unless they are in on it too?). Or maybe there is a team of NSA hackers selectively blocking my messages to and from the people I like the most. Perhaps conducting some kind of vindictive experiment into what happens when you isolate a man from the simple human connection that he craves most. (Is this my cruel and unnatural punishment for sharing too many Edward Snowden stories on Facebook...?)

The silence emanating from my phone is deafening. The absence of noise inescapable. What's worse is that it's not just Ramona who's ignoring me. I've texted four different girls this evening, either past dates or those who were once interested in meeting me for a first, just trying to find some contact to fill this evening's void.

Still my phone sits silent.

Yesterday it had been beeping and buzzing away excitedly with quick fire texts between me and F.R. She was supposed to be studying for an exam, and I said we should meet tonight so I could give her a quiz on her revision notes (by which I meant the fun kind of quiz where wrong answers led to stinging ass cheeks).

She seemed excited by this idea. All that was left to do was to set the time and place. Today though I think I've exhausted my 'non-crazy quota' of three unanswered texts.
'Is three maybe pushing it for 24 hrs?'... 'Shit I'll just send her a :-\ face...:-\ faces don't count towards the crazy quota right?'
'I don't know Timmy, it's your quota. Why are you asking me? '
'Because you're also Timmy.'
'Ok, let's stop this now.'

I'd first met Ramona back in August, over a month ago. She was a West Coaster with wispy brown hair accompanied a wry smile, a dry wit, and a serious interest in getting tied up. When I arrived at the Belfry she was already sitting alone at the bar with an interesting looking cocktail in front of her. I could tell the guy tending bar was disappointed when I sat down beside her. He was cold towards me as I tried to order an Allagash and seemed much more interested in checking on whether R. was enjoying her cocktail.

Conversation flowed between myself and Ramona as if there hadn't been a time when we weren't talking and there'd never be a time when we stopped. Perhaps it was nothing remarkable to write about. I remember her commenting dryly how she kind of hates people, and how that contrasted with her new choice of profession. I talked a bit about my research until she adopted a glazed smile.
"Have I lost you?" I'd asked.
"Yeah, I have no idea what you're saying."
"Ha, sorry."
"It sounds good though! I like hearing people talk who are passionate about what they do, even if it makes no sense to me."

She was confident and her intelligence was self-apparent. Her parents were Jewish and she'd lived the liberal West Coast lifestyle; coop housing, mild drug experimentation, lots of gay friends, beach parties, etc. etc. Cool, smart, hot, mentally together, and interested in kink, and to think I'd almost ignored her first message.

As our lips and bodies conversed I found myself trying to step back, trying to analyse her to check for any insincerity, any clues I'd missed on previous dates that seemed to go well but then led to text silence. All I could see was warmth and flirtation, I made some funny comment and her hand pushed my arm as she laughed. 'No hesitation initiating physical contact there!' I thought to myself, 'surely there is some genuine connection happening here... something strong enough that it won't be broken the minute the subway doors close behind her?'

We talked a bit about online dating. I'd told her how frustrating I found it not getting replies from dates I was into. She commented "Yeah I'd always reply I think, I might not always be that diplomatic, but I usually tell people how I feel."

*

My phone vibrates loudly on the desk.
YES! Maybe it's finally the reply I'm waiting for! I grab it up before the "BEEP-BEEP" alert has even finished.

No, it's a reply from Ashley: *"I'm flattered but I'm just not interested."* Her response to my earlier clumsy proposal for seduction by alcohol, unreliable wit, and promises of sexual gratification.

Shit balls. Well that's one less person I can proposition for casual sex.

I pen a petulant reply: *"Don't be that flattered, you're the fourth girl I've tried for a date tonight. You get points for replying though!"*

Maybe that's a bit much? The wit's not really hiding the petulance. Fuck it. Send. What difference does it make anyway?

Perhaps these evenings of enforced hermitage are part of the reason I'm still single. One girl starts ignoring me and I kick out at the array of dating dominos. A minor hiccup spirals into greater and greater isolation as the subtle aroma of desperation leaches into my messages. I'm not messaging anyone else tonight I tell myself. Besides I don't have the energy.

I watch some gifs of cats doing cute and dumb shit, mixed with footage of idiots falling over onto hard surfaces. Other thoughts that don't involve F.R. occupy me for a while until I get bored of the contents of my Internet happy meal and a prevailing emptiness regains my attention.

I scroll through my Okcupid inbox... Well there was that girl.... She'd probably sleep with me again... Ergh but I find her voice so annoying! Phone off and back down on the table.

F.R. had a nice voice, the low West Coast voice, nothing shrill or piercing about it, and none of those nasal syllables that can scrape at the mind like a cheese grater. My head is back in that bar again.

*

"I could be into that..." F.R. had said after I'd talked about a particularly weird fantasy I have that involves chaining up a girl and covering her in gooey and sticky foodstuffs, (or having a girl subject me to the same humiliating treatment[106]).
"...so long as it wasn't anything too gross or that smells bad!" she added.

---

[106] Referred to as 'sploshing' I think this fantasy comes from when I was a kid. I used to watch lots of shows where my peers competed in various daft challenges and the punishment for failure was to be covered in slime. Not sure why that got to me, but somehow it did.

We were comfortably deep into sex talk. F.R. hadn't experimented seriously with BDSM, though she'd flirted heavily. She described less satisfying boyfriends and more exciting flings. She'd also skirted the San Francisco kink community but not quite been tempted in. I told her I was currently trying to teach myself some rope skills (with the help of the Internet) and I was keen to find a willing volunteer to practice them on.

I first kissed her while we were still sitting at the bar. She was into it, leaning into me and giving as good as she got. Eventually she ran her hand across my face and between our mouths, as if to stop what her lips couldn't. Then keeping her hand on my mouth she turned away to sip her drink with a mischievous smile on her face.

After that date we exchanged no shortage of texts. I sent her a picture of my new pile of ropes, recently arrived in the mail. She'd replied *"Looks like they need breaking in..."* Some gentle sexting and a couple of second date plans were tentatively made, but they fell through as I had a cold and she had a friend visiting.

Then Ramona stopped replying. For the first time.

Eventually, after I had begun to trespass into the psychologically questionable territory of sending unanswered message 4 or 5, she got back in touch. Turned out that her 'visiting friend' had been an ex and old flames had rekindled briefly, only to be extinguished again. We shared a phone call. It was a bit awkward (I am awkward at phone calls), but the channels of communication were opened once again and through them flowed further flirtations, naked pictures, and the resurrected possibility of a second date.

Tonight was almost that night! Except here I am, sitting in my underwear and scratching myself, hands tapping feebly at a plastic keyboard rather than squeezing the reddened ass cheeks of that pretty California girl I so desire.

Perhaps I bore you with my longing... I bore myself but that doesn't allow me to escape the subject. It feels like stoicism is the socially expected male response to emotional challenge, be it rejection, unanswered messages, pet cats getting hit by lawnmowers[107] etc etc. Girls are expected to cry and get emotional and send moderately long strings of obsessive text messages, but if a guy did that, "wow what a loser!" I imagined people would say. Maybe these differences can be explained by chromosomes and hormones or (and I suspect more likely) they're actually mostly a product of our culture's sexist undertows. This might be an interesting debate to research and write about, but I'm talking about ME right now, so let's not get side-tracked!

I mean I think I've gotten pretty good at the whole stoicism thing, I guess it's mostly about controlling expectations and not getting carried away with the possibilities. Repeated exposure to romantic failure has also built up a certain emotional numbness. Perhaps this numbness is a defence mechanism of sorts, the main walls of which were already established before I arrived in New York, and my American experiences have only served to reinforce them. I like to think I have an open gatehouse policy... but now I'm getting lost in my metaphors.

---

[107] This has not happened to me or anyone I know, but it was the most emotionally challenging thing that sprung into my mind, so I went with it.

Stoic or not, I've been on thirty six dates in New York before this evening and I'm still single.

Still single. I may have brushed off each individual failure, but the micro cuts are accumulating and I can't ignore the fact I feel injured. Like any wounded animal, part of me wants to lash out. I want to berate Ramona for fucking me around, for teasing me, for lying to me, for being too cowardly to just tell me what the hell is going on with her. I want to rebuke many other dates for this as well. I want to rage and rant in a self-destructive frenzy of self-righteous admonishment, 'Just because I'm a kinky guy who wants to tie you up and hurt you doesn't mean I don't have god-damned feelings!' I pen the text in my mind's eye.

However, I'm afraid that if I express this anger it will just drive those I crave further away. It would give them ammunition to dismiss me as creepy and excuse themselves of their suppressed guilt. Though perhaps showing them I have strong feelings is actually a good idea? Passion? Isn't that what the movies tell most girls they want to see? Maybe I should enlist a quirky female sidekick and concoct a complex plan to find F.R. and win her over with overt expressions of romantic attraction? Maybe these expressions would involve a marching band and singing? Or filling her lobby with flowers? Or tattooing "For Ramona" onto my penis and sending her Polaroids? I mean if I don't have a quirky female sidekick to provide advice and witticisms, it's possible this whole exercise could just be classified as creepy stalking...

...Yeah, on second thoughts, trying to show her my inner 'passion' is probably not a good plan. Instead, I'm going to go with sitting here, and not doing anything... and hoping she replies.... Actually I'm going go with lying on the bed for a while. That's even better.

Micro cuts. Hooks caught in my flesh. One or two I might shrug off, but now enough barbs have built up and brought me low. I'm lying on my back, staring at the ceiling, transfixed by matters I seem unable to control. I can't blame F.R. alone for this emptiness, it's just that all my strands of bitter existential angst have wrapped around this most recent injury, focusing their drag on that one particular grapnel.

Fucking Ramona.

*

"I get really horny in the mornings for some reason," said Ramona, looking sideways at me, elbows on the bar.
"Oh yeah? I've noticed that's when you seem to be on Fetlife... is that your preferred time for self-pleasure?"
"I guess. But I don't do that much. Normally I just need one good orgasm then I'm good for the week."
"Huh, how very efficient! I guess I'm a once a night kind of guy. Unless I've had too many ales that is"
"Haha! You're ridiculous!" she said, smiling.

*

Ugh lying here is boring. I slide my phone out of my pocket and hold it over my face to replace the view of monotonous ceiling. I press a button and the screen turns on... Ooo there's an exciting envelope sign! Oh no, it's just an email trying to sell me something... Shit.

I scroll through my text message inbox looking at the names, hoping that one will jump out at me as some untapped and reliable source of human connection, but nothing does. I open up Tinder and swipe a few pictures left and right... Ooo she's a really hot match... Oh no she's just advertising some sex chat line. Back to Okcupid, and the sea of face squares that are apparently 'nearby'....

I wonder, in this age of online dating has human contact itself has been commoditized? Perhaps here in New York its value has plummeted due to a perceived glut in supply, and demand seems to wane as we all go about pretending we are immune to our solitude. If New York is really ahead of the cultural curve, is this a chilling vision of a future everywhere? Will all our lives be spent sitting silently in empty rooms in towering apartment buildings where we don't even know the names of our neighbours? Will we all be sitting alone, hunched over our computers, convincing ourselves that technology is keeping us connected? Will we all be sending out countless messages into the digital ether and letting our emotions hang on the silence shattering "beep-beeps" of our cell-phones...?

Already our ears don't cry out for the drumming of fingers on piano keys, or sliding of violin bows on strings, or human breath through resonating instruments. Now all they crave is harsh digital notifications from a tiny speaker translating electrons into a shitty repetitive sound. The siliconized justification for our existence.

I think this city is chewing me up whole, I wonder what will be left when it spits me out again.

*

At an appropriate seeming time on that first date, I'd said to Ramona: "So I don't want to be too forward but you'd be welcome to come back to my place after this if you want... though I know you said you have this party to go to."

"I should probably go to this party, but I am kind of intrigued to see what your place is like though," she replied.

This is where I should have said something like: "Well you can just come for a quick beer and check it out if you like," as it's all about playing the game one step at a time.

However, sadly, I started talking before I finished thinking: "Oh my place is not that exciting, just a regular studio, not some crazy sex dungeon or anything!"
"How disappointing!" she replied, still smiling.

We kissed again and our hands played together some more.

"Yeah my friends will be pissed at me if I don't show up."
Then she looked at me and playfully asked:
"Do you want to come to a party in Bushwick?"
A little surprised by this invitation I took a moment to respond "Erm... maybe? I mean do you want me to come to a party in Bushwick? Wouldn't it be weird for you?"

She thought for a moment.
"Yeah... Yeah it would definitely be weird," she decided .

Shit. I should have just said "Sure!" Why the fuck didn't I just say "Sure"!

I walked R. to the L train stop on Third Avenue and we kissed a passionate goodbye. She made an 'Mmmh' noise as I bit down on her lower lip, then turned and bounced off down the stairs. I stood there motionless, watching her sink down and get further away. Her head turned back to look at me, and her face was alight with her mischievous smile that broadened when she saw I was watching her go. Then she turned away and danced out of sight towards the turnstiles.

Still fixed to that spot I clenched my right hand as it hung beside me, each finger moving in one at a time, starting with the pinkie and making a fist in one smooth movement. They all squeezed together in one brief expression of violent emotion, and then released.

Then my feet walked me home.

*

As I lie here, the black void of a pistol barrel rests beside my ear. "Do it!" it whispers.

I pull the trigger and spray my brains over the wall beside my bed.

"PPPWAAUGH!" I vocalise, because that's what I imagine exploding brains would sound like. I take my forefinger away from my temple and scratch my head.

'I think I'm going to have a little glass of whiskey,' I decide. 'I'm going to have some whiskey because that's what TV says men do when they're existentially challenged and don't know how to deal with all those dreaded 'feelings' they have.'

The cork makes a satisfying whiskey cork noise as it comes out of the bottle. This 12 year old Tomatin has been lasting me well (it must be almost 13 years old by now, but I'm not sure if it works like that). I had mostly been tapping it for a bit of quick pre-date tongue loosening but these days my tongue seems loose enough by itself.

'God, I don't even feel like masturbating,' I think to myself, collapsing back in my desk chair and taking a slow sip of the potent liquid. I check the dreary updates of my Fetlife 'friends', then, uninspired, I find myself leafing through the infinite face collage of Okcupid yet again. I'm just clicking through profiles like an automaton, not even looking, not even liking, not even caring. A moment of utter despair seems close at hand.

Up pops a message at the bottom of my screen: "You have one new message from *cute looking girl*"
"Hey, that's a nice looking Turnip!" it reads (she's referring to a picture on my 'normal' profile where I'm holding a turnip... but this is not even close to being relevant.)

My digital salvation. It hasn't come with beeps, but it'll do for now.

Maybe I'll masturbate after all.

*

The bar where I'd met R. on that first date was quiet when we'd first got there, but by the end it was full to bursting. The music and throng of people was loud and we had to keep our heads close together to hear each other speak.

There was a bachelorette party nearby. They were doing shots. R. and I were chatting away when I felt a tap on my shoulder. I turned to see an attractive member of this party trying to engage me.
"Hi, excuse me." she said.
"Hi," I replied.
"This might sound a bit crazy, but we need you to sing a song to someone," said the party girl.
Then addressing R. she said "I'm so sorry."
"Ha, it's fine!" R. replied.
I maintained an expression of bewilderment.

"You need me to sing a song to someone? Who do you need me to sing to?"

"That girl over there, she's the one getting married. Will you get on your knees and sing to her?"

"Erm that's a strange request..."

"I'm soo sorry to interrupt, but I have to get someone to sing to her!!!" she said, shrilly addressing both me and R.

"Errr, okay..."

Turning to R. I asked her "What do you think?"

"You should do it!" said R.

"Pleeease!" said the party girl

"I mean now I feel like I have to impress you with my confidence by taking up this strange challenge."

"DO IT!" repeated R.

"Ok, ok."

I slid off my bar stool, still hesitating...

"Oh, it's ok, it looks like they've got someone now... Never mind!" said the party girl, distracted and moving away, much to my relief.

The song came on and some poor sap was getting down on his knees and singing 'Build Me Up Buttercup' to a drunk and confused bride to be.

"Wow, I'm glad I didn't do it now. That looks humiliating!" I said

"Haha. It does!" said R.

"...I need you more than anyone, darlin', you know that I have from the start, so build me up, buttercup, don't break my heart!" sang the courageous fellow to a bewildered girl in a tiara. Her friends looked on and laughed. Fortunately, after the first excruciating moments of slightly out of tune solo singing, some other guys started backing him up and his voice was no longer alone.

I was still not quite back on my bar stool and I guess I was a couple of beers to the wind, so I turned to look at Ramona, and then I started to sing:
"Hey! Hey! Hey!... Baby try to find!"

R. smiled and joined in.
"Hey! Hey! Hey!... A little time, and I'll make you happy, Hey! Hey! Hey! I'll be home, I'll be beside the phone waiting for you..."

We lent towards each other, both singing:
"Ooo-oo-ooo!"

We held hands and half danced while still on our stools. Ramona's laughing smile built my confidence and boosted my singing volume.

"Why do you build me up...
Buttercup, baby just to let me down,
And mess me around.
And then worst of all...
You never call baby when you say you will...
But I love you still, I need you...
More than anyone darling.
You know that I have from the sta-ar-ar-rt,
So build me up!
Buttercup!
Don't break my heart!"

Chapter 18 - Date stew

Piss and garbage; these are the inescapable odours that flood Manhattan as summer draws to a close. As I walked to meet Nicole these two aromas alternated and varied in intensity as I passed piles of bulging black plastic and stained concrete. Even when no obvious source was in sight there was no break from the nasal onslaught.

Piss was the scent of the hour in Madison Square Park. Nicole and I sat on a bench and sipped our Argo teas as stale urine wafted past us on the breeze. During a break in conversation I suggested we switched to a different seating area. Getting further away from the doggy play area seemed to improve the smell a bit.

Old ladies with insanely inbred looking dogs circled the park in a kind or narcotised late summer stupor. A young family was pushing a pram past us for a second time and in it their spawn was sat bolt upright, staring directly at me with a singular intensity. He rotated his head slowly as they passed us, eyes locked on me until the hood of the pram blocked his view. I'd already noticed that kid staring at me on his first loop around the park. What was it about me that transfixed him? Could he tell that there was a date going on? Could he see the blackness in my soul? His expression was pretty sour and discouraging. It was as if I had deeply wronged him somehow and he was now my baby nemesis. His eyes looked solid black between his taut lids. I couldn't see any white sclera or coloured irises from this range, just two lumps of piercing coal.

A couple of absurdly small dogs were also attached to the pram and they trotted alongside my new nemesis on their spindly legs. "Those are two ridiculous dogs," I commented to Nicole,

"I mean if you trod on one by mistake it would probably just die instantly. Game over."
She laughed.

*

Many venues are just a bit too quiet for an in depth discussion of BDSM but after a while one gets a little too used to talking about the subject with strangers and you forget that people may be listening in and judging you. Not that it really matters. This is New York and the chances that you're going to come into contact with any eavesdroppers ever again are vanishingly small. Still, if BDSM is a likely topic of date conversation, I recommend picking a venue with at least some background music and a decent number of punters so that your discussion of spanking techniques or kink parties can be absorbed before it travels too far.

One Sunday afternoon I found myself sitting in the back garden of a Soho hotel. The tall tattooed blonde sitting beside me went by Courtney, because that was her name[108]. She sipped her Earl Grey and I slurped my Peroni. The wicker chair creaked underneath me as I shifted position. We were discussing Courtney's intention to try and start a dominatrix business with a friend of hers and chatting about some of the skills that might be involved, as well as my own experience in that area. I couldn't help wishing that she drank alcohol and didn't have to rush off to her hostessing job within the hour. She was quiet yes, but quiet in that cool and good looking way that made you think she secretly had no shortage of interesting things to say, if only you could tease them out of her.

---

[108] Her most distinctive tattoos consisted of vines running up one leg and down the other, I couldn't help but wonder what was tattooed at their apex.

Sparrows frittered and flitted amongst the bamboo in this otherwise tranquil garden. Aside from us there was an Asian couple minding their suitcases, and over in the opposite corner pair of rotund middle aged American tourists having their afternoon tea. I didn't think we were in earshot, but that may have been mis-calibration due to the fact they were sitting in silence (as married couples of a certain age are wont to do). They paid their cheque and started getting up to leave, donning their cameras, fanny packs, and floppy sun-hats. Then, just as they were walking past us, the husband shot us both an extended look of pure unadulterated bile.

"Well he looked kind of judgmental!" I said to Courtney as the doors closed behind them.
"Oh really? I wasn't looking."
"Maybe they overheard us?" I pondered, "oh well."
I took another slurp of my beer.

*

"If you can do anything other than be a writer, do that!" Erin told me.

Erin was a writer. I think her warning was meant to be a general comment on the difficulties of her profession, and not a specific discouragement aimed at me. Although I had been rambling at her with my stream of undeveloped screenplay ideas while I sipped my old fashioned in the bar of Hotel Edison. Some of them seemed to amuse her at least.

I laughed and quizzed her on her career a bit more. 'This girl is definitely out of my league,' I thought to myself as her perfect face smiled at me from amongst her gushing blonde hair. As well as being a successful author she was damned attractive.

Her good looks seemed grounded somehow. They were not those of some anorexic supermodel in danger of evaporating with a strong gust of wind or mild cocaine overdose. I doubted my accent and PhD were going to be enough to cling onto this one, but throwing my kinky side at Erin this early in the game seemed like far too much of a gamble. In fact I was kind of amazed she'd messaged my normal profile without prompting. Perhaps she was conducting research for some piece she was writing on dating weird English scientists?

"How are you guys doing here?" asked the waitress checking in on us. (I'd already complicated my relationship with this member of staff by ordering a drink at the bar and then going and finding a large nice looking table to sit at. This waitress then politely told me that it was actually table service and if a large group of people came in I'd have to move. Just because I had been in New York a while now didn't stop me from committing the occasional faux-pas.).

"Fine thanks!" I replied.

*

I watched an arresting image of lips pressed against a glass sheet, they were heavy with red lipstick and sucking and licking at some syrup substance on the glass. It was unnervingly erotic, and three screens played these clips on loop behind my date as we sat in the bar attached to "the museum of sex".

This venue had been Crystal's suggestion (it won't surprise you that profile number two was what had caught her attention). The weirdest thing about this date so far though was not that it was taking place in the museum of sex with its backdrop of moderately subtle but ever-present Erotica. No, the weirdest thing was that my date seemed to know literally everyone else in this place. Servers passing by us would see her and start up with "Oh my god! Hi Crystal! How are you doo-ing!" And I would sit patiently while they gossiped and the server shot me the occasional quizzical side-glance. She would probably brief them later about how she was on a date with some kinky English guy from Okcupid; "He seemed nice, but wasn't really as dominant as I was expecting," I imagined her saying later, perhaps while the server sat in the very same seat as I was in now.

Once we were left alone again Crystal told me about her day job working in some Tribeca boutique where she never sold anything and just sat around checking Reddit all day. Then she excused herself to go to the bathroom.

"Sorry I didn't realise you know Crystal!" said the bartender.
"Oh, no worries, we only met recently," I replied, deciding that half an hour ago still counted as 'recently'.

*

"How was work today?" I asked Rachel[109].
"Well, I threatened to stab someone if that gives you any idea," she replied.
"Ha! That good? Tell me more!"
"Ergh, there were just two bro-ey guys there that kept bugging me while I was behind the bar, like, trying to chat me up but talking down to me at the same time. I was cutting up fruit, and they were like 'Ooh, be careful, don't cut yourself beautiful!' and just generally being patronising dicks."
"That does sound irritating."

---

[109] Rachel was an aspiring actress who worked in some midtown dive bar to avoid starvation.

"They probably learnt it from one of those awful guides to seducing women; like where it tells you to make a girl feel insecure so she then looks to you for validation."
"Oh yeah, is that what you're supposed to do? Shit maybe that's where I've been going wrong!"
"Ergh, I hate it, it's the worst."
"You didn't stab him though?"
"No, I work in a federal building, so I'd probably get caught."
"Bummer, you should just keep a vat of acid in the back to dissolve the bodies, just in case."
She laughed.
"Wow this is our first conversation and we're already talking about killing people!" I said, "I think this bodes well!"

*

"So what's the weirdest sex toy you own?" Amber asked me while we drank beer in an alcove of a bar called Shoolbred's.

Despite only having seen my normal profile Amber had clearly picked up on my interest in kink prior to messaging me and the subject had already come up a couple of times, in between chat of politics, art, and other more run of the mill dating material.

"Probably my vibrating inflatable butt plug," I replied.
"Oh yeah? That's not that weird."
"How about you?" I asked, almost disappointed she didn't think my butt plug was 'that weird'.
"Well I don't have much now. This one of the problems with breakups... but I did buy my last boyfriend a vacuum bed for our anniversary."
"A what?"
"A vacuum bed. You've not heard of it?"
"Nope."

"Well, it's like a giant rubber zip lock bag that you get inside, and there's a tube you can breathe through, and then you suck all the air out of the bag with a vacuum cleaner and it seals you in place. Kind of like shrink wrap."
"Oh I see, wow, I'll have to Google pictures of that! For some reason I imagined a bed like a reverse air hockey table that just sucked you down onto it."
"Haha, no, I don't know if that would work."
"No neither do I. That's why I was confused! So is it fun?"
"My ex liked it, I get kind of claustrophobic though so I didn't use it much."

*

At the end of Madison Square Park, a stage had been setup and a generic looking assemblage of young hopefuls were strumming guitars and beating drums. A cuteish girl was singing earnestly into a microphone while moving her feet semi-awkwardly in time to the music. Many young and unusually dressed people were in attendance.
"There seems to be some kind of hipster invasion happening here," I commented to Nicole.
"Yeah a lot of flannel shirts that's for sure. Where I come from in Wisconsin the logging industry is still pretty big and I normally just associate checked shirts with Lumberjacks."
"Ha, you must wonder why there are so many lumberjacks in New York then?"
"Yeah, I'm like; 'where are all the trees for them to cut down?'!"

*

"So once you quit your job at this boutique do you have any particular ideas what you want to do with your life?" I asked Crystal after she'd returned from the bathroom.

"I would kind of like to go to med school. I'd love to be a surgeon, although that's probably not going to happen because of my shaky hands..."
"Oh yeah? Are they that bad?"
"Yeah, it's mostly from snorting too much blow."
"Ha! Seriously? How much is too much?"
"Errr, like a lot?...Yeah I do a lot of blow... I probably shouldn't be telling you that."
"I mean it's fine, I won't judge... Although I'm not sure I'd want you as my surgeon now."
"Yeahhh, my doctor said if I keep up like this I'm probably going to die before I reach twenty five."
"Errr, did you just say twenty five or thirty five?"
"Twenty five."
"You're like twenty three now right? So he thinks you only have two years left on the clock?!"
"That's what he said," she replied in a completely upbeat and passé tone of voice, which suggested she was maybe messing with me, or didn't take her doctor seriously, or was in some serene state of acceptance.

"Well if he's right I'm not sure you want to be wasting your time on med school... But you look pretty normal and healthy as far as I can tell! How bad does it get?"
I wasn't lying. She did look together; a perfectly attractive brunette with a strong sense of style and a laid back attitude. I'd go as far as to say that I liked her.

"Ugh, the other week I was in the middle of the Brooklyn Bridge at like 5am and I was sooo high. My heart was racing and I couldn't breathe and I was just freaking out. I rang my mum and I told her: 'I think I'm dying!', but she lives in Maine, so all she could do was freak out and tell me not to die... Yeah it was pretty bad."

"Yup, that does sound pretty bad. I mean my worst drug experience is where I smoked too much weed one time and everything went grey... I mean like solid grey, not that everything went monochrome... Then I threw up in a sink and I was fine."
"Ha, yeah I guess that can happen."
"I've pretty much only tried weed. I might try cocaine if I was in a safe place, just out of curiosity. Although I wouldn't want to get into the habit of it. I'm not rich enough for that!"
She laughed.
"I mean isn't blow meant to be pretty addictive?" I asked, "don't you feel like you're getting hooked on it or something?"
"Not really, no. I don't think it's that addictive. Like, I don't carry my own stuff around with me. I just get it off my rich friends when we're out partying. It's not like I party every night either. I normally go without it for a couple of days in between nights out, and I don't really get, like, cravings."

I didn't comment that a couple of days didn't seem that long. We talked for a while about other things, including the highly visible rack of bondage gear she was setting up in her bedroom. After more cocktails than I'd usually consume on a first date, I told Crystal she could come back and see my toys if she liked.

"Oh, I've got to go give these keys back to my friend soon so she can get into her place. Besides, I'm a classy girl!" was her reply.

*

"Thirty six first dates is a lot!" said my friend, as we lunched on greasy burgers and thick cut fries.
"Yeah, I'm probably doing something wrong if I'm still single right?" I replied after sucking some of my incredibly bubbly coke through an oversized straw.

"I mean, maybe you should stop dating so many people at once?" he suggested

"Maybe... But dating around is what everyone seems to do in this city, and also I feel I need that emotional backup so that when one girl tells me she's found a serious boyfriend, or whatever, then I don't suddenly find myself lost and alone."

"I guess..." he responded, not sounding particularly convinced.

"Also, I think it helps me to play it cool and remain an attractive prospect. I often get bored at work and if I like someone I could easily message them too much. However, if there are multiple people I can message then I can spread out my boredom and avoid sounding needy."

"I suppose that makes sense... but are you really looking for a relationship anyway?"

I wiped the burger grease of my lips with a flimsy paper napkin, and then explained how I was basically still looking for everything.

*

Outside the Hotel Edison, the streets of the Theatre district were flooded with Saturday evening foot traffic. Bright garish signs splashed the names of shows across the fronts of venues. The words 'Jersey Boys' covered the whole building opposite, along with pictures of what I can only assume were boys from Jersey. Punters were streaming out of another theatre down the street from us, escaping a show with its name in black lettering on a large white sign hemmed by a thousand light bulbs.

Erin and I formed an island in this torrent of light-addled people. Somehow she'd already agreed to a second date and I went to hug her goodbye. I was kind of surprised when we kissed... I mean I think I leant in for it first, but despite being friendly in the bar there was a reserve about her, as if she was holding back the most interesting bits of herself. When I leant towards her face I'd half expected a subtle dodge into the hug, but no; we kissed! Even if this girl was out of my league in that moment my lips were on hers and my hands were on her back. 'Should I get feely with them?' I wondered, 'No definitely better not risk that, I'm out on a limb as it is.'

The kiss had poise. The crowds swirled around us and we remained in one place. It was the sort of thing that would look good on the big screen; the crowd sped up to look like a blur, and with us two kissers filmed at normal speed (if we were sped up it might look like we were some kind of possessed demons blurrily attacking each other's faces, which I'm guessing would kill the vibe). She smiled a sweet smile at me after our lips had parted and I bade her a good evening.

I walked back home through Times Square with a smile on my face. No crowd of slow moving zombified tourists was going to kill my buzz that evening[110]. Gigantic screens towered brightly all around me, frenetically beaming their myriad of consumerist messages. Scantily clad fashion models strutted above my head like 10 story giants who could crush me beneath a single well pedicured toe. Perhaps these ads are the incandescent frescos of the new world religion, all trying to fuel the inadequacies of us wee ants below them, forcing us into worship. Dazzling visions that instil needs in us we didn't know we had, creating the holes inside us and at the same time offering to fill them. All for a price of course.

I had just kissed a beautiful woman and tonight none of it could touch me.

---

[110] Except perhaps for a crowd of actual zombies; getting my brain eaten would have probably killed my buzz.

*

I offered to walk Danielle to her block after we'd been drinking in Harlem. I didn't really know this bit of town. It seemed safe enough but had a very different vibe to other parts of the city. For example, there had been couple of families with kids in the bar where we'd met. The kids hadn't been sampling the wide selection of European beers that were on offer but they had been present nevertheless. It hadn't been a long date either. Danielle had told me beforehand that she had to get back for some late night Skype meeting thing. I'm not sure who has Skype meetings late on a Sunday night but I took her word for it.

I've decided that offering to walk a girl to 'her block' rather than her home after a date in her neighbourhood is a good way to be both chivalrous and still avoid giving off creepy stalker vibes that perhaps say 'Hey I want to follow you home so I can find out where you live and then try and sex you'. Danielle had said I could walk her as far as the subway station, which worked for me. The streets were definitely quieter up here. There was hardly anyone around in fact. Some shuffling fellow was coming our way, he locked onto us.
"Do you have 80 cents?" he asked.
"Err sure, one sec..." I fumbled with my wallet.
I gave him a dollar... it seemed like change wasn't really an option, and he shuffled on his way.
"Thanks," said Danielle.
"No worries. I don't normally do that though, so don't think I'm some kind philanthropist! I just made the mistake of making eye contact."

We drew close to the green railings of my subway descent.

"Well this is me," I said. "although if you like I could walk you further? I don't want you to get murdered or anything."
"Oh it's fine. It's only a couple more blocks up."
"Ok. Well it was great meeting you!"
"You too!"

We'd turned to face each other and the kissing started almost as soon as we made eye contact. Soon my hands were moving everywhere just to keep up. We squeezed against each other, mouths furiously engaged. At one point we were so lost in a frenzy of movements that it felt like we were going to fall together and collapse in a heap on the sidewalk. I stuck my leg further out to get some balance.

The kiss ended as suddenly as it had begun, and Danielle began to walk away. One of her hands remained held in mine. Perhaps I should have grasped it and pulled her back to me, but instead our arms reached their maximum extent and our fingers slowly slipped apart.

"See you soon!" she said.
"Yup," was all I could manage as she began walking across the street.
I wanted to call something after her, but she moved fast and 'have a good Skype call' was the only thing I could think of. It didn't seem witty enough to warrant shouting down a Harlem street.

*

I kissed Rachel just inside the subway station. Maybe I should stop leaving it until the very end of dates to kiss girls but, you know, you can't force these things. The perishingly cold wind had caught us off guard and even Rachel's Teddy bear hat was insufficient defence. I'd put my arm around her tentatively.

Helping to keep her marginally warmer seemed as good an excuse as any to initiate physical contact. Winter was coming.

"Well, let's do something again sometime," I'd said, once we were safely in the subterranean warmth of the subway tunnels and about to part ways.

"I'd like that," had been her reply.

I liked Rachel. She'd been the sort to talk a lot and I'd let her, but nothing she said was dull. A hot blonde geeky witty actress/bartender who occasionally threatens to stab people. 'There could be something here,' I'd thought to myself during a discussion about the movie avatar which led to her reaming me for my poor Pocahontas knowledge. I'd told her some of my dating stories but I hadn't risked revealing the true depths of my kinky side. Something told me she might be into it but something else told me I should leave that sort of information for a second date.

As her moist lips moved against mine, my hand ran through her hair, then down over her back... and then further down. It made its presence felt on her rounded yet firm behind. Yes, I wanted to spank it.

But no I didn't get to spank it.

*

"Sooo yeeeaaaahhhh..." said Kayla, ending yet another anecdote with a painfully extended, and Long Island accented enunciation of 'yeah'.

"I'm kind of an asshole," she'd said unrepentantly.

She was kind of correct.

We'd gone back to my place, mainly because she didn't want to drink anything and the bar had gotten loud due to a televised screening of some heavily armoured men running into each other a lot in between adverts. The fact that Kayla was back in my place after one drink might be seen as a positive date development, except for the trifling issue that I wasn't exactly 100% sure I wanted to be dealing with her anymore. I found her perfectly attractive. It was just her personality I was struggling to handle. Its prominent features were a caustic and aggressive attitude combined with taking delight in saying awful things.

"I hate Indian guys," she said (I think she was just referring to her dating preferences, but I wasn't 100% sure), "and I can't stand Asian guys either. Black guys are ok, so long as they're not too ghetto."
"Right... so aside from skin colour what else are you looking for in a guy?"
"A big dick," she replied, without much thought, and then continued, "and not all black guys have big dicks. The stereotype isn't really true. Some do, like the biggest dicks I've seen have been on black guys, but I've also met a couple of black guys with like really embarrassingly small cocks."
"Oh yeah? Do you have a statistically significant sample size?"
"And people underestimate the importance of width," she continued, ignoring my subtle witticism. "The best sex I've had was with people who weren't necessarily long, but... Yeah people who really filled me up laterally speaking. Sooo yeeaahhhhhh..."
"I guess I've never measured my width," I mused, unsure how well I would fare.

She may have then gone on to describe some non-physical attributes she preferred in men, but if she did I have no recollection of what they were. Her legs lay across my lap but she'd already expressed pretty clearly that she wasn't going to sleep with me on a first date. I tried to put some moves on anyway. It seemed like I might as well and at least it stopped her talking.

"You use too much tongue when you kiss," she informed me, "and what's with the teeth?"
Admittedly, my attempt to bite her lower lip hadn't gone to plan when her tongue had got in the way.
"I just want to cause you some pain," I replied nonchalantly.

At this point I had absolutely no idea what we were doing here. Maybe her brashness was a deliberate attempt to try and get a rise out of me so that I would lose my temper and 'put her in her place'. However, while the idea of punishing her body was tempting, this was somewhat outweighed by the clear mound of criticism and bullshit I was going to have to deal with to get to that point.

"I should go," she said, after we'd reached some kind of weird dominance standoff where she was straddling me while I held her wrists pressed firmly against her back.
"Sure," I said. Perhaps I was meant to discourage her from leaving, but if we were playing some kind of game then the rules of it had not been explained to me.

I kissed her again by the door.
"Better," she said, "you've still got to work on that tongue though."
"Ok, get out now," I said, starting to physically push her into the hallway.

*

"I want you to show me!" said Kelly, handing me the lit candle.
"What? You want me to pour the wax on myself?" I asked.

My cardboard box full of sex toys lay open in front of us and chain was snaking around the sofa where we sat. I had used it to tease Kelly by playfully wrapping the links around her clothed body.

"Yeah!" she said.
"I guess I'd better take some clothes off then."
Kelly's hands ran over my jeans and began unzipping them for me as I worked on my shirt.
"Do you want me to drip it on my balls?"
"Yeah I want to see how much it hurts..."

I obliged her, grunting as the string of hot waxy globules made themselves felt. Then Kelly's inquisitive hand joined them... her similarly inquisitive mouth began interrogating other, more tumescent, areas.

At first I gripped the long black hair on the back of her head, pushing her down and forcing my member deep into her mouth. However, she needed no encouragement and I released her, lay back and let her go to work.

Shit. Blow jobs are awesome.

*

"I've now turned thirty and there are a lot of things I've not got to explore that I'd like to," said Rebecca, while swilling her Shiraz in its voluminous glass.

Rebecca worked in media. A self-identified type A personality, a doer, a fixer, a get things done kind of girl.

"Hacked any good celebrity phones lately?" I joked.
"No, we don't do that," she said smiling.
Then she took a long sip of her wine.
"Yeah, that whole News Corps scandal never really got much air time over here did it? I heard a few stories but nothing seemed to take off here like it did in the UK with the whole news of the world thing."
"Yeah, everyone thinks they lost their way a bit there."
"Just a bit... I've been keeping tabs on the Leveson inquiry, it's just terrifying how closely entwined the newspapers are with both governments and their oppositions," I grumbled.

I wondered how much I was preaching to the devil but I was enjoying this date with a big time corporate somebody.

At one point her phone buzzed
"Sorry I just need to reply to this."
"No worries. Anything exciting?"
"Ergh, it's just about some blogger who's trying to sue us for like 5 million dollars."
"Hmm, that's a lot of dollars."
"It's ridiculous. There's no way she'll get that much!"

While Rebecca fingered her iPhone I quaffed my glass of Pino, letting it sit in my mouth, moving it around, sucking air through it like some wino told me to do once. Yup it was definitely red wine. It had all kinds of red wine flavours that I could invent names for; 'red-fruits', 'cherry-notes', 'a chocolatey palate', 'a sandalwood aroma', 'rich in tannins', 'leathery hints', 'the smell you get just before it rains', 'the taste of belly button fluff that's matured in-situ over a month long holiday spent in the Alsace region of France[111]'... Maybe I should just stick with 'red-winey.'

"Sorry, where were we?" she resurfaced.
"You were lamenting all the things you hadn't explored prior to turning 30."
"Yes, I guess I was..."
"So have you never explored any BDSM stuff before? Not been tied up by any ex-boyfriends for example?"
"No, and lately I don't really have enough time for boyfriends. I mean I keep my online dating profile up because that can be fun... but yeah, I don't really know much about that stuff, just kind of intrigued."
"Not been tempted to meet any other kinky people on Okcupid then?"
"No. You're the first. I wouldn't normally respond to someone with just their chest for a profile picture but then you messaged me, and you seemed normal, and you talked about homemade wine, and I was like 'what the hell!'."

After a little more BDSM chat I dropped into conversation that I'd just bought a gas mask.

"A gas mask?! What's that for?"
"Well it was only like $20, and I guess it is multi-use. Firstly if the terrorists decide to gas us all then it could be useful for not dying[112]."
There was a carefully regulated laugh from Rebecca.
"I guess I really got it for kinky reasons though. As well as looking creepy, it's kind of fun to wear and you can use it to do autoerotic asphyxiation relatively safely."

---

[111] I don't actually know what this would taste like, but that's kind of the point.
[112] I do not think this is a likely scenario, but should it occur I'd definitely not regret buying that $20 gas mask!

"What's that?" she asked, looking nervously intrigued. I definitely had her full attention now.

"Oh, it's like where you reduce someone's air supply. It's meant to make you cum harder. It can be kind of dangerous though, and you occasionally hear of people accidentally hanging themselves while doing it alone."

"Wow."

"Yeah. So far I've not done it properly on someone else. I've seen too many episodes of CSI where it goes wrong! I mean, I've put my hands around a girls neck before to sort of half choke her but it's difficult to know the limits of how hard to squeeze, and I worry I might be damaging something vital. Anyway, it's meant to be safer just to restrict someone's air supply and with a gas mask there's a nice single valve you can put your hand over."

"That's faaascinating!" was her response. She took another sip of her wine.

After describing a number of other fun BDSM activities and personal tastes, I went with the soft sell:

"If you were feeling brave you could come back to mine tonight and I could show you the ropes, so to speak."

"Ha, you're ridiculous! But I can't say I'm not tempted..." she replied, her eyes moving around the bar without looking at anything in particular.

*

I let Kelly experience the candle wax first hand, holding her naked body down on my bed as she squirmed beneath me. Her tits, stomach and legs were now textured with the solidified waxy lumps.

It had taken me a while to figure out why she was happy to blow me but reluctant to get naked herself. It turned out this hesitation was because she hadn't had a more conventional waxing in a while and was feeling self-conscious about her lady garden. I'd reassured her that I didn't agree with the harsh standards of pubic grooming that society seems to set for women these days[113] and then finally, after a bit of external massaging, I'd gotten into her pants.

Kelly wasn't quite ready to be tied up on a first meeting but I held her arms down with my hands instead, and once I'd finished the wax torture I fucked her into the mattress. A high pitched stream of "Auh, Auh, Auh, AUH! AUH!" noises were the soundtrack she provided. 'Take that neighbours!' I thought as I thrust again and again, seeing how loud I could make her go.

Eventually I grew tired of that position. I was trying to work towards personal orgasm number 2 and this would probably take a while. Time to change it up. I flipped Kelly over onto her knees and I was just about to get restarted when I noticed something that stopped me...

"Erm, there's something going on back here..." I said, struggling to find a delicate way to describe what I saw.
"What?" questioned Kelly, looking back at me from all fours.
No, there was no delicate way to say this: "Errr, it kind of looks like a little bit of poop has come out..."

It didn't really look like poop, but there was definitely a small lump of something protruding...

---

[113] I mean I appreciate smoothness, but some hair seems perfectly natural to me, I find it hard enough to shave my face on a regular basis so I can't blame a girl for 'letting her garden grow'.

"Oh no, it's not poo. That's just something I have that kinda popped out a while back. I got it when I was with this guy who was really into anal."

"Oooh, I see," I said, glad that it wasn't poop at least, "I have heard of something like that that now you mention it

The word 'prolapse' emerged from my memory. It wasn't a sexy word, so I didn't say it out loud. I mean a little bit of displaced anus wasn't that much of a disfigurement was it? I barely noticed... but then I realized my penis was now at half-mast and drooping fast. Smells of sex and warm latex filled my nostrils. God, I wish condoms smelt better.

"Did we kill the mood?" Kelly asked.
"Yup, sorry, the bum thing just caught me off guard a little!"

*

"How is that? Is that hard enough?" Alyssa asked, having just slapped me solidly across the face.

"Mhmm," I replied, strapped down by my own Velcro cuffs, "maybe you could take your rings off though?"

Alyssa was getting surprisingly into this considering I'd only told her about my kinky side an hour or so ago. In fact she seemed to be enjoying herself a bit too much and my right ear was ringing from the last blow she had dealt me. Even though I could still feel the hard metal on my cheek, I was definitely having fun. It was nice to be strapped down and helpless for a change.

"Can I choke you?" she asked enthusiastically.
"Sure. Just try not to make me black out or anything..."

One hand took a firm hold of my throat and the other continued to slap me across the face as she rode me like a tied down bronco. It was a good evening.

*

I was walking along 34th street. It was coming up to midnight and there was a slight chill in the air. I had been drinking and, despite being in my shirt sleeves, I barely felt the cold. It had been a nice first date. I hoped I'd hear from that girl again but by now I'd learnt not to get my hopes up regardless of how well we seemed to connect. I traipsed across Lexington Avenue while the Chrysler building peered out at me, crowned with its glorious white zigzags.

'Shit, I feel like getting some one dollar pizza!' I thought.
'Hell, I'm going to HAVE some one-dollar pizza!' I decided.
I crossed the street along with some girls who were all dolled up for something and teetering along on their high heels. Much to my disappointment, none of them fell over.

My local $1 pizza joint is deceptively called '99c pizza'. However, this is a relatively minor deception by American standards; with taxes and service charges everything here ends up costing twice as much as it says on the label. Maybe they'll sell you the pizza for 99c if you're a dick about it, but who wants to be that guy?

99c pizza is a tiny place. Just space for a counter with two pizza warming plates, a chiller cabinet with soft drinks, and a couple of stools at the window. I have no idea how they make any money.

"Can I get a slice please?" I said handing a dollar to a gent whose ethnicity I wouldn't want to guess, but I think was talking in Spanish when I came in. A quick twirl of a pizza cutter and he handed me a small white paper plate with a pizza slice balanced on top. Transaction completed, I exited the premises as the two stoned looking dudes held the door open for me, presumably on their way to make their own purchases.

'God damn, this pizza is amazing!' I thought, taking my first bite. I mean I was kind of drunk, so none of this description should be treated as any kind of accurate review. However, maybe a certain amount of intoxication is the best way to open the door to near spiritual culinary experiences.

The crust was thin and light, giving little resistance to my teeth as they bit down. A moist and airy base with an infused greasiness that meant the cheese and tomato free edge bit would not be spared. The warm cheese slid around my tongue as I chewed. All the pizza components began to dissociate and arouse my taste buds with their own flavour spectrums. The modest-but-flavourful coating of tomato sauce filled my mouth instantly with that sweet earthy redness. This richness then formed the backdrop to the firework show of other flavour stimulations. As I chewed on that near-erotic mouthful the lumps of cheese and crust were rent asunder, releasing all the tasty organic molecules and inorganic salts from their prison matrices of casein and carbohydrate. Each closing of teeth realised pure notes of orgasmic flavour. I chewed and chewed, and chewed, and chewed, and chewed until my whole face orifice was filled with a piquant mix of glorious discombobulated pizza essence.

But having it in my mouth was not enough, I needed to CONSUME it. I wanted to force this heavenly mass deep inside my body. And so I swallowed, and the peristaltic muscles of my oesophagus carried it into my stomach. Here it filled a void that had been growing within me, at first unnoticed but then clamouring louder and louder, until I was powerless but to answer. Finally in that triumphant moment of pizza consumption I was complete.

The taste lingered on my cheese-and-tomato moistened lips. My saliva flowed, lubricating my mouth in frenzied anticipation of the next bite. I half folded the pizza to prevent it from flopping and to fit more of it into my voracious face hole. All of life's problems solved or rendered mute for only $1.

So yeah, the pizza was good. I mean I might be over selling it. Sex with my date would still have been better but the pizza was a decent consolation prize. I walked the last couple of blocks to my apartment chomping away, illuminated by the light of hundreds of passing yellow taxi cabs. I felt like Louie CK in the opening credits of 'Louie'... "Timmy, Timmy, Timmy, Timmmmey!" I hummed. Then I muttered to myself though a mouth half full of pizza: "I'm a god damn New Yorker!"

The slice was done. I licked my fingers, crushed my paper plate and dumped it into a nearby trash bin that was already overflowing with god knows what.

Home. Time to sleep now.

VII

T.G.O.M.D.'s nipples rub against my perspiring chest.

Rope from our earlier games lies around the bed like cooked spaghetti but now T.G.O.M.D is free to move as she wishes.

Her fingers dig into the small of my back as I thrust.

Her mouth is open.

Her eyes are closed.

We are both pleased to be there.

Chapter 19 - Infinite wishes!

Glorious autumn colours speed past the bus windows, a blur of yellows, reds and golds that come into crisp focus as my eyes lock onto the details of each passing scene. I gaze at exquisite clapboard houses painted fresh white and with pumpkins on the doorsteps, ready for Halloween. American flags hang gaily beside empty porches, presumably to reassure the passing traveller that they have not yet strayed into Canada. Each diorama breezes into view for a few brief seconds before being obliterated by the next cloud of passing trees.

Iggy pop plays 'I am the passenger' though my headphones. Rivers, bridges, churches, lakes, gas stations, corn silos, and McDonalds all materialise out of the haze of seasonal colour, and then vaporize as fast as they came. I point my camera though the window, snapping occasionally on the off-chance that I can catch some small fragment of each scene and lock it away to look at again someday, when life's colours seem less bright.

My heart sings just to see the swarm of bright lemon-yellow leaves and white trunk of another passing birch tree. It stands out in contrast to the greys of surrounding trunks that strobe in front of this magnificent yellow, all lit by a sun low in the sky. Too much to take in.

*

I was on my way back from a conference in Massachusetts. I would have rated it as a success based on the fact I learned very little science and got to drink a lot of free beer[114] (an increasingly rare feat at conferences these days).

---

[114] I'm normally very studious at conferences but this one didn't

Two beeps suddenly interrupted Iggy's 'la-la-la-la-lalala-la's along with a vibration in my pocket. This signalled a new message from Lauren. We'd been keeping up a steady exchange of texts while I was at the conference and I'd gloated over my free pumpkin beer and sent her a picture of the trees. She was a quick texter and, once we got started, it was almost like having a real conversation. By text we decided that we were both too tired for a first date tonight, plus apparently she 'didn't look good' and was in need of a haircut.
"*I like long hair. It gives me something to grab onto :-P*" I replied.

Through these streams of short messages we were slowly building up a picture of each other's lives. Apparently, Lauren still lived with her ex up on the northern tip of Manhattan. She had numerous pets, earned money mostly through temp jobs, and would rather be spanked over someone's lap than in a more impersonal fashion. While I was riding the bus she was heavily engaged in an Instagram war that was starting to get to her. Someone had called her the C-bomb so I pointed out they were clearly not worth dealing with. Some creative homicide suggestions seemed to cheer her up.

Maybe tomorrow night she'd be free to meet me.
"*There's something I should tell you though,*" she texted.
Then she told me something a little unexpected. I put my head back in my seat and made a "huh" noise. Then, after a minute's thought, I texted her back:

---

feature a lot of science that was relevant to my research. It did, however, feature a lot of free beer and after hours dance parties with the PhD students and smuggled in Whiskey.

"Really? That's very honest of you. Glad you told me, though I won't pretend I don't find that a little scary but I'm totally still up for meeting you!"

By the time the bus was drawing close to the city it was dark outside. The distinctive spires of the Empire State and the Freedom Tower pierced the horizon as we motored though New Jersey. The glowing buildings appeared to do a slow waltz with each other as we got closer to home. The Art Deco pinnacle of the Chrysler building was in the background. Sliding past more lacklustre dancers, it passed hands with the Bank-of-Amercia - Conde-Nanst duo, and then kept moving to stare out over a quieter stretch of the dance floor where the hulking mass of the Empire State stood alone and resolute.

'Somewhere in that tumult is tomorrow's date!' I thought to myself.

Iggy: "Singing la-la-la-la-lalala-la... la-la-la-la-lalala-la... la-la-la-la-lalala-la-lala-la..."

*

"Should there be Korean people everywhere?" read a message from Lauren.
"Yup, this is K-town. You're heading the right direction! I'm just outside the place."

Our date was still on although it had been touch and go for a few hours there. First, Lauren wasn't sure she was in the mood to be spanked and so I reassured her that we could just meet up and chat. Spanking was far from mandatory. Then she had taken a nap and wasn't sure she was feeling up for going out. My internal patience began to wind itself up like a spring but it was a well-conditioned spring by now: "*Ok no worries, but I'd much rather be out drinking with you than sitting at home watching TV...*" I'd texted. This was my subtle way of pointing out how her evening would be similarly boring if she didn't come out.

It had worked, but now she still had to find me.

After a phone call and negotiating a few crowds of Korean people, we finally met each other for the first time. I led her up to the bar in the Hotel Stanford where we ordered two lychee cocktails. They turned out to have real lychees in them on little sticks, (a fruit that always reminds me of testicles for some reason... not that it stops them from tasting good!).

We got into stories of our awkward past dates pretty quickly. Apparently, she'd recently been on one with what turned out to be forty something guy with no teeth and rather striking gold dentures. (She hadn't been into it). Then she told me about the guy with dozens of taxidermied animal heads on his wall who had taken her down to his basement... but surprisingly hadn't murdered her.

Lauren had grown up in New Jersey and didn't really seem to have big aspirations. She later told me "I think the only way I'm going to get rich is if I get lucky gambling, or I win the lottery, or I just marry some rich guy...", but I told her: "That might be the most depressing thing I ever heard."
However, I said this in a kind of playful and light-hearted way that made her smile rather than cry.

We sipped our sugary cocktails and Lauren described living with her ex.

"It's fine though. I couldn't afford to live alone anyway," she said.

"Yeah, I was sleeping with this girl from New Jersey for a while who was sharing a studio with her sort of ex. Later she told me that they had been sharing the same bed as well, which was a bit weird."

"I still share a bed with my ex," said Lauren.

"Oh really?" I said, a little unsure what I had gotten myself into... "Perhaps it's a more common occurrence than I thought!"

"Yeah, we have different blankets though."

"I guess New York property prices tend to force people together."

This bed sharing confession was a symptom of Lauren's near pathological honesty that was twinned with a kind of grim pessimism. She once commented about the weather: "I hate the sun and the heat. I just want to move somewhere where it rains all the time." I found this mix of openness and melancholy to be strangely compelling. I'd not met anyone quite like Lauren before. I wanted to know her. Though the fact that she was also really quite attractive may have played a significant part in this.

After one cocktail, Lauren wanted to go somewhere else and we ended up in a livelier bar drinking tasty beers. In this louder atmosphere she seemed to come out of her shell a bit more and my jokes started to get more genuine laughs and smiles from her. "I love the city and being surrounded by noise," she told me.

For some reason we started talking about dreams (by which I mean the kind of dreams you have when you are sleeping, not the life aspiration ones). We both shared a tendency for weirdness in this department.

"I guess I've been having a lot of dreams with zombies in lately," I said.

"Ergh, I have a massive fear of zombies!" she exclaimed, "in fact I have this recurring dream where I'm on a Ferris wheel and there are zombies swarming everywhere below, and the wheel just keeps turning and I keep getting lower and lower and they keep getting closer..."
"Do you wake up before they get you?"
"Not always."
"Shit. That sounds intense. Most of my zombie dreams aren't that scary. Sometimes I'm trying to protect people from the zombies. I mean, I usually fail and the people usually die, but the zombies don't often get me and if they get too close I wake up. I guess I never actually die in my dreams."
"I die in my dreams all the time!" she said, "I hate it. Sometimes I have dreams where I'm drowning and it feels really real, and they really suck."
"Do you ever have good dreams? Or just nightmares?"
"I'd say I have more nightmares than nice dreams. Though maybe if I have nice dreams I just don't remember them."

"Yeah, I guess, I don't think I have many actual nightmares, I mean a lot of terrible violent shit happens in my dreams but normally I don't feel particularly afraid. Although I did have one dream not long after I moved to New York that really creeped me out."
"Oh yeah, what was it about?"
"Well, I was in the church that my parents always used to take me to when I was growing up. I was just walking down the aisle when suddenly the whole church began to shake, as if a helicopter or something were passing really close overhead. I looked around and everyone in the congregation was frozen somehow, but not as if they were frozen in time. It was like they were conscious and aware, just not moving, and they were all still on their knees praying."
"Creepy."

"Yeah, but when it got really scary was when this figure dressed in black robes emerged from the side chapel. He walked into the centre of the aisle and then he just stared straight at me. There was nothing specifically monstrous about how he looked. He was just a tall bald man in black robes but it was like he exuded the pure essence of evil, and I knew he was either Satan or Death, or both, and I was gripped by this sense of complete terror. Then he beckoned to me and all I wanted to do was run away but it was like there was some invisible force holding my arm behind my back and forcing me towards him. He slowly walked forward and it all just seemed so real, but everyone in the church was just staring straight ahead and doing nothing. Anyway, somehow I knew that if this guy reached me it would be the end of, like, everything. So I tried to gather all my strength, hoping to discover some supernatural powers of my own. He was closing in and closing in with his arm outstretched, and I just released all the energy I had been gathering to try and break free... Then I woke up in a cold sweat."

*

My right hand rested in the small of Lauren's back, palm outstretched as I thrust into her. My eyes traced the violin like curves of her body that were laid out in front of me like some fine antique coffee table[115]. Her hands and knees were entangled in my sheets and her long wavy hair flowed over her shoulders. In my left hand I held my belt, and I hit her with it at my discretion[116].

---

[115] But you know, a sentient coffee table that sexy because it's a person and not just a thing (I call this game objectification dodge ball).
[116] I'd already put her over my knee and spanked her in her preferred fashion.

"You'd better not cum without my permission!" I told her, as we had been at it for a decent amount of time now.

"Don't worry I've got a little way to go yet," she replied a little breathlessly and still moving backwards and forwards in time with my thrusts.

'Shit, having said that I'm not sure I've got much further to go myself,' I thought.

To gain time I attempted to disconnect myself from the situation, trying not to enjoy myself too much. I imagined that I was just a machine conducting rhythmic motions without passion or feeling. It was too late though. I'd already moved onto that downhill slope towards orgasm. Even thinking about Margaret Thatcher naked could only delay the inevitable.

I kept it up as long as I could but then I needed some condom changing time.

Fortunately, my strength quickly recovered and I fingered and slapped Lauren around some more. I put clothes pegs on her nipples and fucked her slowly to conserve my energy. "You have my permission to cum now!" I said, after a quite a few excited moans from her... but the slow ravaging continued without climax... She had already told me that she often found it super hard to cum and reported a high tolerance for pain.

"Ahhh, I'm so turned on and so frustrated!" she moaned, writhing underneath me and reaching up to grasp the metal bed rails above her. She made some sounds that closely resembled sobbing.

"How do you feel about being penetrated by a vibrating butt plug?" I asked, thinking it might bring the additional layer of stimulation that was needed.
"Err, maybe?"

"I'll take that as a yes!" I said, squeezing her thigh and leaning off the edge of the bed to rummage in my box of tricks. After teasing her a little with the vibrations, I let her do the honours with an encouraging command of: "Get it the fuck in there!"

I gave her a quick flogging before returning to the slow ravage. I could feel the vibrations travelling through her, 'Damn this must do the trick...' I thought, 'it's turning me on for sure!'
'Maybe I can pick up the pace a little.'
I took the ravaging up a notch, holding Lauren's arms down by her side: 'Shit that feels good, I should vibrate people's butts more often.'

Another notch up the ravaging scale. Lauren emitted whimpering groans and other positive noises. 'Ok let's just fucking go for it and hope she comes while I fuck her to pieces,' I thought, and I fucked as hard as my stamina would allow. I lost myself in that pool of soft flesh on hard, warm body on warm body, skin touching, rubbing, squeezing, nails digging, cool sweat, breath mixing, lips on skin, teeth on skin, wood on nipple. The buzz of continuous vibration surrounded my cock as it pounded.

'Ruin her!'

I came.

Once I'd regained myself I asked: "How are you doing? Did you cum yet?"
"No! I'm so frustrated!"
"Shit. Well I think you've worn out this guy," I said, indicating my penis, "I might have to work you with my hands for a while"
I lay beside her, running my fingers up and down her clit.
"Can you use some lube?" she asked, "it feels better."

"Sure."

My KY'd fingers slid up and down, and in and out and around and around.

"Mmm, that's the spot. Keep doing that!" she said.

I kept doing that. After a quite a bit of doing that nothing seemed to happen so I did some other things and Lauren kept making happy sounds.

"Can you use more lube?" she said again.

"Mmmm, that's better."

I lay there motionless except for my hand which was repeating the same movements, exploring the same crevices, circling the same bean. My head started to drift elsewhere, sleep held a near-irresistible appeal... 'No, I'm in this now, gotta finish what I started,' I thought, watching Lauren's face through half closed eyelids, willing myself to stay awake.

Time passed. The time for more lube came around.

"Maybe you should have a go with the lube while I punish the rest of you," I said, waking up a little at my own suggestion.

"Sure," she said.

Lauren's hand replaced mine.

"I'm going to keep punishing you until you fucking cum!" I told her, swinging my belt at her legs, hard.

I struck her until she began seriously trying to dodge me. She would be bruised tomorrow.

I lay back alongside her while she continued to moan and rub. My hands twiddled the pegs that were still attached to her nipples, twisting, pulling, stretching, inflicting maximum pain with minimum effort. I started to doze off again while lying there twiddling.

"Auuhh!"
Lauren arched her back, held stiff for a moment and then relaxed.
"Finally!" she said.

*

We both woke up early that Saturday morning and then realised how early it was and went straight back to sleep again. Neither of us had any place to be and the morning could carry on without us. Later an ethereal sound of bagpipes began drifting into my room from somewhere. We couldn't figure out where it was coming from.
"Must be the ghosts of my Scottish ancestors," I said.

Awake now, we lay there talking about whatever popped into our heads.

"This city is so damned noisy," I complained, "I really miss the quiet of the countryside, but here some fucker is always doing something when I want to sleep. I mean, if they're having sex I can deal with that, good for them! That's like a positive sum gain, but in the morning the cleaners always seem to decide to chat right outside my door long before I need to be awake. Then there's the person living above me who seems to like walking around loudly in their high heels at like 3am almost every night."
"What? They can't take off their shoes in their apartment?"
"Exactly. I dunno, now I've actually lived in America I can almost see why people go on killing sprees," I joked.
Lauren laughed and said, "Yeah, I remember the first time I LOST IT in this city. Ergh!"
"What happened?" I asked, a little unsure if Lauren was about to confess to being a mass murderer.

"Ah, there was just this woman who was driving me nuts. She was just, like, completely selfish and taking up three seats on the subway when there were all these people standing. Then we got to my station and across the platform I could SEE the train I needed to change to."
"Ah, I know that stressed out feeling."
"Yeah, I thought it was about to leave, and I was like 'shit I need to run!' But then this lady gets up and she's like physically blocking me and moving super slowly, like almost on purpose, and I just shouted 'Fucking hell'."
"Oh yeah, was that it? You didn't hit her with your knuckle-dusters or something[117]? Right in the kidneys perhaps?"
"No, maybe I should have done," she said, "but yeah, in the end I got on the other train in time, but then I had to wait ages in the station because it turned out that train was being held there for some police investigation or something"
"Hahaha!" (I think I found this story funnier than I was supposed to) "Had someone jumped in front of the train or something?"
"They didn't tell us."

We lay there spooning silently for a moment.

"Like, getting hit by a train is the thing I'm most afraid of," said Lauren, "in most subway stations I stand behind those metal columns in case some crazy person tries to push me onto the tracks."
"I totally do that too... or at least I stand in range of them in case someone pushes me and I need to grab hold of something."

---

[117] Lauren carried knuckle dusters around with her, including on our date...

"Yeah, I've researched this," she said, sounding serious, "and apparently if you fall on the tracks you're just meant to run away from the train."
"Oh yeah? Is it not worth trying to climb out or like lie in the middle of the tracks?"
"No, apparently it's too hard to get up, and if you lie down you'll get electrocuted, but there are ladders at the ends of the platform you should run for."
"Wow, I guess that's useful information if I ever fall on to the subway tracks! Though it's probably still gonna be a pretty shitty day for me if I find myself having to outrun a train."

Beneath the thin sheet my hand rested on her hip and my thumb moved idly up and down against her skin.

After we had been spooning for a while, Lauren turned over to look at me and our horizontal faces lay staring at each other. I silently ran my finger across her face, starting from a small mole on her left cheek, moving slowly, pushing aside some stray hair that was blocking my view of her eyes as they watched mine. I secured those dark blonde strands behind her ear. My finger briefly stroked down to her earlobe and in that moment I couldn't help but think: 'I am pretty content right now.'

"You've got a stray eyelash," she said, picking something off my cheek.
"So have you," I said, raising my hand and gently lifting a rouge lash from her face.
"You have to make a wish then blow it away," she told me.
"Really? Is that a thing?"
"Yup. Make a wish!"

'What to wish for?' I wondered.

The romantic in me was first off the plate and started to come forward with a suggestion: 'I wish to live happily ever after with this...'

'Dude hold up!' Interrupted the rest of me.

'Sure, wishes invented when blowing away eye hair seem unlikely to have any real life consequences but we just learnt about this shit! Let's not rush in with any rash invocations towards this chick who you don't really know and seems a bit crazy (even if she is hot and weirdly compelling). Let's take a second and think of a good wish that still plays it safe, just in case this shit matters!'

I liked Lauren but there were a lot of warning signs that told me this girl might mean trouble and I could be getting myself into dangerous territory. I didn't press her on what had happened in her past, but scars on her body hinted at more in her mind and I got the impression she had been through something pretty bad. In fact on our second date while discussing guns she told me, "I'm probably not allowed to own a gun, even in New Jersey"... Just how crazy do you have to be to not be allowed a gun in America?! Despite many dark confessions, Lauren always seemed totally stable when around me. I would hazard a guess that she'd numbed out some previous hurt and built certain walls around herself to keep her emotions under tight guard. While part of me wanted to break through those barricades, the rest of me was scared of what I might find within.

'I hope whatever this turns out to be, no one gets too badly hurt,' I wished.

We both held our respective eyelashes between thumb and forefinger, bought them to our mouths, closed our eyes, and blew...

We opened our eyes again.
"Did we just blow the eye lashes back onto each other's faces?" I asked.
"Looks like it."
"YES! INFINITE WISHES!"

Chapter 20 - The Republican

Picture a girl looking at you with a heady mixture of disgust and confusion. You are sitting opposite her in a Soho wine bar with a smart varnished-drift-wood kind of vibe. A bottle of Rioja and two half full glasses sit between the pair of you. Her hands push against the table as she leans back in her chair. Her mouth hangs half open. Her thin blonde eyebrows arch up and ride into her crumpled forehead. Her pretty blue eyes dart between you and different patches of the ceiling as she tries to catch sight of all her scandalized thoughts.

This is the situation: I've just told my date something that she has been conditioned to find so abhorrent that she doesn't even know how to react. Her expression changes rapidly as different incensed thoughts flood her head. She starts to recite different condemnatory sentences... However, what I just said has triggered so many potential tirades that she can't choose which one to go with. Instead she ends up spurting disconnected half sentences while her brain tries to figure out the central argument to justify her offence. Perhaps she still wants to leave some room for recovery though, just in case I turn out to be joking or trying to get a rise out of her.

My grossly offending comment was this:
"I'm kind of a socialist."

*

There are definite advantages to using online matching systems that collect info on your personality, political beliefs, toilet paper preferences etc. They may not always be accurate ways of determining a match as I've found I can still have a good time with someone that the computers say is super different from me in lots of ways. However, it's useful to get some kind of heads up as to where your differences may lie. I learnt this in an abrupt fashion when I went out with a girl who I only met through Fetlife, a site where very little personal information is displayed except for an 'about me' section followed by a list of your different kinks and fetishes.

The short dazzling blonde who found me through Fetlife was called Jacqueline. She was fresh out of college and thrilled to be making a new start in the big city. It clearly wasn't just the bright lights that attracted her though. She was on the hunt for a certain type of man. She already knew her way around a lot of the BDSM specific dating sites and as we texted she was very keen to extract information about my dominant proclivities.

We both arrived outside the chosen wine bar at exactly the same time. After we hugged a greeting, Jacqueline told me she was glad I was on time as she always waited outside bars for people as she hated going into places alone. Her nervousness made her seem more adorable somehow and she spoke with a kind of frenzied energy that suggested there was very little filter between what came into her head and what escaped her mouth.

"I was thinking about a career in teaching," she said, once we were ensconced and chatting, "maybe I could teach science... no I couldn't, actually maybe I could... no... well maybe I could teach some science, but not all of it..."

We ordered a small platter of meats and cheeses to accompany our wine and this got us onto the subject of food in general.

"I love sweet things," said Jacqueline, without any particular prompting, "I like chocolate, candy, cupcakes... actually we had cupcakes at work today and I've decided I don't like cupcakes."

"Wait, what? Now you're saying you don't like cupcakes?" I asked, trying to keep up with this information stream.
"No, I think they're over-rated! I don't get what the big deal is!"
"But you like all other sweet things?" I said, making sure I maintained a handle on the conversation
"Yeah. I like candy, I like chocolate, I like cakes, I like cookies, I like sweets, I like Haribo, I like ice cream, I like apple pie... I just don't like cupcakes!"

"Ok, got it. But do you like your job apart from the terrible cupcakes?"
"Yeah, I think so... well it's pretty intense."

Jacqueline had just started a job as a client manager at some technology firm and seemed to be finding it a tad stressful.
"I've found myself a good rooftop crying space!" she said, earnestly
"Really?"
"Yeah, I probably only go there once a day... or maybe twice if it's a bad one, and a client seems super angry. I hope they don't lock that door..."
"Man, I'm glad my work doesn't get that bad!" I said, "I mean I get frustrated with the science or myself sometimes, but I haven't had to find a crying space yet."

This date seemed to be going well. Jacqueline kept smiling and giving off nervously-into-me vibes. However, the first big clue that her world view might not necessarily align with my own was when I made some comment about evolution and her face pulled an oddly sour expression.
"Wait, you're not one of those crazy people who doesn't believe in Evolution are you?" I asked.
"I'm not opposed to evolution," she replied, suddenly hesitant and for once taking care how she chose her words, "but I just don't think it explains everything."

'Uh oh,' I thought, making a quick value judgement, 'do I challenge what on earth she means by that? Or do I continue trying to get this hot girl to like me?'
"Uh huh. So are you quite religious then?" I asked, gently probing the minefield.
"Yeah, I'm Catholic. A lot of my family are very strict Catholics."

'Yup, potential area of friction identified!' I decided not to talk about how I was a godless heathen and steered the conversation away from religion.
"And are you close to your family?" I asked.
"Yeah, I talk about everything with them... well not everything... but yeah, like, everything not to do with sex stuff! I'm particularly close to my mum. I mean she calls me fat all the time, but you know, like in a friendly way!"

*

It wasn't until we got talking about Mad Men and advertising that I let loose with my "I'm kind of a socialist" comment and the tectonic scale of the rift between us became fully apparent.

"...Obamacare is so annoying... and like communism just didn't work... and Medicare... and like social security is like, ugh... and I hate having to pay so many taxes," rambled Jacqueline in response to my socialist revelation. Her hands were now waving around instead of holding onto the table. Her shocked expression had diminished and was replaced with one of concerted disapproval.

I think one of the reasons Jacqueline was struggling to figure out what to say is that she had heard so many things criticised for being 'socialist', but she wasn't actually sure what the arguments against socialism were. Consequently, in order to try and describe why she hated socialism, she was now attempting to switch it around and use all the things that were bad because they were socialist as reasons why socialism was bad.

"So I'm guessing you're a Republican then?" I asked.
"Yeah, well my whole family is," she replied, "my mum is in the Republican party, so we kind of have to be!"
"Your mum is in politics?"
"Yeah, she holds a seat where I grew up in Wyoming."
"Huh," I replied, making a mental note never to visit that particular state if I ever got to dominate Jacqueline.

"So you're not a fan of taxes then?" I asked.
"No!"
"I mean I can empathise with that," I said, trying to see if there were any bridges to be built.
"Yeah. It really pisses me off that I'm working and my money is paying for lazy people's benefits so they just get to sit around on their asses all day."

"Yeah I guess that's an understandable feeling," I said, "and when I say I'm kind of a socialist, I only mean it from an American perspective. It's not like I want to overthrow capitalism or anything. But I do think there are some big problems with like the neo-liberal, deregulated, ultra-capitalism that has a stranglehold on America and is taking over the UK and Europe."
"How do you mean?"
"Well it's like these days 'productivity' and 'GDP' are revered as these big 'be all and end all' goals of our society, which our governments blindly focus on. Then there's this narrative that tells us that if we work harder, and work more hours, and buy the more things, then the better our lives will be. Which I think is kind of fucked up."

"Why is it fucked up?"

"So it may have made sense for a lot of the last century where all the stuff we needed in our lives had to be made by human hands at some stage. Now though technology and robots are taking over a lot of basic jobs that humans used to have, and so there is just becoming less and less stuff for everyone to actually DO. Anyway, as I see it, either you need to give people shorter working weeks or more holiday, and so spread the remaining jobs around between more people, or you can just accept that there aren't always going to be enough unskilled jobs for everyone and that if you don't want the unemployed to starve to death then there needs to be a system to take care of them, and it needs to be run with some of the money from those of us that are lucky enough to have jobs."

"Huh," said Jacqueline, not sounding convinced

"Or I guess we can just keep doing what we're doing and keep creating pointless jobs, and keep fucking over a whole bunch of people who aren't skilled enough to get good work, and then just hope they all don't rise up and break shit."

I paused to sip my wine. Jacqueline made as if to say something but then didn't. I continued, "But yeah, if those at the bottom of the ladder do get pissed off and start breaking shit, then the damage they could do to society might prove way more costly to us than those social security payments, and we'll wish we hadn't made all of those people so desperate in the first place[118]."

Jacqueline thought about this for a moment.

---

[118] This is one of many theories and reasons why I identify as 'kind-of-but-not-really a socialist'. However, this is meant to be a book about my dating exploits and not my weakly-informed political and economic theories, so let's not get too distracted with how wrong I may or may not be.

"Ahhh, everything is going to go to shit isn't it," she said, with a defeated expression. Apocalyptic thoughts scrolled across her eyes.

"Yup, the robots are gonna take over!"

I seemed to reconnect with her through fears of a robot apocalypse / general apocalypse and, having smoothed over the rather large fracture of our political differences, conversation moved onto doomsday prepping, bomb shelters, gas masks, and how bomb shelters and gas masks could also be repurposed for kinky fun times...

*

So from our first date I could tell that Jacqueline was clearly nuts. However, she was also really pretty... and had a nice smile... and so of course I kept talking to her.

Jacqueline herself didn't seem too put off by our political differences and, even though she didn't want to go home with me on that first date, we stayed in close contact afterwards.

*

"Beep-Beep!" Went my phone one Friday evening/ Saturday morning, just as I was lying in bed and about to go to sleep.
Jacqueline: 1.26 am : *"You awake?????"*
    Me: 1.27 am: *"Yup. Got enough question marks there? :-P"*
Jacqueline: *1.30 am: "haha sorry I'm drunk and I kinda wanna see you"*
    Me: 1.31 am: "Oh do you now? Whereabouts are you?"
    Me: 1.33 am: "I may be in my pyjamas but I expect you could persuade me..."

Jacqueline: *1.32 am:* "In Hoboken but I wanna come back to the city"
    Me: *1:33 am* "Wow. How'd you get there? Well I'm at: *my address* if you think you can make it here before you fall asleep :-p"
Jacqueline: *1.34 am:* "Don't fall asleep!!!!!!!!!"
    Me: *1:34 am:* "How long do you think it will take you to get here so I know when to change out of my pjs?"
Jacqueline: *1:42 am:* "I'll be there in 30"
    Me: *1:42 am:* "Cool, buzz me when you get here and I'll come down and let you in"
Jacqueline: *1:43 am:* "Ok I'll call you when I leave NJ"
Jacqueline: *1:58 am:* "Hey can I come over???"
    Me: *1.59 am:* "Yes sure..."
Jacqueline: *2.00 am:* "I'm getting in a cab now"
    Me: *2.01 am:* "Cool, I have clothes on and everything :)"
Jacqueline: *2:07 am:* "Hhahahha ok just took my friend home about to hop in a cab. Stay awake!!!"
    Me: *2.08 am:* "Will do my best"
Jacqueline: *2.09 am:* "Hey don't fuck me over"
    Me: *2.09 am:* "Don't worry I wouldn't dare leave you standing in the cold"
Jacqueline: *2:13 am:* "Let's go out?"
    Me: *2:14 am:* "Out? where's still open?"
Jacqueline: *2:14 am:* "Hey trying to get in a cab"
    Me: *2:15 am:* "I guess it's not super late yet. Still used to UK closing times"
    Me: *2:15 am:* "I think you should come here and drink wine then we can make a plan . Don't worry I won't take advantage of you :)"
Jacqueline: *2.18 am:* "I might meet my brother"
Jacqueline: *2.18 am:* "Maybe idk"
    Me: *2.20 am* "Dude don't be that chick who just got me out of my pjs at 2am only to flake out on me!"

Jacqueline: 2.22 am: "I'm not flanking out I'm just fucked up"
    Me: 2:23 am: "If you just want to have a drink and sleep on my futon that's fine"
    Me: 2.24 am: "Or if you want me to tie you down and give you a solid spanking that's also fine"
    Me 2.24 am: ":)"
Jacqueline: 2.24 am: "hahahaha what do you want?"
    Me: 2.25 am "You to get your ass here sharpish!"
    Me: 2.27 am: "But if you want to chicken out promise me a drink tomorrow evening then I wont make you feel too guilty about this"
    Me:2.28 am: "but decide soon so I know whether to keep drinking this tea or not..."
...
    Me: 2.35 am "5mins to decide then I'm going back to bed and you're getting a serious black mark"
Jacqueline: 2.41 am: "I'm in a car right now"
    Me 2.41 am: "Going where?"
Jacqueline: 2.42 am: "To yours"
    Me: 2.43 am: "Ok good, I almost gave up on you there!"
Jacqueline: 2.44 am: "Well I'm really fucked up so idk"
    Me: 2.45 am: "Drunk fucked up you mean?"
Jacqueline: 2.53 am "Yes no idk a little haha"
    Me: 2:54 am: "Well I guess I'll figure that out when you get here. Where are you now?
Jacqueline: 2:55 am "In a cab coming from New Jersey"
    Me: 2.56 am "In the city yet?"
    Me: 3.03 am: "I'm fading, you should still come but"

That last text message was unfinished because I had to break away to answer a phone call from Jacqueline. She tried to drunkenly explain her plight to me while simultaneously negotiating with a New Jersey cab driver who was kicking her out somewhere in the Lower East side. The call concluded with her saying she needed to get into another cab and reassuring me she was on her way.

Time passed. I tried to ring her again. Voicemail.

> Me: 3.20 am: "How are you doing? Just tried ringing and got your voicemail. Hope your phone hasn't died!"
> Me: 3.33 am: "You ok? I'd come find you but I don't know where to look!"

...

> Me: 3.40 am "My body if forcing me to sleep. If you're still coming here you can wake me up, but plz let me know you are ok ASAP!"

Jacqueline: 3:45 am: "Okay okay with my brother right now so sorry"
> Me: 3:46 am: "Ok glad you're safe! Night."

Jacqueline: 4:59 am: "Hey Timmy baby you awake??????"
I was not awake
Jacqueline: 7:30 am: "Come over and cuddle babe I'm home alone."
I was still not awake

*

Despite this farcical attempt at a booty call, I eventually replied to those last texts from Jacqueline and that Sunday I found myself walking to the subway station to pick her up (for some reason she was afraid of getting lost and murdered in Midtown). She was on her way back from some family thing and so wasn't 'made up' but still looked hot walking beside me as I led her back to my place while we chatted about her Saturday hangover.

It wasn't long though before Jacqueline returned to form. We were approaching my block when she started talking about how she wanted to get married, be a housewife, and live to please her husband's kinky fantasies.

"I just want to be a homemaker, put food on the table, get fucked on the table, you know... just live to serve my man!" she said.

"I guess there's a certain appeal to having someone who exists to serve me," I said, "but I mean I consider myself a feminist, and if I ever get married I want it to be like an alliance with someone, not just bending someone to my will"

"I hate feminism," she said.

"You hate feminism?" I said, chewing the absurdity of that statement in my mouth.

"Yeah, feminists want all women to be, like, these independent hard working money makers! I just want to stay at home and raise kids and take care of my man, and they don't want me to do that[119]!"

"I think we must hang out with different feminists..." I said, unsure where to start. "As I understand it feminism is at its core just believing that women should have the same rights as men. That means both having the right to get high paying jobs if you have the skills, or the right to settle down and have a family if you want that instead. It's just about having the right to choose."

"Well, feminists hate men and I like men! They're always making out that if a guy comes onto a girl that he doesn't know he is, like, almost a rapist. So they're just making it harder for me to get guys to talk to me!"

'Yup, this girl is a lost cause,' I thought to myself.
'She is pretty though and I do REALLY want to hurt her.'

---

[119] I know, but I can't hit her yet, we're still in the street at this point.

*

Once in my apartment I made her tea and after some more innocuous chat Jacqueline started being offensive again.

"I don't get bisexual people. I feel like they should just decide to be one thing or the other," she said.

"I think bisexual people would disagree," I replied.

"No. You either like penis or you like vagina. That's just how it is!"

"Why is that how it is?"

"Because that's how I say it should be! You like PENIS or you like VAGINA," she said, while looking at me with an expression that exuded a bizarre confidence, almost as if she thought that the louder she said the words 'penis' or 'vagina' the more right that made her.

A picture was emerging where Jacqueline seemed to confuse 'actual facts about reality' with 'short sentences pronounced loudly and with conviction'. No discussion of the Kinsey scale or presentation of peer reviewed evidence seemed likely to sway her on that subject. Then Jacqueline talked about how she made out with girls sometimes; "but just to get the attention of guys!" she insisted. Apparently she had done that on Friday, but the guy she was trying to impress had got pissed off at her for some reason and then stopped talking to her. "I was just too much for him," she said. I could only imagine.

*

"Well here comes Dr Jekyll!" said Jacqueline, after I'd pulled her shirt and cardigan over her head, stripped off her bra, and pushed her down into the couch. Then she said: "Or is it Dr Hyde who's the bad one?"

"I have no fucking clue!" I replied, gripping her wrists harder and then assaulting her tits with my mouth.

Jeans off and only her undies left, I flipped her on her front and had at her with my spanking hand. At last my patience was paying off. I wanted to make that smooth white butt sing. 'God she deserves this!' I thought.

My red cotton ropes snaked their way around her wrists as I held them together behind her back. Then, after making sure she was tightly bound I lifted her up off the sofa and pushed her down so her knees were on the floor.

"How sensitive are those nipples?" I asked.

"I don't know..."

"Well then I guess we'll find out," I said, holding a clothes peg in each hand and squeezing them rapidly in front of her like two little ravenous piranhas ready to attack.

"Fuck!" she said, as the first one took hold.

"Auuh! Shhhit!" she whispered as the second piranha bit down. Jacqueline gnawed on her lower lip and her crumpled eyebrows expressed her significant nipple pain.

"There you go, take your punishment like a good girl!" I said, and then tried not to think about how creepily paternalistic that just sounded.

I unbuckled my belt and pulled down my trousers. "Now for your reward," I said, sitting in front of her with my erect phallus waving towards her face. I took hold of her scrunched up blonde hair and began to pull her head towards my cock.

However, rather than opening her mouth and obediently accepting what she was offered, Jacqueline kept her lips firmly closed and dodged her head to the side.

'Hmmm, that's not happened before,' I thought, 'maybe this is some kind of game where she wants me to force her somehow?'

"Get my cock in your mouth!" I instructed.

She shook her head. This was an unexpected setback.

"Those pegs aren't coming off your nipples until you suck it!"
She writhed a little, clearly upset at the idea but keeping her lips firmly closed.
"Ok I don't get it? Do you want me to force you or something? I'm not going to force you without your consent."
"No, I'm not going to have sex with you," she said.

...

'Huh, well that kind of throws a spanner in the works,' I thought, feeling remarkably impotent all of a sudden, especially considering this pretty girl was, for all intents and purposes, tied up and at my mercy.
"Okaay..." I said.
"I mean you can do other things to me, but I don't want to have sex[120]."
"Well that's kind of interrupted my flow a little... I mean it's fine, but... Yeah."
I leaned back in the couch for a moment and looked at her with a quizzical expression, my penis nodded down a bit, clearly confused as to why it was still waving around fruitlessly in the un-stimulating air.
"Could you perhaps take these pegs off now though? They REALLY hurt," she whined.
"Ok, ok, but they're gonna hurt more when I take them off, so prepare yourself."
After I de-pegged her, she cursed and tried to hug my leg, although her hands were still tied behind her back so it was more like she just leant against my knee in an imploring fashion.

---

[120] I assumed she was going by the definition of sexual relations that had been used to impeach a certain former democratic president.

When she had recovered from her nipple crippling, I walked her onto the bed and spanked her some more. I held her half upside-down, her weight resting on her upper back and shoulders while I held her legs under my left arm, ass in the air. My right had slapped away as if it was playing a bongo drum.

"Ah! Ah! AH! AH! AHHH! Maybe could you switch to a different cheek?" she said after I had given one spot a prolonged thwacking. I gave that pink butt area one more solid swipe before switching, just to show her who was boss.

I tried to tempt her with my cock again, rubbing it over her face and up and down across her lips to make a "flub-bulb-blb-blblb-blb" noise as she exhaled.
I left it resting under her nose as she squirmed.
"Do you like the smell of cock in your nose?"
"Err... not really," she replied, "also your balls are kind of hairy," she added.
"Fine!" I said, slumping on the bed beside her.

"You can jerk off onto my tits if you want," she muttered.
I entertained a vision of me masturbating awkwardly over her for a prolonged period.
"No, that's ok. Is there anything specific you want me to do to you?"
"I don't know... Is there anything you want to do to me?... Besides sex?"

I'm sure there were a lot more painful things I could have done to her at that point, but my inspiration was drained by the futility of my erection, and so I accepted defeat and untied her arms[121].

---

[121] Later Jacqueline kept texting me about how sorry she was for

*

After walking Jacqueline back to the subway I went home and stripped off. I took a pair of scissors from the medicine cabinet and positioned myself over the toilet, one foot resting on the seat. Then, very gingerly, I began to trim my ball hair.

---

leading me on and not having sex with me, even though I said nothing to try and make her feel bad. It was almost as if she was getting off on the feeling of guilt she thought she should have.

VIII

T.G.O.M.D. nestles in the spoon of my body, her smooth hair gently moving against my cheek as she breathes. I've held many girls like this before. I want to say this felt different but that implies all those other spooning experiences were the same on some level, and they weren't. Maybe it just feels MORE different because I'm living it in this moment. Who knows how I'll remember it weeks from now.

It is morning and my thin curtains are doing a poor job of holding back the bright daylight that's saturating the outside world. We've both been awake and talking for a while now, and despite not really being a morning person I'm enjoying the sound of every word she says.

"You don't have anywhere you need to be, do you?" she asks, after I've checked the time on my phone.
"Nope. Here is good," I reply.
"Ok, but I want to try being the big spoon now," she says, wiggling around to face me.
"Really? That seems weird... but whatever," I reply, rolling into position and submitting to her encircling arms.

I feel her warm lips on my shoulder.

"This feels odd somehow," I comment.
"Why does it feel odd?" she asks.
"I don't know. It's like I feel more exposed or something," I reply, "... like you could stick something in my bum at any moment"
"Ha, and is that a good or a bad feeling?"

"I'm not sure..."

Aside 3 - New York New York New York New York... New York

New York New York New York New York New York New York New York...

Manhattan...

It's tempting to keep saying its name just to circumnavigate the difficult task of trying to describe a place so multifaceted that it defies all description. When I arrived in 2012 there were 1.6 million people squeezed onto this 33.8 sq. mile lump of mud and rock[122]. Apparently, it was in 1626 that the island of Manna-hata was bought off a forgotten tribe of Native Americans by Dutch settlers in exchange for items worth 60 guilders. According to Wikipedia, this is equivalent to around $1050 in 2014, and it would be neither the first nor the last time that the Native Americans got short changed in a real estate transaction.

In my first year here my feelings towards this city fluctuated with a wild intensity depending on four main factors. These were: 1- How shitty the weather was, 2- How badly work was sucking, 3- How lonely and isolated I felt, and 4- How much I was getting laid.

I still remember my first weekend here, walking around beneath great skyscrapers with a sense of awe and possibility, meeting some friends from Oxford down in the East Village and being surrounded by life and excitement. Every street was

---

[122] I sometimes wonder what would happen if everyone left their tower blocks and went down into the street at the same time. Would there be some kind of awful sardine like crush? How many would die as they were forced off the sidewalks and into moving traffic?

new, every face fascinating, and every scene a photograph just waiting to be taken. Then I remember how these feelings were rapidly replaced by feelings of "Oh shit, a Hurricane!' "Oh shit, no power!" "Oh shit, no Internet or cell phone reception!" "Oh shit, no running water" "Oh shit, my laptop battery is dead and I can't watch any more Breaking Bad!"

Thus my New York pendulum was set in motion.

The intricate collage of life in this city contains many features that can be inspiring one day and enraging the next. One's reaction can depend on personal circumstance and just how much of a dick the city decides to be to you on that particular day. However, to keep this description on track, I thought I'd pick three features of big city life to structure this ramble around and we'll just have to see where they take us.

The People

I think I may have mentioned that New York contains a lot of people. At the end of the day it is the people that make a city, and nowhere can a more diverse and eclectic mixture of humans be found than in New York. As well as providing a near limitless supply of single women to date, this overpopulation has a number of other advantages. Firstly, you can find pretty much any shop or service you could possibly imagine, because somewhere in this vast creative melting pot there will be someone with a novel skill or idea, and other people that will pay for it.

People rave about the food in New York, and they are right to; it is pretty damn good! This is probably down to the combination of cultural diversity, lots of discerning mouths to feed, and heavy competition between feeders. However, good food is only one example of the innumerable benefits of populousness and multiculturalism. All the different people from all different cultures mean the city is like a distillate of the best things from all over the planet. New York is a giant pool of energy and creativity where all the best new ideas can feed off each other and the future is born.

Everyone in New York is doing different things too. It's not like Oxford, where everyone is either a student, or an academic, or someone who hates students and academics. Almost every profession flocks to the big city; accountants, lawyers, strippers, investment bankers, models, photographers, actors, musicians, scientists, artists, street sweepers, mixologists, con men, teachers, writers, and so on and so forth. The only people that might stay away are farmers and agoraphobics and, even without those merrymakers, New York could still be considered the biggest party on the planet. (Well at least it would be if everyone didn't have to work every waking hour in order to pay their rent.)

I'm told New York is considered unfriendly, even hostile, compared to the rest of America. However, to me it still seems like a positively affable place when contrasted with English cities. It's not that English cities are especially hostile, but the British reserve dictates that we don't talk to strangers unless there is some big occurrence that clearly deserves comment. For example, "I think that escaped bull is charging in our direction!" or "That toddler just stole your purse!" are acceptable comments to make to strangers[123], whereas "Hi! Are you visiting or do you live around here?" or "That's a nice coat you're wearing!" are entirely unacceptable and immediately single out the commenter as either a foreigner or a mentalist[124].

---

[123] Assuming there is actually an angry bull or thieving toddler in the vicinity.

[124] Perhaps this is why we are known for always talking about the

In New York though, even a mildly introverted Englishman like me can still find himself talking to interesting strangers on occasion and not really know how he got there. Whether it's chatting to an old lady who's complaining about the price of ham in the supermarket, or explaining my research to some over enthusiastic teenagers[125] on the subway, or commenting on the joys of being English to some drunk NYU girls queuing for $1 pizza, I have found myself seamlessly wandering into random chats without even having to use the English classic "Looks like it's about to rain soon!" as an icebreaker.

While there are endless possibilities for human connection in this city, these interactions are usually fleeting. In England there is a significant possibility that if you escaped a stampeding bull with someone they could become your friend for life, but in NY the odds are you wouldn't even exchange numbers. Herein begins the flip side. Despite being packed to the brim with interesting people, New York can still be a very lonely place. Sure, it might be easy enough to meet people and chat to them, but actually forming genuine friendships is much harder. You might think it's my standoffish English attitude getting in the way but I swear it's not just me! Lots of other people, including many sociable Americans, have told me that they find New York to be a lonely place as well.

Perhaps having lots of people in one small area not only stimulates economic competition but also social competition, as those of us with only a moderate social energies find ourselves alone because we assume that everyone else has

---

weather, even with people we know, as we don't want to start a conversation with any dangerously personal questions or observations.
[125] And by 'over enthusiastic' I mean they were either high or remarkably excited about the world.

better things to be doing with their other friends instead of hanging out with us. These thoughts probably aren't limited to people with a low opinion of their social skills because socialising isn't just a selfish act. Part of the reason we do it is because, as well as not wanting to be alone ourselves, we don't want our friends to be alone either. When you move to a bustling place like New York it seems like no one else could ever be lonely in this city, and this may undermine our motivation to socialise, which ironically makes it easier to end up alone[126].

While I love making friends and being around interesting people, I'm not someone who's afraid of solitude for the most part. However, New York solitude is perhaps the worst kind of solitude because wherever you go, you still can't escape other people's shit. There is no space to breathe in and be quietly alone. Even Central Park is clogged full of tourists, joggers and other miscellaneous humans. You'd be hard pressed to take a piss behind a tree in the verdant ramble[127] without accidentally shocking some old lady distributing bird seed, or spooking some stoned teenagers, or interrupting a Grindr date.

It's also hard to find a quiet patch of grass to lie on without having to listen to some obnoxious bro brag loudly to his buddy about how he banged a hot chick last night, or some Manhattan princess complain on the phone about how she is "Soooo over it!" (despite having talked about "it" loudly for the last 15 minutes). Being surrounded by the buzz of other people and their social lives can make the loneliness of the city more

---

[126] Oh and the fact that it's a big city doesn't help either. Friends can have the annoying tendency to live on the other side of it.
[127] The ramble is a particularly overgrown and wild area in the middle of central park. You can almost get lost there, but there will still be plenty of other people lost with you.

intense, even if those social lives do sound truly god-awful to be part of.

Still, there's always something going on, whether it's a flash mob of rollerbladers somehow not dying on 1st Avenue.... Or a homeless dude yelling that he's al Qaeda's spokesperson on E14th Street... Or a 'performance artist' clad in mankini and lucha libre mask dancing with buckets in Astor Place... Or some dude hitting full cartons of milk with a golf club into Petroniso Square... Or an incredible four man a-cappella group serenading you on the 1 train... Or a man walking around Bryant Park with a cat on his head... Or one of the so many other bizarre things I've seen here that I have actually started to forget them.

However you look at it, there's never a dull moment in this city and always a good story to tell.

Attitudes

With a lot of different people come a lot of different attitudes, but there is something about all these people being forced to live with each other in such close proximity that can shape these attitudes in certain ways. Cities on the whole tend to be more progressive places, perhaps because exposure to different ideas and people breeds a better collective understanding of each other[128]. New York is no exception. It still maintains some conservative trappings, probably because it is mostly controlled by lots of stupidly rich people, but there is enough youthful energy in the place to look past niggles like not being allowed to drink a beer in a public park[129].

---

[128] Or perhaps cities are generally more progressive because you have to be pretty smart to get a good job and afford to live in them, (and yes I am inferring smart people are generally more progressive.)

A significant amount of New York's 'energy' is less positive though. If you stand and listen to the sounds of the city, there is one frequently heard noise that will soon cut through all others. It's a noise which I think most embodies the dark side of New York's personality; the blaring ear punch of a car horn. These blasts are rarely heard in isolation either. It sometimes seems like the gaggle of car tooting is the city's substitute for a dawn chorus... and an evening chorus, and a generally-anytime-there's-traffic chorus.

There are of course many legitimate reasons one can use one's car horn, but I still think that the melody of "Beeeep" "BEEP-BEEP" "BEEEEEEEEEEEP"-ing that often erupts from the city's streets and intersections tells of something more than a city full of bad drivers. It's particularly well symbolised by the douchebag or douchebaguette who blares on their horn when sitting in the middle of a stationary traffic jam where it is obvious that no one is moving and loud noises serve no purpose except to make everyone else less happy.

Most New Yorkers don't actually drive cars and so can't rave on their horns, but the same impatient attitude of "You're either helping me get somewhere or you're in my way!" can be found everywhere you look in this city. Whether it's people barging into a subway car before the occupants can escape, or some lady leaving her dog's shit on the sidewalk for someone else to slip on, or the bus driver taking off at speed when clearly you're running to get there and only need 5 more seconds to reach those closing doors. All these small acts of unkindness add up and can result in a maddening despair for humanity. NYC is a

---

[129] Though there is a paper bag etiquette thing... but as a resident alien with minimal constitutional rights I've not taken the risk!

place where selfishness and impatience are the norm. Hell, they are even expected.

Perhaps part of the reason for the city's impatient selfitude is that there are so many people in this place that you are unlikely to run into any given person more than once. Therefore it seems like being a bit of a dick to a stranger is unlikely to detrimentally affect your own life in any way[130]. This, combined with the American propensity for being 'outspoken' (which is my English way of saying 'loud and obnoxious'[131]), can generate a heady cocktail of poisonous human-human interactions.

Maybe truly destructive NY selfishness is only endemic in a few bad apples, but it spreads and infects, and the few truly rotten fruit blemish and corrupt those they come into contact with. If some ne'er-do-well doesn't get their comeuppance for publicly acting like an asshole, then initially decent people may observe this as and become more prone to shitty behaviour themselves[132].

New Yorkers quickly become cynical and tired of being taken advantage of, and the city becomes a pit where human generosity, goodness, and empathy are all gradually eroded to dust. To illustrate this point with personal experience; I once watched a blind man standing on a street corner audibly asking for help crossing the road. "Can somebody help me cross the road?" he said, several times, waving his big white stick that

---

[130] This of course ignores the collective damage done by selfish acts, and while personally I don't believe in karma, I do believe we are all connected in that we all share the same planet and all interact in the same society, and so bad actions hurt us all one way or another.
[131] And yes, that was my New York way of saying it.
[132] After perhaps first making some self-righteous declaration of despair.

highlights him as someone who doesn't just wear big sunglasses because it's kind of sunny out. Three or four people walked straight past him without even slowing down (perhaps they thought 'I'm not an asshole if he can't see me being an asshole?'). Anyway in the end I walked over and helped him across the street. It cost me nothing and I got to feel smug about myself. (Although I did first wonder if it might be some kind of 'blind man scam' and I checked my wallet was securely buried in my pocket before going to help.)

My acts of NY 'generosity' did not always go quite so smoothly though. I still have a random bucket of tools in my apartment after some guy dressed as a construction worker told me his van had been towed with his wallet inside and then asked me if he could borrow $20 to get back to New Jersey. He left me his tools and his mobile number as 'security' but I never heard from him again. I mean it wasn't really a very forward thinking scam considering the tools look like they're worth way more than $20, but I'm kind of afraid to sell them in case they were stolen to begin with.

As well as selfishness and impatience, there are probably a lot of other negative attitudes that swirl around in the New York maelstrom, but the end result is that this city can begin to feel like a pretty dehumanizing place. That said, continued exposure to this social tornado has a certain character building quality. You start to reach a more Zen-like state of acceptance and perhaps gain a better insight into people in general. Well, either that or you find your peace by blaring on your car horn and yelling "motherfucker" a lot.

Tall shit

One final undeniable fact about New York is that it contains a lot of big stuff.

Giant monoliths, of near inconceivable size, tower over you in midtown and the financial district, and even in the low rise areas tall brownstones and other terraced conglomerations still blot out an unnaturally large amount of the sky. In this city you can forget that the horizon is a big wide line that stretches 360 degrees, instead it becomes a distant streak at the end of a long ravine of concrete, a one dimensional light at the end of a nearly endless three dimensional tunnel.

There is an undeniable grandeur to New York's architectural immensity. This forest of pillars and spires is one of the greatest physical testaments to the power of the American dream. The haphazard diversity in NY building style tells its own story. This city was not built to a grand plan and it is not the product of one designer's imagination. Instead, it has grown from the inspiration of thousands. New York is almost biological. It is a city that has evolved and is always evolving. Classical columns, gothic brickwork, minimalist blocks of concrete, futurist angles of glass, it's all here. There are all the details too. Details that tell stories in plaques, frescos, and sculpture. Patriotic stories about the history of America, vainglorious accounts of corporate empire, and even quaint little tales about everyday people who maybe did something interesting one time.

All these gigantic feats of construction can embolden the human spirit.
"We built this!" I might find myself thinking, "not gods, or giants, or aliens from outer space, but us!"

New York was built by little tiny people just like you and me. They built these towers of babel with regular hands and regular feet and regular backbones. Undoubtedly it took a lot of those hands and feet[133], and still needed the help of a lot of smart minds and cunning machines but, at the end of the day, the achievement is all human. No supernatural mythology or marvels of Mother Nature are required to explain it. Being surrounded by this testament to the capabilities of man can be inspirational. If we did all this, then anything might be possible! If you want to build something with your life then this might seem like a damn good place to start.

However, along with the grandeur of New York comes the less compelling architectural metaphors of closed doors and glass ceilings. A great multitude of people built this city, but a much smaller number of people actually own it. Put on some more cynical glasses and Manhattan's grand edifices are transformed from symbols of collective achievement into phallic embodiments of the shameless concentration of power and wealth in the hands of the few. The Rockefellers, the Donald Trumps, the Chryslers, and all those other profiteers and dynasties, each burning through immeasurable human energy just to square off over who has the biggest or prettiest dong in the sky.

This city may well help inspire a plucky individual to build his own fortune, but it can also be brutally discouraging when the monopolistic empires of others already stare down at you from crushingly impossible heights. Sure, if you want to gaze from on high yourself you can pay the man your ~$27 dollars to stand on one of his tall buildings and take in the view. Although it's hard to pretend that you're really standing in a spot that's meant for your feet. You are merely renting that

---

[133] And broke a disturbing number of backbones.

space for a few minutes; a brief lacuna of awe and grandiosity before you get bored or need to pee, and then you'll be ushered into a crowded elevator by a man wearing an excessively smart uniform, and sent back down to earth.

There are many who slip on the New York ladder of career success or bang their sweaty scalps on impenetrable glass ceilings. To the cynical eyes of the downtrodden, the gigantic towers of this city can become like the towers of a prison; frightful reminders of your economic subservience to a vast and unstoppable capitalist machine; the American dream turned nightmare. Perhaps for many of us the American dream is one of those nightmares where you are running away from some undefined terror towards an imagined safety, but part of you just knows you are never going to make it in time.

*

While I walked along the bottom of New York's glass canyons I could usually maintain a healthy balance of awe and cynicism. Casting myself as the observer in a foreign land, I always had the option of retreat. However, by the late autumn of 2013 the city was starting to make me feel small. I had been in my job over a year and what had been a promising scientific career before I left Oxford had hit a solid wall of misfortune and demotivation. I wasn't researching what I wanted to research, and I felt I no longer had the academic freedom I had gotten used to in Oxford. I had applied for my own funding to help with that, but I had had one fellowship proposal rejected, and a second one hung in the balance. I poured my energy into this second proposal as it seemed like the last glimmer of hope in a sea of failed experiments and bureaucratic time wasting. If I won the money I might once again soar on my own updraft but until then I was stuck beneath unscalable walls, and watched over by great towers that belonged to people who could probably fund years of my research with less money than they spent on a weekend of cocaine and prostitutes.

Of course, I did not go into science for the money. Science degrees might be a sound undergraduate investment but if you want to 'make bank', then staying in academia is a poor gamble to make. However, money seemed like a particularly frivolous consideration when I was studying at Oxford and surrounded by intelligent people who valued knowledge above all else. To most Oxford academics, solving the mysteries of the universe was their passion and guiding mission (although most of them were far too modest to ever put it like that). Amongst Oxford's dreaming spires someone who had an excessively fancy car or flashed other displays of wealth might be looked down upon or subtly mocked for their insecurity. In New York, however, dollar signs, and those who flaunt them, are worshipped like deities... and it is a decidedly infectious religion.

I have clearly been corrupted by this place. Perhaps the corruption is not absolute, and perhaps it has been somewhat to my own betterment, but I am corrupted. There's no doubt about it. Whatever my conclusions on New York end up being, this city has changed me, tested me, enriched me, and almost broken me. At the end of the day, I'm glad I took the chance of moving here and I'd probably do it all again[134].

---

[134] Especially the bits where I got have sex with pretty girls.

Chapter 21 - I'm in trouble!

Sexting is an odd sport; there is undoubtedly a subtle art to it that requires one to try and second guess the recipient's state of mind, and then to say something sufficiently unexpected to excite the hell out of them, but not so shocking that it freaks them out and they decide to throw their phone down a well and run for the hills.

I did a lot of sexting over the summer of 2013 and I'd go as far as to say that I got good at it. The 'giving orders and obeying them' aspect of BDSM can translate quite well into a text format, and the fact that both parties are usually comfortably situated in their own homes allows more scope for getting freaky while feeling safe. I liked telling girls to do weird shit to themselves. I made several girls insert vibrating toothbrushes into unhygienic places. I got one girl to cover herself in honey in her bathroom. I got another girl to write "SLUT" above her pussy in permanent marker, and I got almost all of them to send me photographic evidence of their misdeeds. Another good trick I 'invented' was to make a girl stick her phone down her pants and rest it on her clit while I sent her a long stream of one word texts; vibration at my discretion. When the time felt right I might tell them they were sluts, or tell them they were dirty whores, or tell them they were worthless pieces of meat who needed to be fucked until they couldn't even remember that they had a name[135]. I told them to call me sir, I told them

---

[135] With regards to the awful objectification on display here; awful objectification is part of the game for some people. Of course I didn't think that any of these girls were worthless sluts when I called them that, but good sexting is about articulating each other's fantasies in a way that might be super awkward in person. Also if anyone took offence at being called mean things I was quick to reassure them that I was not projecting any real world opinions.

to tell me what disgusting whores they were, and I made them yell things like 'I'm a dirty slut!' out loud again and again so that their roommates might hear.

So yes, in conclusion, you can have a surprising amount of fun via text. I could almost make a girl cum remotely more easily than I could in person. The only problem with this strategy was that giving someone an orgasm via text doesn't seem to translate into an increased chance of actually getting a date with them in the real world. Also, while sexting was fun for me to some extent, I found it tricky to multi-task typing and self-pleasure, and so I would normally wait until afterwards to masturbate when I could quietly reflect on the seedy pictures I had been sent. Anyway after that first summer of sexting shenanigans I decided it was better to keep more of a lid on these digital sex fantasies, at least until after I'd been on an actual date with the girl. Sometimes though opportunities present themselves that you just can't resist...

*

A texted mirror selfie appeared on my phone. It was from a girl called Katie who I'd been chatting to for a week or so but not yet met. She's was in a washroom at some airport in North Carolina and about to head back to the city. Her bright red hair streamed out from behind her iPhone as she held it in front of her face.

"*Ha looks like some inspiring surroundings :-P*" I replied.
"*Right. Philosophers paradise*" she texted.
Feeling like this bathroom selfie was an invitation to naughtiness I asked her: "*Got enough time to get yourself off in a cubicle?*"
Katie: "*There's no cubicles, but it's pretty empty if you want to send me some dirty thoughts?*"

I had a flood of dirty thoughts... I tried to think of a good place to start...

Katie: "*I pretty frequently get off in public places without people noticing. I mean not level 10 orgasms but nice all the same.*"
"*dirty, dirty girl*"
"*Guilty*"
"*You definitely deserve some serious punishment for that kind of disgraceful behaviour...*" (A fairly clichéd opener, but every sextcapade has got to start somewhere...)
"*Anything you can imagine me tying you to in that wash room?*" I asked.

"*It's pretty sparse. You could always just tie my hands behind my back, I like that...*" she texted, and then followed it up with, "*Tie my hands behind my back and slip your fingers up under my cocktail dress and into my underwear... you probably won't be surprised by what you'll find... (I only like black lace lingerie by the way.)*"

Me: "*Bend you over the sink so your ass is mine to play with*"
Her: "*Pull my hair to arch me up?*"
Me: "*Tug your hair with one hand while the other pulls that black lace down to your knees*"
Her: "*I have a tight pussy but get very wet... very quickly*"
Me: "*Maybe I'll toy with your clit a little first*"
Her: "*I'd love to taste myself from your fingers when you shut me up*"
Me: "*Then whip that dress up and give you a stern strike with my hand...* "
Her: "*Mmm I'd like that. Turn my pale skin bright red!*"

Damn she was good at this. She was in my head as much as I was in hers.

Me: *"I'll strike you again and again until you can't take it anymore and try to move your ass away...*
...but I'll just push you harder against the sinks and keep going until every inch of your ass glows and tingles"

"I'm playing with myself in the washroom" she texted
"Damn right you are!"
"Please keep it coming... I'm fingering myself now"
"When your ass is nice and red I'll run my nails over it tenderly... squeeze it firmly, and then finger fuck you until you're gasping!"
"But will you let me suck your cock...?"
"When you're good and wet I'll reach forward and stick my fingers in your mouth. Make you suck them. Then holding you by the mouth I'll pull you around and down..."
"I'm yours to play with"
"Now stick this down your fucking throat!"
"Timmy please I'm getting close"
"Please sir!" I correct her
"Please sir!" she texts
"A hard slap in the face for that disrespect. You better not cum without my permission."
"Please sir can I cum?" she begged
"I board in 5..." she added
"Not until I've blown my load all over your face. Nice and juicy for the plane."
"Oh yeah I like that"
"Ok now you can come slut :-P"

Then just in case she needed a little help with that last step I texted; *"I hope you're imagining my cum all over your cheeks,* eyelids and nose. *Not to mention it seeping in through those slutty lips. ;)"*

"That was great :)" came her response.

We chatted normally for a little longer and she agreed a possible day to meet. Then she had to switch off her phone so the plane didn't crash. I wished her a pleasant flight.

*

It was raining when I walked to meet Katie for the first time. It was a certain kind of rain that reminded me of England. I don't often feel homesick but the particular smell of the air, along with a specific size and density of the water droplets falling from a distinct greyness of cloud, all conspired to bring up a buried longing for England's pastures green.

I shook off this feeling of nostalgia and then jumped to avoid a large puddle at the corner of E32nd and 3rd. Water was running down gutters and falling on concrete with a continuous succession of 'splat-splat-splat-splat-splat" noises. Streets shone with bright red and white reflections, diffusing the glaring head and tail lights of cars that passed with the crackling hissing noises of sticky tyres on wet asphalt.

I waited outside my local speakeasy with raindrops running off my umbrella. Muffled sounds of live jazz and laughter drifted out through the frosted windows and the ghoulishly distorted shadow of a musician with a double bass could just about be made out on the glass. Droplets pitter-pattered around my feet sending up tall crowns of spray that moistened my shoes and trousers. A little later than expected, Katie appeared. Umbrella-less and with her head wrapped in a shawl. Her ginger hair had that sexy-darkened-and-definitely-been-in-the-rain look but she wore a broad smile as she approached me and we hugged a greeting. We squeezed into the bar and my glasses steamed up instantly. After waiting a little while to get a cocktail, we found some standing space and some hooks where we could hang our damp coats.

Katie was new to Okcupid and wanted to know what I thought of her profile. This immediately got me on to thin ice as it had been a week or so since I'd looked at it and my memory for online dating profiles had definitely faded with repeated exposure. Fortunately, she didn't press me too hard and conversation moved on the generalities of dating in the city, her degree in far-eastern studies, and her new job at a non-profit. Katie was smart and vivacious, a 'free spirit' (whatever that means) but definitely the kind of person I could see organizing the revolution with a joint hanging from her lips and war paint on her face. She told me she wanted to save some money from her job so she could buy some land out West and start a weed plantation. While I wasn't 100% sure she was serious, I didn't doubt for a minute that she could make it happen.

After one cocktail we decided to try somewhere a bit quieter with room to sit down, so I led her across the street to a different bar.
"I like your jeans," she commented.
"Thanks! This is one of my limited number of date outfits," I confessed as we crossed the street in the drizzle.
"I could take you clothes shopping if you'd like!" she said, "I love shopping for guys!"
It made me happy to think that after one drink I might have already found a new friend who wanted to go shopping with me. This date seemed to be going well and it got better when we had seats and a bottle of wine to share. Katie certainly wasn't shy. Her parents were nudist academics who lived out in

Oregon, so she grew up in a very free spirited household where sex and drugs were open topics of conversation and naked relatives could often be found in the hot tub.

"Wow, yeah that's about the polar opposite of my parents," I said, "I remember when I went off to university, my dad gave me a box of condoms that he'd hand wrapped in brown paper as if they were some big shameful thing I couldn't buy myself."
"Aww, that's adorable!"
"Yeah maybe... I guess as far as they know I've never had sex. It's not a subject we've ever talked about."
"Ha, I've been on the pill since I was fifteen."
"Oh yeah?"
"Yeah. Some people come off it when they're single and then go back on when they have a boyfriend, but that's bad for your body, and besides, what if you just want to have a one night stand?"
"Yeah, it's not like you know when these opportunities will present themselves!" I said, trying to manoeuvre my leg towards hers but getting blocked by the base of our table.

I shared some of my better dating anecdotes including my recent experience with a hot Republican.

"Yeah my ex-girlfriend was really hot but really crazy," she said, "sorry, I know you're not supposed to talk about exs on a first date."
"Oh no, do go on. I'm intrigued to hear about this ex-girlfriend!"
"You would be!" she said, grinning at me, "well she had two kids with two different guys because she didn't 'believe' in condoms, and then was really bad at taking the pill"
"Ah, man, that's another reason I always use condoms! Can't imagine having a surprise kid to deal with."

"Yeah, she was still technically married to one of the guys when we were dating. We had some threesomes. It was kind of fun, but yeah... It got too crazy even for me!"
"Ha, you don't seem that crazy! In fact you seem kind of down to earth in a weird, super liberal, kind of way."
"Thanks, you don't seem crazy either, which I guess is good considering how I found you..."

*

"Looks like it's still raining," I commented as we exited the bar, momentarily sheltering under some scaffolding.
"Yep."
"So are you up for coming back to my place?" I asked.
"Yeah?" she replied, seeming surprised that I had even asked the question.
"Well you can share my umbrella then!" I said, putting my arm around her before we crossed the threshold into that wet night.

It wasn't a big umbrella and I tried to hold it more over Katie than myself, but we were both pretty damp by the time we got back to my apartment. I only got around to switching on the hallway light. We were kissing and stripping off each other's wet clothes before I had a chance to switch on any more. Rain still pattered on the window, and gave my dark room that warm feeling of refuge.

"Take a shower with me?" Katie said, after I'd stripped her down and fingered her a little.
"Sure!" I said, more than willing to go along with whatever the hot naked chick was saying.

She took my hand and led me to my bathroom. I turned the tap, pulled the lever and the shower head erupted with warm gushing water that thundered into the bath and against my bamboo-effect shower curtain. (Man was I glad that I'd thrown away that first shower curtain that had gone mouldy, it would have totally ruined the mood.)

Water spattered off our bare bodies as they pressed together. Shiny warm droplets sat on her shoulders as the shower's spray bounced off her back. Those animated sparkling drops coalesced, ran in thin streams over her clavicles and breasts, and then flooded the ravines we formed as my torso pressed against her soft tits. We kissed, warm wet skin on warm wet skin. I held her close and my fingers toyed.

Katie put out a hand to steady herself against the tiles. Her second hand went out as I pushed her against them. I stepped into full bore of the shower stream, one of my hands pressed on Katie's back, squishing her against the cold wet tiles, the other massaged between her legs... a smack... then back between the legs. I leaned over her, moving one hand up her back and into her wet red hair, two fingers in her pussy now. I thrust them hard and fast... Holding her by the hair I turned her head towards me and smooshed her cheek against those smooth ceramic squares. She groaned and made other noises that indicated her body was fully under my control. Her hands still pressed out, palms against the tiles, legs spread apart with water cascading down them. My cock rubbed against her thigh; my god I wanted to fuck her right there in the shower, to hell with the risk of slippage! However, we had already discussed the importance of protection and I was able to restrain myself. "Let's get you back into bed" I said, releasing her from the wall and holding her against me again.

A quick towel off but not enough time to get dry before I was pushing her down and wrapping Velcro cuffs around her wrists.

"Can you leave my legs free?" she said, "I want to be able to grab onto you when we fuck."
"Sure," I said, "now what toys should we play with..."
"Ooo do you have one of those mouth ball things?"
"A ball gag? Yup."
"I want to try one of those! Not done that before."

There was no doubt that Katie knew what she wanted and wasn't afraid to ask for it. I liked that, even if it undermined my attempts to dominate her a little. I gagged her as she lay there and slapped her exposed legs. I thought about getting my flogger and toying with her more but I was too eager to bury myself inside her... I discovered she was as tight and wet as promised.

After a solid period of rough sex, it seemed like Katie was trying to say something... I un-gagged her...
"Can you un-tie one of my hands? I really want to rub my clit while you fuck me..."
"Fine..." I said, a little begrudgingly as I was unsure if it even really counted as bondage when a girl is only held down by a single hand.

"You should come first though," she gasped, her knuckles now rubbing against my abs.
"No, you should come first. Otherwise I'll lose my energy!" I wheezed.
"Besides I'm enjoying fucking you too much!"
She seemed to do as she was told.

A brief break in proceedings, a fresh condom, and then a lesson in how blowjobs through latex are way less awesome than regular blow jobs. Still I was ready for more and Katie was on top of me now, her red hair backlit in the light coming from the hallway; a hot young Boadicea riding me for all I was worth. It wasn't 100% clear who was dominating who at this point, but whatever was happening I definitely didn't want it to stop.

"Call me a slut!" she cried, bouncing up and down on me, fully in the moment.

I was equally in the moment and my burst of verbal abuse would have perhaps benefited from more scripting: "You're a disgusting shitting slut!!... Shitting disgusting slutty slut!"
"Auh! YES! I'm such a disgusting slut!" she responded.
I tried to think of some other abusive words that weren't 'disgusting' 'shitting' or 'slut'.
"You fucking dirty whore!" I said breathlessly (sticking with a classic 'whore' based comment there.)
"Mmmm yeauh!"
She didn't really speed up with that one, I needed to show some more imagination...
"Fuck my fucking cock you fucking slut!!"
"Yeah!"
"Don't think you can slow down slut! I'm just going to keep fucking you until you can't even remember a time when you weren't being fucked, and you can't imagine a time when it will stop!!"

The dirty talk may have gotten a little kafkaesque, but it seemed to do the trick as she pummelled and grinded as hard as she could. She threw her head back, her tits stuck out, one hand pressed down on my chest, the other ran through her hair; the perfect sculpture of passion. I rose up to meet her, one hand grasping her shoulder and pushing her down onto me even harder. Her energy slackened, but I kept going, now lost in my new ability to control her rhythm. My fingers dug into her back while my thumb squeezed her collarbone... So close to that ecstasy...
"I'm in trouble," Katie moaned. Her tone was still sexual but exhausted somehow. I wasn't quite sure what she meant, and I

didn't stop to find out as I was so deep in the zone I just fucked and fucked and pushed and squeezed and thrusted and grunted and sweated and shoved and gripped and came.

*

"Cuddle with me!" said Katie as I returned to the bed.
"Most definitely!" I replied, collapsing with her into that warm afterglow.

Before we could doze off fully though the glow was interrupted:
"I should go," she said, moving to escape my arms that were folded around her.
"Mmnh?... Are you sure?" I said, already half asleep, "you're very welcome to stay the night."
"No, I should get going," she said, moving with surprising speed and quickly retrieving her various clothes from where-so-ever they had been flung.

By the time I had blinked the sleep out of my eyes she was almost dressed.
"What time is it?" I asked, groping for my bedside clock.
"It's almost two," I said, answering my own question, "are you going to be ok getting back?"
"Yeah, I'll take a taxi."
"Ok, that makes sense," I said, trying to hide my disappointment by lying star-shaped and spreading my arms over that space that Boadicea had now left empty. 'Didn't she say she had the day off tomorrow?' I thought, pondering over her rapid exit.
"You can come wait for a taxi with me if you want?" she said, wiggling into her shoes as her shawl draped down from her neck.
"Blarg... naked... sleepy," I said, still gripped in the comfort of my mattress. I was about to persuade myself that I should put

on clothes and go down with her (even though there would be a million taxis zooming past and my role would be merely ceremonial).

"Ha! That's fine," she said, before my chivalry had a chance to win out.

I rose from the bed, kissed her one last time, and then she marched down my hallway and out through the door.

*

The next day I texted an apology for not walking her to a taxi. "*No worries, totally understand!*" she replied, although this didn't entirely relieve my sense that I had faux-pas-ed. After a day or so I texted her again to see if she wanted to hang out at the weekend and "*...get properly dominated this time?*"

She replied: "*Hey Timmy. I had a good week thanks. So I enjoyed meeting you but I didn't really feel a spark. I hope you find another playmate soon.*"

That stung a little.

I took a moment to swallow, but when I replied I shrugged off her rejection with a joke about electrosex and admitting that I already had the playmate thing covered. A couple of further texts and she seemed up for just getting a friendly drink sometime.

It was fair enough if she just wanted to leave it as a one night thing. It had seemed implicit that our meeting was about no strings attached fun, almost a model for how a casual hook-up should be, with a clean exit and no expectations raised or quashed. However, for me a sense of loss still crept in. I had had an incredible night with an interesting person and I wanted more like it. I wanted to reach after Katie, to keep her in my life somehow, but I knew now that the harder I tried to grasp onto her the faster she would slip through my fingers.

I played it cool. I waited a week and then shot Katie another text to see if she felt like a drink that weekend... She thanked me for thinking of her, but apparently she now had met Mr Boyfriend material and was spending the weekend with him.

The game seemed up. With nothing to lose from looking insecure I asked her why she didn't think we had a spark and if she could give me any tips for my future dating endeavours. She replied that she didn't think we had many similar interests and that she preferred to date guys who were heavier set than me (which I read as 'more muscle bound'). Apparently she thought I was "super nice" and didn't think I should change anything... "...*Keep doing your thing!*" she concluded. I guess that would have been more encouraging if "my thing" didn't seem to be leaving me perpetually single.

IX

My knees are resting on plastic sheeting and as I shift my weight it makes a certain kind of crunkling plastic sheeting noise that I don't believe the English language has a good word for.

I am entirely naked. My own ball gag is stuffed in my mouth. My arms are restrained behind me by several weighty loops of cold chain that are padlocked tightly around my wrists and ankles, and then linked to each other by another length of my awkward hardware store purchase. If I want to move from this spot I will need to first fall over, and then wriggle.

I am helpless.

I am also very turned on.

T.G.O.M.D stands over me and in her hands she is cradling a fluffy lemon-meringue number that I shall inaccurately refer to as a custard pie. Beside me on the plastic sheeting sit several more custard pies, chocolate syrup, whipping cream and a bucket full of homemade slime. This is the realisation of one of my more logistically challenging fantasies. The clean-up will undoubtedly be a bitch, but in a way that is part of the thrill.

"Are you ready?" she asks.

After a brief pause I nod, and try to say "Mmm hmm," but the ball gag gets in the way and adds some guttural syllables.

Then she hits me in the face with the pie.

It is glorious.

Chapter 22 - What is Love? Baby don't hurt me. Don't hurt me...

On a quiet Monday evening, I composed a new text to Lauren (you remember, that girl from a few chapters back who was afraid of subway death). Our third date plans had been delayed and our texts had grown less frequent over the last few weeks. She had been busy starting a new job and then had been unwell for a bit. I, meanwhile, had been busy getting my second fellowship application rejected, having a general existential crisis, and meeting Katie and Jacqueline[136].

"Feeling better yet? How's the new secretary job going?" I texted.
Lauren: *"Yea, things are ok"*

Not much to work with there. I texted back: *"Don't sound too enthusiastic! :-P Sorry I have been quiet, I have been sulking because they didn't give me money... And also being a bit of a man slut :-/"*

No response. Bringing up the fact I had been sleeping around was probably not such a smooth move, but Lauren and I hadn't made any exclusive commitments to each other, and I wanted to keep being honest with her to check what page we were on.

I let a day pass without a reply. Then on Wednesday I texted her again: *"I probably shouldn't have mentioned the man slut thing huh?"*

A quick reply this time: *"It doesn't bother me, I'm just not sure I want to meet up again."*

---

[136] Plus a couple of others girls that I mentioned in the date stew.

After a little bit of thought I decided to try and text her a frank explanation of my feelings.

"*I understand. I like you (and not just because you're hot), but I'm not sure I can see us being a serious thing. Let me know if you change your mind and want to hang out sometime as friends (with or without benefits)*"

"*I will :-)*" was her pithy reply.

And so, with that final smiley face, passed another thing that might have been, but wasn't. No one seemed to get hurt though, so maybe wishes made when blowing away eyelashes really do come true? Next time I'm going to wish for a beach house in the Hamptons.

*

By now you may have noticed my tendency towards placid euthanasia when it comes to my New York proto-relationships. A gentle reduction in oxygen leading to a peaceful sleep. Perhaps there is some painful self-analysis to be done at this point (if the rest of this book wasn't already enough). How though to make it less painful for the reader? You may well have come to your own conclusions about how I am 'emotionally withdrawn', 'commitment-phobic' or some other pleasantly succinct diagnosis. It may also seem to some that there has been a shortage of romance in these here tales of derring-doin-it. I may pass the blame for my continual singleness back and forth between my own deficiencies, my bizarre dating strategies, and the fact that New York dating is hard. Whatever my reasons, the fact remains that after a year of dating I had not yet had a real chance to fall in Love.

Love is a word that gets thrown around a lot. Of course it means different things in different contexts. The ancient Greeks had different words for different types of love, which was thoroughly sensible of them. However, I don't want this chapter to start sounding like some GCSE 'religious education' essay, so let's not get bogged down there. We English speakers just have the word 'love' to deal with and, despite its profligate meanings, most of the time everyone seems to know what they're talking about when they use it. For example, it seems easy to distinguish the different emotions at play when someone says 'I love fried chicken' vs. 'I love my fiancée'.

The kind of love that just means 'liking something a lot' is easy enough to explain and understand. However, there seems to be a particularly mysterious quality about the idea of romantic love that defies definition...

...or at least we like to believe there is, because to most people not knowing quite what 'love' is makes it better and more magical somehow. Unfortunately though this lack of definition also means there is no simple system of tick boxes that one can refer to determine whether "Yes, one is in love, go bake a cake!", or "No, one is not in love, better luck next time!"

Despite this ambiguity I'm pretty sure I was in love once. I make this claim because it felt like I was going fucking crazy over an extended period and, as I had no previous history of mental illness and I hadn't been ingesting any psychoactive drugs, I decided that being 'in love' was the most appropriate diagnosis.

Symptoms included:

- Constant mental re-playing of all interactions with the unfortunate individual I fell for.

- A surreal feeling of content-ness when I was around them, which allowed me to forget all other concerns and just be happy to be in their presence. (A popular analogy might be 'feeling like I was walking on air' but without any immediate concern that physics would catch up with me).
- The tiniest things they did or said could fill me with elation or completely shatter me.
- Feeling complete freedom to tell that person all of my weirdest and darkest thoughts without fear of judgment or misunderstanding. (Although forgetting this fear was perhaps unwise).
- Inability to sleep due to constantly pondering what my next move should be in trying to seduce her (even though my next move should clearly have been to sleep).
- Irrational excitement over the green dot that appeared whenever she came online on G-chat or Skype. (Green dots should really never be allowed to adopt such emotional significance).
- Frequent mind blowing moments of happiness when she would message "Hey!" to me unprompted, (even though I had been staring at that green dot for ages already, hoping she'd message me first in a mildly excruciating act of self-control).
- Constantly trying to find a way around the fact that the girl I'd fallen for had a boyfriend and things were clearly never going to work out between us.

Some might pose the objection that displaying these symptoms of cognitive disruption didn't necessarily mean I was 'in love'. A lot of people like to maintain a fairy tale idea of love, believing that 'true love conquers all' and if some insurmountable challenge comes along they will then tell you, 'It's just not meant to be'[137]. They may then belittle your feelings of love, as they wish to preserve their own magical gold standard idea of love-that-always-works-out, so they'll say: "You're not in love, you're just infatuated!" If what they mean by 'infatuated' is: "You're crazy in a bad kind of way" instead of "You're crazy in a good/cute kind of way" they could well be right, but to the infatuated it still feels like the same kind of crazy.

The phrase "it wasn't meant to be" always infuriates me as it doesn't square with the way I see the world. I don't believe in fate, I don't believe in a higher power, and I don't believe there's any grand plan that keeps the world ticking. I think the universe is just a jumble of matter and energy bouncing around in accordance with certain physical laws that we are still gradually figuring out. Galaxies, planets, life forms, people, thoughts, and fleeting romances are all little more than the flickering of an imperfect candle flame. A dance of entropy and enthalpy where the combined amount of mass and energy always stays the same, and whatever the dance moves turn out to be, disorder always reigns[138].

Perhaps I found this view of the universe depressing at first as I had been brought up by Anglican parents and learnt to assign value and beauty through a system inspired by a Christian morality. In this higher-power-centric value system, it seems like everything good and beautiful should have meaning and purpose as if it's the fulfilment of some meticulous plan. Now though, I see a chaotic universe to be just as amazing and beautiful as any mythology, even if it does put the

---

[137] These are perhaps among the worst people to discuss your romantic problems with.
[138] Yes, if you don't understand what I'm talking about you should have paid more attention in science class!

responsibility for the world's ills somewhat squarely in our own hands.

Consequently I do not see love as some magical pre-ordained calling but rather a rare chance event where two people with sufficient compatibilities come together under the right circumstances and then some 'magic' happens (but this 'magic' has a physical and chemical basis in reality, even if it's not fully understood). The upshot of this philosophy is that I don't believe there is only one person for everyone, or that we only get one chance to fall in love. Clutching at that straw kept me on the functional side of crazy when drowning in the hopelessness of my first serious infatuation. It also seemed to me that there was a line in the sand past which crazy romantic gestures or overly passionate remarks would just alienate me from the person I most desired. Actors in Hollywood movies may often ignore this line in the sand, but then the love stories that end with restraining orders don't normally make it into successful screenplays. Anyway, I got through failed falling in love attempt no 1 without a restraining order and I didn't do this by recognising that 'it wasn't meant to be', but just by realising that nothing I could do was going to make it happen. I finished my PhD on time, I bade farewell to Oxford's cobbled streets and their bittersweet reminiscences, and then I moved to America.

When I first moved to New York, the faded memories of that first deranged love still clung to me like flecks of used tissue paper, but after less than a year they had mostly washed away. Perhaps my longing had been split through the prism of over 40 dates; transferring, diluting, and dissolving, until I could safely say I was 'Sooo over it'.

However, I think I must disagree with Shakespeare when he says "it is better to have loved and to have lost than to have never loved at all" because A) loving and losing really fucking sucks, and B) once you know what love tastes like it makes it that much harder to settle for anything less.

*

"You're living the dream!" various male friends would say to me when I described some of my NY dating antics. I'd smile and say something like: "It's alright I guess!"... I'm not sure you can really ever 'live a dream' though, because then it's not technically a dream anymore.

Maybe fucking a near constant stream of different people doesn't sound that romantic or conducive to developing 'true love', but for me sleeping with a lot of different girls didn't really make any individual girl less special or interesting. I certainly didn't act the slut out of some macho desire to notch up my bedpost. I went on all those dates because I was curious to meet those people, and then I slept with a bunch of them because sex is fun.

I did sometimes wonder whether the thick skin I was building up was making it harder for me to truly connect with the girls I met, and if all these encounters were reducing my capacity for love, or at least the capacity for the naïve fairy-tale kind of love that a part of me still craved despite my cynicism. I don't know the answer to that question, but I still met girls during my New York dating adventures for whom feelings began to take root. Those little emotional overreactions started to creep in: excessive excitement over a message, or that sense of warmth when I looked at their smile, or a reflection of hope glanced in their eyes. Those feelings, given time, could perhaps have grown into something wonderful, but unfortunately they were mostly for girls that I never got a second or third date with.

There were other girls who were keener to reply to me. Girls who I liked, but who maybe liked me a little more than I liked them. Were it not for my frenzied over analysis of interpersonal differences and irresolvable sources of future friction (i.e. picky-ness), I might have found myself in actual relationships with one of these perfectly nice ladies. However, I wasn't going to start rolling down a hill with someone when I could already see the rocks at the bottom, and so I would end up telling them something along the lines of "Let's not do this. I can see rocks down there and I don't want to push you on them."

And so some girls vanished, some drifted, and others I cast off. I stayed friends with a few dates I met through the Internet and that was always rewarding. It was good to see a friendly face and have company for some minor NY adventure. Still, I lost many exciting connections to the NY vortex and all those girls left their impressions on me. Impressions that turned to empty hollows when contact was broken. However, I wouldn't feel like I was missing something if I hadn't experienced something good that was worth missing in the first place. I'm glad that I got to meet so many interesting people and snatch thin glimpses of their lives, and even though I will probably never see most of them again, they still left me more enriched than they found me.

Unfortunately my first year of New York dating has not followed a nice narrative parabola. Rather it has continued along an unending curve, like a rocket that has escaped the expected gravity of resolution and instead orbits, pensive, in the vacuum of space. Maybe you'd prefer it if I invented a happy ending for you, with rainbows, daises, fluffy animals, and all of that shit... Too bad this is life and not some fairy-tale.

If you're looking for a simple lesson from my NY experiences it might be this: Yes you can sleep with a lot of girls with an English accent in New York, and yes you can do it in a broadly ethical way, and yes it can be fun. However, with everything comes a cost. Not some grand 'fire and brimstone' type of cost of course, and indeed the price may turn out to be extremely reasonable, but it is still a cost that must be paid. My own bill has not yet been finalised, and hidden charges could yet be revealed. However, should you wish to follow in my footsteps, you should budget for these two considerations: your fantasies may lose some of their thrill and future solitude may gain a darker shade. (Oh, and if you're a guy you'll also spend a painful amount of money buying drinks for girls who then won't so much as text you to say thank you.)

To those people who will simply accuse me of being immoral for sleeping with a lot of women and not marrying them, my response is: "That's just like… your opinion man!"

In this modern age we have abandoned many conservative values, mostly to our betterment. The phrase "Well why not?" is perhaps a slogan of our time, a time when we are less afraid to question meaningless dogma. However, there may sometimes be hidden reasons 'why not', and with promiscuity these might be more than just the (highly manageable) risks of sexually transmitted diseases[139]. There could be reasonable social and psychological arguments for 'keeping it in your pants', but whatever those arguments are they have been completely lost in the stream of idiotic hate that spews from the political right. Even if the sensible arguments are comprehensively assessed and fairly presented, the down-sides of sleeping around are perhaps insufficient detractors to

---

[139] And no, despite my 2013 antics I came up clean on all available STD tests! Protection ftw!

prevent a logical, interested, and informed mind from ploughing a new course. However, they should be weighed in nevertheless.

Would I like to have a traditional family someday? Probably. Could I also be happy in a variety of unconventional relationships? Quite possibly. Could I even be satisfied if I ended up perpetually single but surrounded by good friends? Perhaps.

As my generation struggles to build new moralities from the burnt out moral wreckage of the past, we may easily get lost in a world full of false gods and enduring hypocrisy. We will sometimes get it wrong and take bad paths, but there's no way to know for sure if a road is right for us until we try to walk down it. I don't think there should be shame in trying new directions, but nor should there be shame in turning back if we find ourselves lost.

I could not say if I was really lost as that balmy New York autumn gave way to the frigid East Coast winter. The winds blew in and dead brown leaves swept across dirty streets, collected in gutters and danced in eddies beneath shop fronts. Discarded paper cups rolled along sidewalks towards no destination of their own, but still they announced their movement with a gravelly and monotonous song. V-shaped formations of migratory geese cut through the sky, squawking to each other as they travelled hundreds of miles to escape the winter's cold. Many of them would not make it but all of them seemed to know exactly where they were going.

As for me, I was at sea beneath unfamiliar stars. Nothing to guide me but the memory of a blinking lighthouse that I'd once spotted somewhere on the horizon.

But it was the brightest thing I had ever seen and there was no turning back now.

X

I can't speak.

T.G.O.M.D. looks at me with an expression of confused pity. My mouth opens: "It's just that... Err... Well... Ha. Why is this hard?"

...

"It's just that I think I kind of might be falling for you," I blurt.

It wasn't the smoothly delivered 'I'm falling in love with you' line I had been planning, but it would have to do.

"You're sweet!" she says, smiling in a way that tells me she was pleased to hear it. Still I fear that the next word she says will be the knife point of 'But...'

Instead though she is leaning towards me, reaching up and running her hands through my hair. My arms are around her now as we pull ourselves into each other.

This is the kiss. This is the moment. This is it.

*

Having realised that perfect moment I know something bad has to happen next. I try to fight my own imagination, but this means I just lose the moment faster. There is now a cold feeling in the pit of my spine.

"How did it get dark so quickly?" I ask T.G.O.M.D. "I could swear it was daytime just a moment ago."

A purposeful wind bends the high branches. 'Is this Central Park?' I wonder, 'it looks different somehow... like something is missing that I can't put my finger on...'

Suddenly the menacing shadows of hunched figures are appearing through the trees and across the grass. I instinctively know that they mean us harm. I scan behind me but hundreds of lurching corpses are approaching from every angle. The undead have us surrounded.

Fear is useless now. Accepting that there is no escape, I pull the girl of my dreams in close for a final death-defying kiss while the zombie horde converges on us with unexpected speed.

They are upon us. The press of their violent bodies thrusts us to the ground, forcing us apart. Teeth sink into my back and arms. Despite the pain and fear I clutch the hand of The Girl Of My Dreams... but it is torn out of mine.

I wake up alone and sweaty beneath my heavy duvet.

Conscious now I try to recall her face... But it has already gone.

Another epilogue, but in the right place this time

As I trudged up First Avenue I noticed my reflection in the shiny one-way glass of an office building. I looked sufficiently ridiculous that I started laughing to myself. Two suitcases dragged behind me, one in each hand, and my hiking backpack bulged on my back. I was a one man caravan and it was far too warm for this shit.

I went to turn left onto 41st Street and discovered there was no left turn onto 41st Street. Instead, there was just a bench and a tree with a concrete wall behind it, and so I kept walking. I paused by another bench, took off my jacket and rearranged my luggage. A little further along some homeless guy was doing much the same thing, except he had less baggage than I did. Across the street, the monolith of the United Nations stood in relief against the East River. Presumably there were lots of people in there trying to make the world a better place... or a worse place... I was never quite clear on that point. It also seemed possible that the monolith was entirely empty and just there to make us feel better about ourselves, like some functionless obelisk.

As I turned and rumbled down 42nd Street, the United Nations building diminished behind me and people in suits started to zoom past. Most of them were glued to their cell-phones and supping on takeaway coffees. I took a certain amount of pleasure from the fact that my personal suitcase rollercade kept getting in their way.

The Chrysler building dominated the view along 42nd, and soon its shining gargoyles were overhead and peering down at me; the outsider in a city full of misfits. In the distance I could see the arching bridge that went into Grand Central station. At certain times of year the sun lines up with this street and sets right beneath that bridge. 'Manhattan-henge' they call it. I'd tried to go see this once but a cloud over New Jersey hid the sun, so I just took pictures of disappointed tourists instead.

I trundled back south onto 41st Street where I found a bus stop and two promising looking queues of people. A girl in a white suit was waiting at the back of the queue nearest to me, her maroon suitcase looking like it came straight out of a shop window where all they sold was class.

"Is this the line for JFK?" I asked her.

"Yes, I think so," she replied in a gorgeous Italian accent.

"Cool. Thanks," I smiled at her and propped my bags upright.

She smiled back and then turned away. Her long blonde hair was tied in a plait that hung down over her shoulders and almost reached her taut hips. I had some inappropriate thoughts.

The other queue seemed to be growing but no one was joining ours. Doubt overcame me.

"Do you mind watching my bags for a second?" I asked the Italian girl, "I'll just go check we're in the right place..."
"Sure, no problem," she replied and I wandered towards a guy with a ticket machine who looked as if he knew what was what. I hoped this pretty girl wasn't going to peek inside my bags, if she did there were quite a lot of sex and bondage toys she might discover...

A few moments later I walked back to my spot in the queue and gave her a thumbs-up.

"See! I told you, but you didn't believe me," she said playfully. "I'm sorry! I never should have doubted you!" I replied.

This seemed like a promising interaction, and something told me this girl might like it if I kept talking to her...

I stood quietly by my suitcases for a moment. 'Come on Timmy, after all this time in New York you ought to be able to start a conversation with a pretty girl you've just met!'

I shifted the weight of my backpack.

I looked around the street.

Steam was emanating from a nearby drain and also from a nearby hot dog stand. One smelled good, the other not so much.

'Come on Timmy, now or never...'

I caught her eye again.

"So do you live in New York or are you just visiting?" I asked.

Her blue eyes flirted with possibility as she answered. Our conversation grew from a spark to a blaze in no time at all.

As we boarded the bus and found seats together I caught myself wondering 'Who knows? Maybe this one could be the girl of my dreams...'

END OF BOOK

Acknowledgements

Firstly I would like to thank you, the reader for finishing my book! I would also like to presumptuously thank you for reviewing this book on Amazon and telling your friends about it! At the moment this is my first book and I'm running this show solo without a publisher or publicist and so if you think this book is worth reading I need your help to get it out there. If you're interested in keeping up to date with my writing projects I have a rag-tag blog that can be found here:
http://sexlovebdsm.blogspot.com/

I would also like to thank the following anonymous initials for their help and advice with this undertaking:

A.M. for the confidence boost that got this book train rolling,
P.P. for early encouragement and critical advice,
O.R. for ripping into it,
C.G. for critical comments and advice on the ending,
P.Z. for the advice on how to open the show,
L.G. for reading the whole thing on a plane and giving me great advice to tie the story together,
L.B. for advice and typo spotting,
D.C. for patient corrections and edits,
S.W. for even more typo spotting,
And everyone else who read it and gave me feedback!

Finally thanks to all the dates featured in this book, I couldn't have done it without you!

Printed in Great Britain
by Amazon.co.uk, Ltd.,
Marston Gate.